Japanese Loyalism Reconstrued

VOID

Japanese Loyalism Reconstrued

Yamagata Daini's *Ryūshi shinron* of 1759

BOB TADASHI WAKABAYASHI

 University of Hawai'i Press

Honolulu

Library of Congress Cataloging-in-Publication Data
Wakabayashi, Bob Tadashi, 1950–
  Japanese loyalism reconstrued : Yamagata Daini's Ryūshi shinron of
1759 / Bob Tadashi Wakabayashi.
    p.   cm.
  Includes bibliographical references and index.
  ISBN 0-8248-1667-6 (alk. paper)
    1. Yamagata, Daini, 1725–1767, Ryūshi Shinron.   2. Emperor
worship—Japan—History.   3. Japan—Politics and
government—1600–1868.   4. Japan—Intellectual life—1600–1868.
5. Royalists—Japan—Biography.
DS843.W25   1995
952'.025'092—dc20   94-30662
                                                          CIP

Frontispiece: Portrait of Yamagata Daini by Muraoka
Antō. Date unknown. Reprinted from Kōno Yukitaka,
ed., *Yamagata jinji shi* (Tokyo: Tsukagawa meibun
sha, 1972).

University of Hawai'i Press books are printed on acid-
free paper and meet the guidelines for permanence and
durability of the Council on Library Resources

Designed by Paula Newcomb

For Professor Ienaga Saburō,

a scholar of courage and conviction

Contents

Acknowledgments

I am responsible for all shortcomings in this book. But it could never have been written without generous support from many quarters. So it is a pleasure to acknowledge my debts by thanking the people and institutions who so kindly assisted me. First, this study is dedicated to Professor Ienaga Saburō, my graduate supervisor at Tokyo Kyōiku University. In challenging the dogma of Japanese government authority and braving death threats from right-wing terrorists, he has never wavered in pursuing the truth as a scholar and teacher.

The Social Sciences and Humanities Research Council of Canada provided generous financial support from July 1990 to February 1992 that allowed me to work on this project in Toronto and in Japan. As well, the SSHRC granted a time-release stipend that, coupled with funding from York University's Faculty of Arts, gave me what amounted to an extra year of sabbatical in 1990–1991. Supportive colleagues in the History Department, particularly Peter Mitchell, Margo Gewurtz, Bernard Luk, and Sydney Kanya-Forstner, graciously picked up the teaching and administrative slack caused by my three-year leave of absence from 1990 to 1993. Russ Chace placed his computer skills at my service, and Paul Lovejoy gave me a crash course in the art of composing grant proposals. It should be noted that the York History Department has fostered a nurturing atmosphere for junior faculty such as myself despite gruesome fiscal stringencies over the past several years.

Mr. Ichiba Seiichi, his wife Tomoko, and members of their family provided lodgings and gentle hospitality on my research trip to Japan in the wretchedly hot summer of 1990. At that time, I also imposed on Professor Yorifuji Michio, Chair of the English Department at Tsuru Bunka University and an old friend. A knowledgeable amateur historian in his own right, he cheerfully took time from his busy schedule to chauffeur me about various historical sites in Kōfu and its environs. Professor Yorifuji was also instrumental in gaining access to people and source materials. Through him I contacted Professors Menju Shin'ichirō and Matsuzawa Hidenori of Yamanashi University, who in turn introduced me to their colleague, Professor Iida Bunya. An expert in local history and the Tokugawa period, Professor Iida allowed me to locate and photocopy rare materials on Daini in the Yamanashi Prefectural Library; without these, my insights on Daini's thought would be far poorer.

Mr. Tsukagawa Norimasa, head priest at the Yamagata Shrine in Ryūō, shared his knowledge of its history and Daini's life. He also showed me unpublished primary sources housed in the shrine. The library staffs at Hiroshima Shūdō University and Tsuru Bunka University helped me locate materials. Dr. Ishii Katsumi of Kitasato University and his wife Noriko provided emergency medical care in 1990 to cure the most miserable summer of my life. Professors Ichikawa Ta'ichi, Kikkawa Gen, Hirayama Kazuhiko, Hama Hideo, and Kobayashi Tazuko made that trip—as well as subsequent stays in Japan—both pleasant and productive.

Prior to my 1990 research trip, I was able to air some of my ideas by giving papers at two academic conferences in North America. One panel was organized by George Wilson for the Association for Asian Studies in Washington in March 1989, where Harry Harootunian served as discussant. The other was organized by Susan Long for the AAS Midwest Regional Conference and Midwest Japan Seminar in East Lansing in October 1989, where Jackson Bailey made helpful suggestions. Diana Wright-Foss of the University of Toronto commented on my work at an early stage; and, in a different capacity, Professor Harold Bolitho of Harvard University later gave me insightful suggestions to improve the manuscript. I have taken his criticisms to heart—in a way that only he knows—to my great profit.

Despite "feudal" connotations, the *gakubatsu,* or Japanese school clique, has its positive features. Indeed, that old-boy network fostered years ago at Kyōikudai came through for me yet again. A former graduate mentor there, Professor Matsumoto Sannosuke, now at Surugadai University, and an upperclassman,

Yoshida Toshizumi, who now teaches at Tokyo Kasei Gakuin, have patiently answered my queries about the *Ryūshi shinron* and Tokugawa-era views of Yamagata Daini. Old school chums Eizawa Kōji, Kurihara Takashi, and Igarashi Akio—now professors in their own right—tracked down and photocopied more than a few obscure journal articles for me. Professor Igarashi, his wife Atsuko, and their daughters Yuki and Eri have lodged and entertained me in their Urawa home several times.

Elsewhere, Professor Watanabe Hiroshi of Tokyo University kindly photographed sources on Yamagata Daini for me at his own expense. These rare documents—not readily accessible to non-Tōdai personnel—proved crucial to my understanding of how the "Daini image" changed over time. It was Professor Watanabe as well who first informed me about the Kawaura edition of Daini's *Ryūshi shinron*. And it was he who steered me to a little-known Kanda secondhand bookshop specializing in paperbacks. There I was able to pick up a cheap copy of this out-of-print book, which became the main source for this study and translation.

Such friendship and assistance are absolutely invaluable on brief research trips when time is of the essence. But no matter how hard one may try, one can never obtain all the necessary materials during a single short stay in Japan. That is why I wish to acknowledge Clark Taber of J. P. Morgan Trust, Professor Janice Matsumura of the University of Montreal, and Professor Honda Itsuo of Kyūshū Kōgyō University, who secured books and articles related to Daini after my return to Canada.

Patricia Crosby, Cheri Dunn, Don Yoder, and staff members of the University of Hawai'i Press deserve special thanks for their meticulous editing and scrupulous attention to detail at all stages of the manuscript's review and preparation for publication. Anonymous readers provided valuable comments to strengthen the manuscript as well. Because of the efforts expended by all these persons, the final product is far better than what it otherwise would have been. Nothing could make an author happier than to acknowledge that fact.

Finally, I wish to mention two other people: a sweet but impish little girl named Megumi, who did all she could to keep me from writing this book, and my long-suffering wife Yumiko who forced me to get it done.

A Note on Transliteration and Dates

Transliteration. My romanization of classical Chinese terms follows a modified Wade-Giles system that omits diacritical marks such as umlauts over vowels. Following standard practice, I have dropped macrons from vowels in well-known Japanese place-names such as Kyoto and in terms such as "daimyo" and "shogun" that have made their way into English. To benefit readers with a background in Chinese history and language but not Japanese, or vice versa, the glossary offers a list of Chinese ideographs for important terms and personal names that appear in this book.

Dates. With the exception of the eleventh day of February 660 B.C., all dates cited in the main text and notes follow the traditional Japanese lunar calendar; none are converted to the Gregorian calendar. Thus, 11/1767 denotes the second lunar month of 1767. No intercalary months or years are given.

PART ONE

Yamagata Daini

CHAPTER 1

Ghosts of Daini Past

Early in 1759, a samurai-physician, master tactician, Confucian scholar, and classical Chinese poet completed a polemical tract on sociopolitical reform entitled *Ryūshi shinron* (Master Ryū's New Thesis). This man, known to history as Yamagata Daini (1725–1767), never published or widely circulated his polemic because it included harsh criticism of warrior regimes in Japan since the twelfth century. But eight years later, the Tokugawa bakufu in Edo arraigned Yamagata, his student Fujii Umon (1720–1767), and another Confucian scholar named Takenouchi Shikibu (1712–1767) on charges of lese majesty in the 1767 Meiwa Incident. Yamagata Daini and Fujii Umon were beheaded for their sacrilege. Takenouchi Shikibu was ordered into remote exile but died en route. These sentencings took place nine years after the Hōreki Incident of 1758—a disturbance instigated by conservative leaders at the imperial court in Kyoto, who asked the Edo bakufu to punish Takenouchi for having lectured to low-ranking nobles on the Shinto-Confucian syncretist thought of Yamazaki Ansai (1618–1682).

Up to now, the consensus among Japanese and Western historians of the Tokugawa, or Edo, period (1600–1868) has been to link these eighteenth-century Hōreki and Meiwa Incidents and to view Yamagata, Fujii, and Takenouchi as prototypes of later loyalist martyrs victimized by a tainted shogunal government. The highly authoritarian Tokugawa military regime, it is said, was bent on crushing any sign of popular dissent or opposition—especially if motivated by incipient restorationist sentiments. Yamagata Daini in particular has been glorified as part of a grand myth that has grievously marred our understanding of his life and thought. That myth comes in two basic versions, pre-1945 and post-1945, but both depict him as a revolutionary idol and a fervid visionary. Daini's cutting invective, we are told, laid bare the moral bankruptcy of Tokugawa feudalism and urged that it be destroyed and replaced by a superior form of government under restored imperial aegis.

Most prewar and wartime Japanese scholars expounded the pre-1945 version of this myth in line with the state orthodoxy of their day. They sought to establish a hallowed pedigree for the ultranationalist ideal of "revering the emperor" *(sonnō, kinnō)*— the defining core of their "national essence or polity" *(kokutai)*. That search for a hallowed pedigree led them to idolize any historical figure who could be portrayed as having remotely inspired the Meiji Restoration. Thus the nativist but still pro-Tokugawa Kokugaku and Mitogaku schools were misrepresented as hotbeds of restorationist sentiment. Kokugaku scholars such as Motoori Norinaga (1730–1801) and Mitogaku thinker-activists such as Fujita Tōko (1806–1855) won high state honors and wide public acclaim as "loyalists" when in fact neither man wished to end shogunal rule or return power to the emperor. As Matsumoto Sannosuke, a prominent postwar Japanese intellectual historian points out, any critical "scientific" inquiry about Japan's *kokutai* was tabooed before 1945; and Japanese scholars who published in fields such as Kokugaku were, in his words, "nothing but consorts of the emperor state and its theology."[1]

Then came Japan's ignoble defeat and surrender in August 1945, soon followed by war crimes trials and a purge of ultranationalists under the Allied Occupation. After that, right-wing values and the emperor system fell into sordid disrepute among mainstream Japanese academics and the general public. Largely but not solely under iconoclastic Marxist influence, a postwar revisionist school of interpretation in Japan strove to debunk this myth of "revolutionary imperial loyalism leading to the Meiji Restoration." As a result, both Marxist and non-Marxist historians in Japan and the West now stress the "limits" of Tokugawa loyalism by underscoring its highly conservative, hierarchy-affirming nature—at least with regard to Kokugaku and Mitogaku. The now-accepted view holds that loyalist thinkers such as Motoori Norinaga and Fujita Tōko tried to shore the bakufu up—not tear it down—by borrowing prestige and spiritual authority from the imperial court and national deities.[2]

But in Yamagata Daini's case, this myth of revolutionary loyalism remains firmly intact—although it has been suitably revamped by postwar leftist historians who see themselves as desecrators, not consorts, of the old emperor state. Whereas prewar and wartime nationalist scholars construed Yamagata Daini's loyalism as being inspired by his love of the emperor, postwar humanist scholars ascribe it to his concern for the oppressed masses. In the post-1945 version of the myth, Daini has become an avatar of humanism, democracy, and egalitarianism. Now he is portrayed as wanting to destroy the Tokugawa military regime (tōbaku), not as an end in itself, but as the best way to implement radical populist ideals that would liberate downtrodden Japanese commoners.

In the following pages, I hope to carry on this revisionism in Tokugawa political thought by showing that Yamagata Daini, no less than Kokugaku or Mitogaku figures, must be cast in a more historically accurate light. At the same time, I seek to avoid the excesses inherent in this revisionist interpretation and to correct the distorted postwar image of Daini it has created. In short, it is time for the ghosts of Daini past—both pre-1945 and post-1945—to be exorcised. My main contention is that Daini was not a loyalist in the "restorationist" or "revolutionary" sense usually ascribed to him. That is, Daini never sought to reinstate direct imperial rule by destroying the bakufu and abolishing warrior supremacy and domain ownership, the cardinal principles on which the Edo regime was based. Yamagata Daini's loyalism was of another variety—one that is admittedly less exciting but perhaps more important. Daini's main thesis, implicitly advanced in his Ryūshi shinron of 1759, held that the shogun and daimyo were imperial regents or ministers of state who—as long as they took sagely counsel from Confucian scholar-advisors such as Master Ryū—should enjoy de facto autonomy in "assisting" (hohitsu) political administration under figurehead emperors.

In order to substantiate this reinterpretation of "Tokugawa loyalism as imperial assistance" and identify its significance in the history of Japanese political thought overall, I adopt the following approach. First, I introduce some basic yet little-known information about Yamagata Daini's life, describe the corpus of his scholarly writings, and critically reexamine the Meiwa Incident to

separate fact from legend about his role in it. Beyond that, I outline certain key issues of the day that Daini disputed through
Master Ryū, his polemical mouthpiece. This effort should reveal
how Daini's contemporaries—as opposed to latter-day interpreters—construed his ideas. By doing all of this, I hope to show
how the "Daini image" changed over time in line with political
exigencies. But integral to this approach is the need to translate
his *Ryūshi shinron* in full. A close reading of this text *as a whole*
—plus rigorous philological explication of its historical and literary allusions—will disclose its unstated assumptions and underlying logic; and that in turn will radically alter received wisdom as
to Daini's socio-political thought. In sum, I am convinced that a
thoroughgoing reinterpretation of Yamagata Daini's life and letters will uncover a very different tradition of Japanese imperial
loyalism—one we have missed up to now in our haste to see the
bakufu fall.

The National Essence View

Prewar and wartime Japanese scholars eagerly advanced—or at
least could not publicly disclaim—an ultranationalistic emperor-
centered view of their nation's past now disparagingly labeled
kōkoku shikan, or "the national essence conception of Japanese
history." It is only within this overall thesis that the Daini myth in
its pre-1945 version is fully comprehensible. This "emperor-state
theology" as mocked by Matsumoto Sannosuke had many early
adherents who urged the imperial government to promote what
they called Japan's "national morality" in Meiji and Taishō times
(1868–1925). But this interpretation did not become an all-perva-
sive dogma enforced in torture chambers under police-state
powers until the early Shōwa era (1926–1945). To cite a relatively
benign example, Minister of Commerce Nakajima Kumakichi
was publicly hounded and forced from office in February 1932
for reprinting an article on Ashikaga Takauji (1305–1358) published eleven years before. In it Nakajima was so indiscreet as to
express a brief note of admiration for the character of this medieval figure who crushed the first imperial restoration in 1336 and
went on to found the Muromachi bakufu.[3] But probably the crucial event in establishing the *kōkoku shikan* as a state orthodoxy

came in 1935, when the renowned legal scholar Minobe Tatsuki-chi (1873–1948) suffered prosecution on charges of lese majesty in the "Emperor Organ Incident." The very nature of these grave charges against Minobe impinged on the Peace Preservation Law as revised seven years before. This law prescribed a maximum sentence of death for any imperial subject who called for, or even discussed the merits of, altering Japan's *kokutai*—the "national essence or polity." But given the vagueness and ambiguity of that term, the cabinet of Okada Keisuke deemed it wise to launch a "Campaign to Clarify Our National Essence." Then everyone could be sure of what was being imperiled with alteration.

Two of the major figures in this government-directed clarification campaign were professors of Japanese history and literature: Hiraizumi Kiyoshi at Tokyo Imperial University and Yamada Yoshio at Tōhoku Imperial University. Hiraizumi Kiyoshi enjoyed deity-like influence with, and ample funding from, right-wing army extremists and violent ultranationalist societies. He and his university teaching assistants underscored points in lecture by brandishing samurai swords or daggers; and, we should note, some of those Hiraizumi protégés went on to censor textbooks in the postwar Ministry of Education.[4] Prominent left-wing historians today who studied under Hiraizumi back then still remember him for banning their use of *"kimi"* or *"X-kun"*—an informal "you" or "Mr. X"—in class. Hiraizumi's reason was: "that appellation [also meaning 'sovereign'] is reserved solely for His August Majesty, the Emperor."[5] Yamada Yoshio, an undisputed authority on Japanese language and literature, largely wrote the Ministry of Education's *Kokutai no hongi* (Principles of Our National Essence). This treatise, meant as a guide for teachers, was published in 1937, the year that Japan launched its full-scale invasion of China.[6] *Kokutai no hongi*—along with the ministry's *Kokushi gaisetsu* (Outline of Japanese History) written in 1943—enshrined the *kōkoku shikan* orthodoxy in all Japanese public and private elementary and middle schools.

Professors such as Hiraizumi and Yamada earned the derisive postwar epithet "consorts of the emperor state" for having led government efforts to inculcate the national essence through primary and secondary school instruction in Japanese history, language, and literature. The aim of such educators was as much political as pedagogical: to dispel confusion about proper "national morality" by refuting dangerous foreign ideas. This specification of moral correctness would forge a consensus at home to support military expansion abroad. These educators admitted that assimilating Western thought and institutions had done much to strengthen Japan after 1868. But they believed that liberalism, democracy, and bolshevism were based on alien ideals of individual freedom and a faith in reason that were incompatible with, and inimical to, Japan's national essence.[7] Their *kōkoku shikan* thesis clarified this national essence by casting Japanese historical development along teleological lines attesting to the gods' will. In brief, that divine will was for imperial loyalism to overcome treachery and thereby revive the pristine and only proper form of Japan's government—the "national polity," as *kokutai* is often translated. More specifically, this national polity took the form of "direct rule by emperors" *(tennō shinsei)* in the dynastic line descended from the Sun Goddess Amaterasu. This one and only Japanese dynasty began with Jimmu's accession on 11 February 660 B.C., and celebrated its twenty-six-hundredth anniversary in A.D. 1940 under its hundred and twenty-fourth Emperor Shōwa, or Hirohito as he is known in the West.

The *kōkoku shikan* ideologues would phrase their interpretation somewhat as follows. The Fujiwara and Hōjō regents and the Kamakura, Ashikaga, and Tokugawa shoguns never dared to kill an emperor or usurp his sovereign title outright. But these nefarious subjects deviously expropriated the emperor's sovereign powers from the ninth through nineteenth centuries A.D. Exemplars of loyalty and patriotism could be found even in those dark ages—as evinced by patriots such as Kusunoki Masashige (d. 1336) and Nitta Yoshisada (1301—1338) during the fourteenth-century Northern and Southern Courts period. These men and their descendants destroyed the Kamakura bakufu in 1333, faithfully served Emperor Godaigo during his ill-starred Kemmu Restoration *(chūkō)* from 1333 to 1336, and remained steadfast in their loyalty to his Southern Court until its tragic demise in 1392. Muromachi bakufu leaders such as Shogun Ashikaga Takauji—who treacherously foiled that first imperial restoration—acted from evil motives to be sure. (Takauji's very name was vilified; the character *"Taka"* meaning "exalted" was replaced with that for "high," as in "high-handed.") But apart from such factors of human wickedness, scholars like Hiraizumi argued, there were basic institutional problems in those dark ages. The national polity was deformed in that the loyalist aspirations of true and good Japanese subjects were blocked by political inter-mediaries—land stewards, estate managers, court regents or min-isters, regional daimyo, and shogunal officials. These political intermediaries parceled out imperial lands among themselves, cut imperial subjects off from the emperor's will, and so divided impe-rial sovereign authority. This system of private rule by intermedi-aries was certainly abnormal and violated the *kokutai*; yet most Japanese subjects were blind to that fact because it had gone on for so long.

Thus, the argument went, the national essence became obfus-cated and remained so until it was rediscovered, mainly during the Tokugawa era. Imperial loyalists such as Motoori Norinaga in the Kokugaku school and Yamazaki Ansai, Takenouchi Shikibu, Yamagata Daini, and Fujii Umon in various Confucian schools bravely defied Edo bakufu suppression. All strove to clarify the *kokutai* through their research, teaching, and writing; but these last four scholar-activists went even further. They pursued their lofty goal through a well-conceived, if badly executed, restora-tionist coup manifested in the Hōreki and Meiwa Incidents between 1758 and 1767. Their mid-Tokugawa attempt at impe-rial restoration met with defeat, but their valiant efforts would bear fruit after the coming of Perry's Black Ships in the Baku-matsu era (1853–1868) at the end of the Tokugawa. Like those fourteenth-century patriots who overthrew the Kamakura bakufu and restored Emperor Godaigo, Bakumatsu loyalist heroes *(shi-shi)* toppled the Edo bakufu *(tōbaku)* and revived direct rule by Emperor Meiji. That revolutionary event, the Meiji Restora-tion *(ishin)*, ended more than seven centuries of misrule by war-rior intermediaries that had begun in 1185, and it reestablished Japan's national polity in its proper original form. For the first time since 1336, the emperor combined sovereign authority with real power to exercise it. Japanese subjects were liberated from "feudal" oppression at home, saved from imminent enslave-ment by the white colonial powers, and given a stable foundation from which to discharge their divine mission of Asian leadership against the West.[8]

The government sponsors of this *kōkoku shikan* thesis prescribed a loyalist canon appropriate for it; and that canon rarely excluded Yamagata Daini's *Ryūshi shinron*. This set of venerable classics began with the eighth-century *Kojiki* and *Nihon shoki*, those veritable records compiled by the Yamato imperial court that revealed Sun Goddess Amaterasu's divine decree *(shinchoku):* "Japan is the land over which my descendants shall be sovereign. Go to rule it, my imperial grandson. Your dynastic line shall flourish coeval with heaven and earth."[9] This divine decree stipulated a categorical imperative in the *kokutai:* Amaterasu's offspring would enjoy dominion over Japan forever. And the officially prescribed loyalist canon generally ended with Emperor Meiji's 1890 "Rescript on Education" and 1908 "Boshin Edict." These sacred texts exhorted subjects to obey Amaterasu's decree through loyal and filial devotion to Japan's family state, headed by her descendants in the imperial line.

Prominent Japanese scholars and writers recruited a pantheon of loyalist heroes to go with this canon. Hayashi Fusao, for example, a well-known proletarian novelist turned ultranationalist, nominated the following Tokugawa stalwarts in 1940: the forty-seven Akō retainers of *Chūshingura* fame, Yamaga Sokō, Yamagata Daini, Keichū, Kamo no Mabuchi, Motoori Norinaga, Matsuo Bashō, Yosa Buson, Rai Sanyō, Fujita Tōko, and Yoshida Shōin.[10] These men and their works had clarified the national essence so long obscured; thus they cleared the way for uprooting warrior rule and achieving the Meiji Restoration. Beyond that, men like Hayashi argued, imperial subjects in the 1930s and 1940s could overcome their current national crisis by assiduously studying these same loyalist writers; for this crisis too stemmed from ignorance of the *kokutai* and correct Japanese values.

Another prominent *kōkoku shikan* spokesman was Mikami Sanji, the eminent Tokugawa history specialist at Tokyo Imperial University. A perennial candidate for education minister, he was member of the House of Peers from 1932 until his death in 1939. In fact, Mikami inadvertently helped trigger the 1935 Emperor Organ Incident in the House of Peers when he chided the Okada cabinet for neglecting to show proper reverence for the national gods.[11] One of Mikami's best-known works, his posthumously published *Sonnōron hattatsu shi* (The Historical Development of Imperial Loyalism), was compiled from university lecture notes.

Its first chapter concisely outlines the national essence conception of Japanese history, and the book goes on to describe both the Meiwa Incident and Yamagata Daini's loyalist thought within that general thesis.[12] Together with the government's multivolume *Ishin shi* (Restoration History) of 1941–1943 and Watsuji Tetsuro's *Sonnō shisō to sono dentō* (The Evolution of Imperial Loyalism) of 1943, Mikami's book certainly contributed to wartime historical scholarship. To be fair, it should be stated that these works retain a measure of scholarly value even by present-day standards. But in their own day they lent unquestioned academic credence to an emperor-centered view of history, to its corollary thesis of Tokugawa revolutionary loyalism, and to the Yamagata Daini myth in its pre-1945 version.

To sum up, then, most prewar and wartime Japanese scholars interpreted Yamagata Daini, his *Ryūshi shinron,* and the Meiwa Incident as part of this politically inspired, state-sponsored *kōkoku shikan* theology of history. According to it, the unique national essence and polity of Japan, the *kokutai,* was revealed at the dawn of time in Sun Goddess Amaterasu's decree that her offspring would hold sway over the divine land forever. Hence "the Way of the subject," "one's ultimate duty," "the national morality," and "the Japanese spirit," as these were conceived, called for absolute compliance with Amaterasu's divine decree through selfless devotion to her imperial dynasty in succeeding generations and beyond.

For an emperor to reign but not rule, or for subjects to serve any master except His Majesty, blatantly contradicted Japan's *kokutai.* Nevertheless, certain subjects dared to violate the national essence and alter the national polity by setting up privately run national and local regimes from the Heian through Edo periods—save for Godaigo's three-year Kemmu Restoration. However, revolutionary loyalists such as Yamagata Daini reclarified and rearticulated the *kokutai* in classics such as the *Ryūshi shinron.* What is more, Yamagata Daini, Takenouchi Shikibu, and Fujii Umon spearheaded a movement to revive imperial rule midway through the Tokugawa period: the Hōreki and Meiwa Incidents. Their visionary endeavor failed—much as Nitta Yoshisada and Kusunoki Masashige had failed four hundred years before. But the Hōreki and Meiwa Incidents, plus writings like the *Ryūshi shinron,* eventually inspired patriotic Bakumatsu *shishi* to over-throw warrior government under the Edo bakufu and to revive direct imperial rule under Emperor Meiji. In that sense, Yamagata Daini, his life, and his work presaged the Meiji Restoration that took place a century later.

The Postwar Western View

Postwar Western scholars, of course, have rejected the main tenets and conclusions of this prewar and wartime Japanese government dogma. Even so, a few of its presuppositions and assertions about Tokugawa loyalism have slipped through and endure to this day. Let us, then, examine non-Japanese appraisals of Yamagata Daini, his *Ryūshi shinron,* and the Meiwa Incident in relation to the issue of imperial loyalism in the Edo period.

In an influential three-volume history of Japan, George B. Sansom argues that Takenouchi Shikibu and Yamagata Daini espoused "anti-Bakufu sentiment" in a premature "loyalist move-ment," which the "Leviathan" Edo regime was "determined to suppress." More specifically, maintains Sansom, Yamagata Daini's "teaching was hostile to the absolute rule of the Bakufu, which depended upon force. He . . . was in favour of the 'Kingly Way' (Ōdō), that is to say of Imperial rule."[13] Delmer M. Brown's his-torical outline of Japanese nationalism locates Takenouchi Shikibu and Yamagata Daini in a "Revere the Emperor *(Sonnō)* movement" that was reemerging during Tokugawa times. Wors-ening socioeconomic conditions all over Japan, says Brown, "were causing more of the court nobility to think that there might soon be another opportunity, like the one that had arisen in the fourteenth century, for the Imperial Court to throw off the shackles of the military regime." According to Brown, Yamagata Daini forcefully argued that "the country should be under one ruler" and hoped that "strong leaders would emerge to rectify this situation." After giving lectures on the "means by which the Edo castle could be seized," he was "convicted of organizing a plot to overthrow the Bakufu."[14]

Edwin O. Reischauer and John K. Fairbank—who produced a classic East Asian history text still in wide use—place the "loyalist teacher" Yamagata Daini in a tradition of "National Learning," or Kokugaku. That school of thought, they note, "revived interest in the imperial line which was to prove highly subversive to the Tokugawa in their last years of rule."[15] This view of Yamagata Daini as a loyalist thinker affiliated with or influenced by Kokugaku has won support from some Western scholars. But others dispute any links to that school and instead argue that his loyalism was inspired by the Shinto-Confucian syncretism of Yamazaki Ansai. Thus, in an authoritative survey of eighteenth-century nativism, Peter Nosco does not identify Yamagata Daini and Takenouchi Shikibu as Kokugaku adherents per se; but Nosco does disclose a latent potential to undermine the Edo regime that these two "proponents of imperial loyalism *(sonnō ron)*" shared with such men as Motoori Norinaga in the Kokugaku school. In Nosco's view, the *Ryūshi shinron* contains "unambiguous challenges to the legitimacy of bakufu rule . . . couched within the context of a discourse on the imperial court." Hence, Nosco concludes, "the bakufu was justified in regarding the work as subversive of its rule, and Yamagata Daini was executed some years later in 1767 for his active involvement in an anti-bakufu plot."[16]

By contrast, William G. Beasley argues that Takenouchi Shikibu and Yamagata Daini drew their loyalism from Yamazaki Ansai's amalgam of Shinto and Confucian ideas. In what is generally regarded as the standard Western-language account of the Meiji Restoration, Beasley contends that the Edo bakufu executed Daini "for pointing out the potential conflict between loyalty to Emperor and loyalty to Shogun, and claiming that loyalty to the Emperor took first place."[17] Harry D. Harootunian takes an eclectic stance, arguing that the concept of imperial loyalism was originally Confucian in nature but later assumed militant Kokugaku overtones. As early as the eighteenth century, Harootunian maintains, "*sonnō* had been something of a subversive idea in the hands of courtiers such as Yamagata Daini and Takenouchi Shikibu." But when later combined with the nativism of Motoori Norinaga's Kokugaku, their stripe of imperial loyalism became more violent. It roused Bakumatsu *shishi* to stage revolutionary coups in a "rehearsal for restoration" that Ii Naosuke's Edo regime ruthlessly suppressed in its 1859 Ansei Purge.[18]

Herschel Webb cautions us that Yamagata Daini and Takenouchi Shikibu "were not spokesmen for their own age, but were prophets of an age to come." Still, he cites Mikami Sanji to claim that Daini "wrote a book which could only have been intended as subversive of shogunal rule." Webb goes further, to claim that Yamagata Daini "was not only an anti-shogunal polemicist, but also an active plotter against the shogun's government" who "planned some sort of military uprising" and "was executed for his activities."[19] As well, Webb argues, Daini berated post-1185 warrior rule on two specific counts: abrogating imperial prerogatives and upholding martial law in eras of peace. To substantiate these points, Webb translates and quotes a passage from Section I of the *Ryūshi shinron:*

> The universal principle of ancient and modern times for achieving good government is that the civil order should defend the country in ordinary circumstances and the military order should attend to occasions of crisis. In the present government there is no discrimination between civil and military affairs. Those who attend to times of crisis also defend the country in ordinary times.[20]

Like Beasley, David M. Earl affirms the thesis that Yamagata Daini followed Yamazaki Ansai, not Kokugaku. But Earl differs by asserting that any charge of plotting a revolt "would have been militarily absurd for anyone as unimportant as Daini in the feudal hierarchy." After all, Daini was a *rōnin,* or samurai at large without domain affiliation. Still, in Earl's mind, Yamagata Daini's thought was "impregnated with loyalty to the emperor," and the *Ryūshi shinron* was nothing less than a "published advocacy of imperial restoration."[21] To support these contentions, Earl submits the following précis of Section I in Daini's work. According to Earl, Master Ryū argued

> that divine emperors were the foundation of the country, [and] that they had created the Way for the prosperity and welfare of the people and had established civilization and order. Their government had continued for over two thousand years; their virtue had permeated the hearts of the people; no one remained unaffected by their influence. Their power was temporarily in a state of decline, but "if the efforts of one or two loyal subjects could be obtained, it is probable that their position could easily be restored."[22]

As Earl notes, this précis derives from a Japanese-language article written in 1935 to expound "Yamagata Daini's Views on *Koku-*

tai."[23] Earl winds up his account of Takenouchi Shikibu and Yamagata Daini by calling them "the first martyrs of the imperial restoration movement."[24]

These postwar non-Japanese scholars give Yamagata Daini, the *Ryūshi shinron,* and the Meiwa Incident passing reference in general histories or in monographs devoted to Tokugawa thought and institutions. Only one Western scholar, the intellectual historian Tetsuo Najita, has produced an in-depth, article-length study of Daini and his thought.[25] Najita places Yamagata Daini in the context of emerging Japanese nationalism. But it is a polemical and historicist form of nationalism—not the prewar *kokutai* variety. For Najita, the key to understanding Yamagata Daini's thought is the concept of "restorationism." Najita argues that Daini's restorationism was nationalist in justifying violent overthrow of the current political system for the greater good of society, and it was historicist in purporting to show why the present had devolved from past political ideals and how this condition should be rectified.[26]

Yamagata Daini, says Najita, did not necessarily advocate restoration in the literal sense of recapturing imperial rule as it existed in high antiquity; rather, Daini advocated the idea as a polemical device. That is, Yamagata Daini idealized imperial government in the remote past as a "true tradition" in order to contrast it with, and deny legitimacy to, warrior rule dating from a more recent past.[27] By positing conventionally accepted Confucian norms such as "names," "merit," or "culture" against the harsh reality of bakufu rule, Daini exposed its hypocritical and exploitive nature. For example, Tokugawa bakufu rulers purported to reward talent when they in fact perpetuated rule by hereditary status. Or they claimed to represent culture and civilization but in fact used the wartime expedient of naked power to extend and reinforce their sway in an era of peace. In other words, this warrior regime used the mantle of Confucian benevolence to disguise brutal exploitation. But Najita further asserts that Yamagata Daini argued for a radical restructuring of existing sociopolitical institutions because "even moral men cannot make faulty structures function in an ethical way." Thus the military aristocracy should be dissolved and warriors should be returned to the soil; then "talent among the poor and lowly of status would be tapped" in order to set up a sociopolitical system based on merit.[28] But in the end, Daini came to realize that "the only recourse was to raise an army . . . to overthrow the Bakufu."[29]

Tetsuo Najita's essay is a closely argued, well-documented exercise in intellectual history. With good reason, it has remained the standard Western account of Yamagata Daini ever since it appeared in 1971. Najita's groundbreaking works have stimulated much interest in Tokugawa thought, and he has been instrumental in establishing this field as a discipline within Japan studies in North America. But the very quality of his article has had the unforeseen and unfortunate consequence of stifling debate on Daini among non-Japanese scholars for a quarter-century. Let us for the moment grant Najita's claim that Yamagata Daini advocated a "military overthrow of the very Bakufu he served."[30] But if Daini did not necessarily call for a restoration of imperial rule as it actually existed in antiquity, just what did he envision taking the place of warrior government under the Tokugawa house? Viewed together with Najita's other writings on Japanese thought, it appears that he places Daini in a tradition of "loyalism as rebellion" directly linked with such figures as Ōshio Heihachirō, the Bakumatsu *shishi*, Nakano Seigō, and Shōwa restorationists like Kita Ikki who inspired the 26 February Incident of 1936.[31]

Thus, Najita seems to argue that Yamagata Daini—like the right-wing terrorists or "young officers" in the 1930s—just wanted to tear down the present evil system by evoking ancient imperial ideals of benevolent rule, and then left the concrete tasks of planning and construction to those who would come later. In sum, Tetsuo Najita has advanced a powerful thesis and provoked an arresting question. But sadly, no Western scholar has carried on his groundbreaking work to address this problem plus other key issues concerning Daini and his significance for the overall history of Japanese political thought.

Although strictly limited to the early Tokugawa period, studies by Kate Wildman Nakai and Joyce Ackroyd shed light on the ancillary issue of Tokugawa loyalism as revealed in Confucian historiography. Thus their work warrants mention here even though it does not relate directly to Yamagata Daini or the Meiwa Incident. Nakai examines the thought of the Hayashi school, bakufu advisor Arai Hakuseki, and early Mitogaku figures. In brief, her findings corroborate the main conclusions of postwar Japanese historians to show that Confucian-inspired loyalism in the Tokugawa period posed no danger to Edo bakufu supremacy; indeed, such loyalism ably served to legitimize that supremacy by endorsing the merits of warrior rule over and against the imperial court.[32] Joyce Ackroyd, whose work centers on the historiography of Arai Hakuseki, is less clear-cut. She fully agrees that Hakuseki justified bakufu rule by outlining the history of warrior-courtier relations to show why the imperial court could not but lose power in Japan during medieval times. Yet at the same time, Ackroyd seems drawn to a certain strain of prewar Japanese scholarship when she insists that Hakuseki embraced "reverence for pure imperial rule" and that he firmly regarded the shogun's self-proclaimed status, "King of Japan," to be "one step below" the emperor in Kyoto.[33]

The Postwar Japanese View

As noted above, postwar Japanese historians showed their revulsion for prewar and wartime patriotic excesses by striving to refute the "national essence conception of history." Their scholarly revisionism now reigns unchallenged in the fields of Kokugaku and Mitogaku. But surprisingly enough, few Japanese historians since 1945 have produced detailed critical analyses of Yamagata Daini, his *Ryūshi shinron*, and the Meiwa Incident as these relate to the issue of imperial loyalism. Below, I examine only the most important and influential of these postwar Japanese studies.

One scholar who has examined Daini is Maruyama Masao. He has pioneered studies in—indeed, he established the field of—the history of political ideas in Japan. In a seminal work, Maruyama briefly treats Daini's thought in the context of Ogyū Sorai's conception of "nature and invention."[34] According to Maruyama, Ogyū Sorai repudiated Chu Hsi's claim that ethical norms, sociopolitical institutions, and the existing status order were inherent in nature and hence unchangeable. Instead, Ogyū Sorai claimed that the sage-kings of ancient China had invented these norms and institutions in the form of rites and music for the express purpose of expediting political administration. Sorai further maintained that these sagely created rites and music had fallen to decay in Japan; and so shogunal authorities had to create new institutions based on their present needs: to rule effectively as a central government. Maruyama asserted that Yamagata Daini took over this "logic of invention for practical purposes" from Ogyū Sorai but applied it to the imperial court, not the Edo bakufu.[35]

Maruyama suppresses any hint of prewar-style approbation; but he still sees Yamagata Daini as an imperial loyalist, defines his thought as incompatible with bakufu hegemony over the court, and places him in a tradition of potential revolutionary opposition to the existing order. Maruyama's main aim was to trace the change from "medieval" to "modern" modes of thought in Japan by showing how individuals consciously came to alter their moral or political environment—just as they would alter the physical world—in the light of practically perceived secular needs. He portrays Ogyū Sorai and Yamagata Daini as groping toward the future by freeing themselves from the shackles of medieval fatalism and the dead hand of Chu Hsi scholasticism.

In 1963, historian Hayashi Motoi submitted an influential thesis related to Yamagata Daini. It focused on the socioeconomic dimensions that Maruyama had largely omitted. Hayashi may be considered an early advocate of the "history of the masses" (minshūshi) genre popular in the 1970s and 1980s. His orthodox Marxist analysis argues that Daini and his tract represented nascent bourgeois-democratic opposition to the Tokugawa feudal order.[36] Hayashi hypothesizes that the era 1751 to 1788 brought unprecedented crises to bakufu and daimyo rulers and so marked a watershed in Japanese social history. Unable to bear further exploitation under the oppressive bakufu and daimyo landowning system, rural proletarians were emerging throughout Japan; and they began to launch massive revolts that were far more violent, organized, sustained, and geographically extensive than earlier peasant uprisings. As well, urban-based bourgeois elements joined forces to foment anti-bakufu protodemocratic movements such as the Hōreki and Meiwa Incidents.

According to Hayashi, prewar historians (whatever their motives) had been wrong to accept the rhetoric of these incidents at face value. The loyalist slogans of that day did not signify any groundswell of yearning for direct imperial rule designed to restore Japan's *kokutai*. Instead, those slogans were the only expressions of dissent available to the Japanese masses, who were just beginning their struggle to acquire political and class consciousness. Hence, in Hayashi's eyes, the rhetoric of mid-Tokugawa imperial loyalism was really a means to attain revolutionary ends in the Marxist sense of ending feudal exploitation and advancing to the next stage of history: bourgeois democracy under capitalism. The main points of this radical program in the Hōreki and Meiwa eras, Hayashi argues, found definite if vague articulation in such works as Yamagata Daini's *Ryūshi shinron* and Andō Shōeki's *Shizen shin'ei dō*.[37]

Thus Maruyama Masao sees Yamagata Daini conveying the revolutionary idea that modern individuals create moral norms and sociopolitical institutions based on their own practically perceived needs whereas Hayashi Motoi sees him deftly manipulating loyalist slogans to veil revolutionary Marxist ends. Ichii Saburō, a prominent non-Marxist professor of Western philosophy, synthesizes and further develops these two strands of interpretation in Hegelian fashion. As we shall see, Ichii argues that Yamagata Daini espoused a form of radical populism—based on a democratic respect for the will of the people—that called for leveling all hereditary social classes in order to attain egalitarian ends.

Political considerations were hardly absent in the postwar Japanese debate over Yamagata Daini's loyalism. Despite important ideological and political differences, Maruyama, Hayashi, and Ichii all supported mass protests against renewing and revising the U.S.–Japan Security Pact in 1960. And all three opposed the government's Meiji Centennial of 1968. They saw this campaign as a devious distortion of historical truth designed by a reactionary Satō Eisaku regime bent on glorifying the imperial institution and its role in Japan's "modernization"—a flawed, if not fraudulent, theoretical model supplied by abetting American scholars.[38] This harshly critical spirit is readily apparent in Ichii Saburō's academic and semipopular writings on Yamagata Daini published between 1965 and 1967. That is perhaps most true of Ichii's intensely personal *Meiji ishin no tetsugaku* (A Philosophy of the Meiji Restoration), wherein he searches for a humanist vision of the past in order to champion avowedly presentist aims. Today Ichii's humanist thesis remains the standard postwar Japanese interpretation of Yamagata Daini, the *Ryūshi shinron,* and the Meiwa Incident as these relate to Confucian-inspired Tokugawa imperial loyalism. For that reason, Ichii's *problematik* and findings warrant detailed exposition.[39]

Ichii Saburō is quite candid about his presuppositions and motives for depicting Daini as a revolutionary martyr who inspired the Meiji Restoration to be achieved one century later. Ichii begins his account by declaring two related assumptions: people who lack an acute concern for sociopolitical problems in their own age do not care about history; and those who do care choose certain historical events as especially worth studying in order to gain encouragement for their current endeavors. Ichii then cites the example of fierce antigovernment and anti-American opposition to revision of the U.S.–Japan Security Pact in 1960. Over ten thousand young Japanese men and women risked life and limb in those massive protests, all seemingly for naught, and their poignant sense of failure led them to examine history as a source of inspiration and sustenance.[40] But, Ichii wrote, the young protesters were wrong to feel disillusioned over their setback. In point of historical fact, mass protests twice as big as the 1960 anti–Security Pact demonstrations had taken place in the mid-Tokugawa period when modern technology and the mass media were totally lacking; and those protests went on to win ultimate success despite early failures.

Indeed, radical populist consciousness in modern Japan could be traced directly to Yamagata Daini's *Ryūshi shinron* of 1759 and the Meiwa Incident of 1767; so, one could derive hope and strength by studying these topics. Here were the first steps toward the Meiji Restoration, which Ichii sees as roughly analogous to the Puritan and French Revolutions. None of these three struggles was complete in itself. The British and French peoples had to overcome even more obstacles and setbacks before creating a fully egalitarian society in the nineteenth century; the Japanese people would have to do much the same after 1960. Nevertheless, these three events were the initial phases in a worldwide democratic revolution and so constitute milestones in the history of human progress. In that specific sense, then, certain aspects of Yamagata Daini's Confucianism correspond to "modern thought" as it had developed in Western Europe.[41]

How does Ichii Saburō measure this modern spirit of demo-cratic human progress in contemporary times? And how does he apply such a standard to Yamagata Daini's life and thought? Ichii's central criterion is avowedly normative—namely, "the degree to which individuals are not forced to suffer for things not of their own making." By "things not of their own making," he means "objective sociopolitical factors" such as discrimination imposed by hereditary status under feudalism or restricted access to higher education under capitalism, and "subjective moral fac-tors" such as fatalistic religious or ethical systems designed to convince each individual that artificially imposed limitations are unalterable and must be resigned to.[42] Yamagata Daini, contends Ichii, died in the Meiwa Incident striving to eliminate both sets of factors. According to Ichii, Daini realized that some twenty thou-sand peasants in and around Obata domain, where he was employed, were about to stage an uprising; and he knew it would easily be quashed. Still he struggled to provide guiding principles for turning those seemingly futile popular efforts into a power capable of transforming the existing sociopolitical order later on. Daini knew that peace was normally an ethical good, but vowed that if any government upheld that ethical good at the expense of its people's happiness and livelihood, that regime had to be altered or removed—by force if need be.

Daini also realized the practical difficulties posed by any imme-diate attempt to destroy the bakufu through violent means. So he chose a gradualist approach that relied on the power of the people and on long-term efforts at edification spread over decades or "even a century." That is why he erected monuments to Prince Yamatotakeru and Princess Ototachibana, legendary figures con-nected with the imperial house. Daini's inscriptions on these mon-uments would enlighten commoners about the glories of imperial rule in antiquity, long before the rise of warrior government. Once edified, the people would rise up and overthrow the bakufu some time in the future; yet Daini was sure that event would take "ten years at the very least."[43]

Like brutally oppressive regimes everywhere, the Tokugawa bakufu buttressed its rule with an orthodox morality. Therefore, Yamagata Daini had to devise a counterideology of popular well-being to justify violent revolution. Ichii contends that Daini did this by shrewdly distorting two normative conventions—usually employed by feudal rulers to legitimize their authority—in seditious ways. One of these was the idealized pre-Tokugawa system of a warrior-peasantry *(nōhei)* living on the land; the other was Mencius' classical concept of "deposing" *(hōbatsu)* evil rulers.

Earlier Confucian reformers had advocated reviving the pre-Tokugawa system of a nondifferentiated warrior-peasantry by returning daimyo and samurai from castle towns to the countryside. But the aim was to wean warriors from consumption in the marketplace, boost their economic self-sufficiency, and so buttress their supremacy over peasants under the established order. Yamagata Daini's idea worked in the opposite direction: lower taxes and leave peasants with the time and resources to become literate, purchase arms, and train in their use. He did not advocate this measure because it existed in antiquity. He advocated it because a peasant militia logically precluded the hereditary privileges then enjoyed by daimyo and samurai rulers—rooted as these were in their monopoly over the means of violence in society. As well, Daini believed that peasant militia could eventually be used to overthrow the bakufu. And, according to Ichii, Daini's revolutionary idea for arming commoners later inspired the *kiheitai*: mixed brigades of peasants and low-ranking samurai that spearheaded Chōshū's restoration army.

Likewise, earlier Confucian thinkers in the Edo period had praised Mencius' idea of "deposing" *(hōbatsu)* evil rulers through violent means. But they did so to legitimize Tokugawa hegemony over and against other daimyo houses. Yamagata Daini applied that classical idea in a radically new fashion: to justify popular revolution against the Edo bakufu in the emperor's name. But Ichii insists that Daini saw nothing valuable in imperial rule as such; it was good only for having been more benevolent to the common people in antiquity compared with warrior regimes in later ages.[44]

Thus, Ichii maintains, Yamagata Daini's imperial loyalism shared little with that of Yamazaki Ansai or the Kokugaku and Mitogaku scholars. They steeped themselves in irrational ethnocentric biases to argue that the emperor was truly a descendant of the Sun Goddess whose unbroken dynastic line proved Japanese moral eminence in the world. Daini had studied both the Yamazaki Ansai and Ogyū Sorai schools, but he owed far more to Sorai's rationalism and universalism than to Ansai's nativism. In the *Ryūshi shinron,* Daini refers to divine Japanese emperors only once; and that, by Ichii's reckoning, shows him to be free of nativist prejudice. What is more, Daini extolls Japan's ancient dynasty because its rule by civil officials recruited for ability was superior to rule by a latter-day military aristocracy who enjoyed privilege commensurate with pedigree. Daini was especially ahead of his time in claiming that all men are born equal and that the only valid status rankings in society are those that derive from occupations and government offices based on individual merit.[45]

In sum, Ichii portrays Yamagata Daini as a revolutionary ideologue, humanist visionary, and social leveler whose brand of imperial loyalism was unlike that found in other Tokugawa schools. Daini was liberal, cosmopolitan, and progressive—not bigoted, xenophobic, and reactionary. His popular egalitarianism and love of emperor would be conveyed to Yoshida Shōin (1830–1859) in the 1850s by the hearing-and-speech-impaired itinerant priest Utsunomiya Mokurin (1824–1897). And those ideals would in turn inspire Shōin's students such as Kusaka Genzui (1840–1864) to rebel against the Tokugawa regime and overthrow it. Daini advanced pro-court, anti-bakufu arguments in the genuine belief that emperors had dispensed virtuous government in high antiquity. Moreover, he believed, restoring that ancient system of civil rule based on merit would abolish the discrimination based on bloodline and lineage that he so detested in his own day.

Ichii Saburō's works enjoyed considerable influence among Japanese intellectuals and activists in the 1960s and 1970s. For example, the left-wing social critic and outspoken Vietnam War protester Oda Makoto enthusiastically cited Ichii's definition of human progress in history to support his own "ethics and logic of revolutionary world renewal" *(yonaoshi)* in 1971. Based in part on Ichii's work, Oda reinterpreted this Tokugawa-era concept of revolutionary social upheaval and proposed it as an alternative to the sterile and inhuman Marxist-Leninist theories then current among student radicals.[46] On a more popular level, the people of Yamagata Daini's native Yamanashi prefecture (formerly Kai province) have drawn on Ichii Saburō's findings to idolize their local son as a Tokugawa harbinger of freedom, democracy, and social equality. Yamanashi schoolchildren sing the praises of Daini and his famous tract in no uncertain terms:

> Reading *Master Ryū's New Thesis*,
> we learn that all men are equal.
> There should be no discrimination of noble or base
> due to the occupational class in which one is born,
> whether samurai, peasant, artisan, or merchant.
> Never wavering in his democratic ideas,
> he cried, "Freedom can never be violated!"[47]

Toward a New View

Above, I have briefly surveyed the salient prewar and postwar interpretations of Yamagata Daini and his thought, including views of prominent Japanese scholars whose findings are unavailable in English. The overall consensus is that the *Ryūshi shinron* was a subversive loyalist tract whose author staunchly advocated destroying the Tokugawa military regime one century too soon and therefore suffered execution at its hands. But within that general consensus, scholarly opinion is divided on at least three crucial issues.

First, prewar and postwar Japanese and Western historians dispute whether Daini was just a thinker or an activist too—that is, did he simply call for an armed rebellion against Edo or actually plot to carry one out? Second, historians debate whether Daini's imperial loyalism was inspired by the Ansai, Sorai, or Kokugaku schools. Third, and above all, they disagree over why Daini sought to end Tokugawa rule. *Kōkoku shikan* adherents, who usually quote from Section I of the *Ryūshi shinron*, contend that Daini raged indignant over warrior usurpation of imperial prerogatives, that he truly revered the emperor in Kyoto, and that he longed to remake the emperor into the ruler of Japan in fact as well as name. Postwar humanist scholars, who usually cite his idea of deposing evil rulers found in Sections XII and XIII of the *Ryūshi shinron*, maintain that Daini shrewdly exploited loyalist rhetoric and the imperial symbol to mask democratic goals far in advance of his time. In other words, Daini's imperial loyalism was not intended to restore imperial rule per se; it was designed to implement a modern form of popular egalitarianism by leveling the Tokugawa feudal class hierarchy.

Apart from Tetsuo Najita's pioneering article in 1971, Western historians have produced no in-depth studies of Yamagata Daini despite his importance as a Tokugawa thinker. And, as we have seen, prewar and postwar Japanese historians alike have tended to search for something positive in Daini's life and thought—something to treasure as a cultural legacy and draw inspiration from in their current-day struggles. That quest has perforce caused Japanese historians to judge Yamagata Daini by the values and perceived needs of the era in which they themselves lived. Perhaps nothing better reflects this prewar-to-postwar shift in Japanese interpretation than the chameleonlike change in image achieved by Daini's shrine, the Yamagata *jinja,* located in the town of Ryūō near Kōfu city in Yamanashi prefecture.

Daini had received the posthumous honor of senior fourth rank from the imperial court in 1891, and prominent local leaders soon launched a campaign to gain government support for a Shinto shrine dedicated to him. The shrine was finally constructed between 1921 and 1928 at a cost of 38,380 yen, or about seventy years' wages for an average worker at the time.[48] It soon became a mecca for patriots and right-wing zealots of all stripes; in 1924, it even boasted a visit by Crown Prince Hirohito, then acting emperor. Like state Shinto shrines all over Japan, the Yamagata *jinja* sponsored youth rallies to send local recruits off to the front and organized lantern parades to celebrate Japanese victories in battle. But Occupation officials stripped the Yamagata *jinja* of state funding after the war, and private patronage declined owing to popular enthusiasm for democracy—plus a newfound revulsion with militaristic emperor-centered ultranationalism. In a bid to survive, shrine priests shed its now-discredited pre-1945 image and recast their patron deity as a rival to Tenjin-sama, or Sugawara no Michizane, the traditional god of learning in Japan. So, whereas prewar and wartime worshipers tossed coins into shrine coffers to pray for Imperial Army triumphs, postwar worshipers do so to pray for high marks in school or success in university entrance examinations.

In other words, the image of Yamagata Daini gained from secondary Japanese scholarship suffers from pendulumlike swings in interpretation, and these in turn reflect fundamental changes in central Japanese values and beliefs. Clearly we need to achieve a more historically grounded understanding of Daini's life, his role in the Meiwa Incident, his thought as revealed in the *Ryūshi shinron,* and the significance that all of these have for the history of Japanese political thought.

Virtually all historians assume that the 1758 Hōreki and 1767 Meiwa Incidents were inseparably linked; most of them argue that Takenouchi Shikibu, Fujii Umon, and Yamagata Daini were cohorts in sedition who provoked a coordinated bakufu retaliation. The Edo regime did punish them in 1767. But beyond that, connections between these three men and two events are far from crystal clear. All accounts hold that Fujii Umon served as the chief liaison responsible for establishing and maintaining contact between Yamagata Daini, who was in Edo, and Takenouchi Shikibu, who was then in exile in Ise. Thus Fujii is reputed to be the key agent linking the two incidents. But in truth his identity is highly suspect; for although Fujii himself claimed to be Takenouchi's trusted aide, that relationship cannot be substantiated by other extant sources. Takenouchi Shikibu and Yamagata Daini are known for sure to have met only once—when they erected a monument to Yamatotakeru in 1763—and that was *before* Fujii Umon came to study with Daini. It is also true that Takenouchi Shikibu was arraigned and punished in Kyoto in the 1758 Hōreki Incident; but that was not because Edo officials knew of his alleged activities and were bent on crushing them from the start. Instead, conservative high-ranking nobles in Kyoto informed on him; and in fact their tattling owed more to factional court squabbles than to a genuine fear that heterodox thought would incur bakufu wrath. As we shall see, the Meiwa Incident too was instigated by informers who, in effect, forced Edo bakufu officials to take punitive action.

These considerations lead me to conclude that Takenouchi Shikibu and Yamagata Daini did meet at least once before the Meiwa Incident of 1867. But it is highly implausible that they planned or joined any full-blown conspiracy to subvert and overthrow Tokugawa rule. Hence there could be no concerted, ideologically motivated bakufu crackdown against them. And what is more, the onus of proof should fall on those historians who claim the opposite. Even if not totally unconnected, the Hōreki and Meiwa Incidents took place nine years apart in Kyoto and in Edo. As such, the two historical events may be considered as separate and need not be treated in tandem. My aims in the present study stem from that conviction. These aims are threefold: to explain Yamagata Daini's role in the Meiwa Incident, to show what the *Ryūshi shinron* reveals about his political thought, and to place that thought within an alternative tradition of Japanese loyalist thinking.

On these issues I submit the following contentions. First, Yamagata Daini was in fact harshly critical of bakufu governments dating from 1185, including the Tokugawa. So if we grant the nondemocratic and authoritarian premise—common in premodern non-Western societies—that gratuitous criticism of a regime in power warrants the death sentence, then Edo leaders had ample grounds for executing Daini. But this does not make him a "revolutionary" loyalist or a "restorationist" in the sense of wishing to end all forms of warrior rule and domain ownership in order to restore the emperor and court to ruling power. Second, in viewing the imperial court as a "fallen dynasty" barely surviving from the past, and also in formulating sociopolitical reforms for his own day, Yamagata Daini followed the Ogyū Sorai school far more than either the Yamazaki Ansai or the Kokugaku schools. And, precisely because of this allegiance to certain tenets in Sorai Learning, Daini's proposed reforms called for strengthening and perpetuating—not ending—socioeconomic discrimination based on hereditary class privilege under the existing political order. Third, Yamagata Daini held two key implicit assumptions that can only be flushed out through close textual and contextual analysis of the *Ryūshi shinron*. These two assumptions are that the imperial house would reign forever but emperors were not fit to rule, and that emperors therefore should emulate Chinese exemplars by delegating power to loyal state ministers—the shogun and daimyo—who in turn would seek out harsh criticism and enlightened counsel from scholar-advisors such as Master Ryū. Fourth, and above all, Daini's brand of loyalism lies in the tradition of "imperial assistance" that was inspired by the Fujiwara regents and articulated in medieval histories such as Jien's *Gukan-*

shō and Kitabatake Chikafusa's *Jinnō shōtōki*—works which extolled the principle of ministerial autonomy exercised on behalf of figurehead emperors. The main historical significance of Yamagata Daini's political thought lies here, not in his anti-bakufu criticism or his putative restorationist aims.

CHAPTER 2

Life, Letters, and Illusion

Like most prominent Japanese historical figures, Yamagata Daini assumed several names during his lifetime. Born Yamagata Masasada in 1725, he went by the surname Murase between 1745 and 1751 while serving as a bakufu police constable in Kōfu. Later he abandoned Masasada sometime in the mid-1760s when he acquired the imperial court title "Governor-General of the Thirty-Three Eastern Provinces."[1] Only then—several years after composing the *Ryūshi shinron*—did he begin to call himself "Daini," an office title in the ancient Ritsu-Ryō government. In fact, while he was alive his best-known nom de plume was "Yamagata Masasada." Nevertheless, "Daini" is how he comes down to us in history. So, for reasons of convenience and easy identification, I refer to him by that name throughout this introduction. But I also employ the literary device of elegant variation on occasion to call him "Master Ryū," author of the *Ryūshi shinron*.

Biographical Background

The Yamagatas were medieval warrior chieftains in Kai province, now Yamanashi prefecture, where they served as hereditary retainers to the powerful Takeda.[2] The Yamagata family suffered extinction in the 1450s, but a certain Sakatomi Masakage restored it in the Eiroku era (1558–1569). He died in the 1575 Battle of Nagashino, leaving two natural sons and one adopted son named Tarōzaemon, who hailed from the Nozawa family in Shinano province. As Genji, the Nozawa boasted descent from Emperor Seiwa (r. 858–876), a crucially important consideration in status-conscious Japanese society. Nozawa Tarōzaemon settled in Shinohara village in the Koma district of Kai. Under his great-grandson, Sawaemon, the Nozawa prospered as a wealthy peasant household *(gōnō),* but they remained strongly conscious of their noble lineage. Sawaemon reassumed the Yamagata surname and adopted a promising village lad named Yamasaburō, who in turn had three sons, Masaki, Masasada (Daini), and Bumon.

In the Hōei era (1704–1710), Yamasaburō purchased the bakufu post of police constable *(yoriki)* held by a certain Murase family who had fallen on hard times. He moved to the castle town of Kōfu in order to take up this position, which carried an income of eighty *koku,* and he assumed the name Murase Kiyozaemon Tamenobu. When he died in 1738, his eldest son Masaki inherited the post as Murase Kiyozaemon Tamekiyo. Masaki fell ill and relinquished the post in 1745 to Masasada (Daini), who then became Police Constable Murase Gunji. His official duties were light, requiring service only every fifth day, so Daini had much spare time in which to study medicine or to lecture on military science and the Confucian classics.

This secure life as a petty bakufu official ended in 1750, when Daini's younger brother Bumon allegedly killed a peasant and fled the scene of his crime. Daini was ordered to house confinement, and six months later, in 1751, he was stripped of his post and Murase surname. According to one primary source, this was because he and Masaki were suspected of having helped Bumon escape.[3] In any case, Murase Gunji went back to being Yamagata Masasada in 1751; and under that name, Daini left Kōfu to practice medicine in the Yotsuya district of Edo. Life there was miserably poor, but his fortunes improved three years later. In late 1754, Daini became a retainer of Ōoka Tadamitsu, who had just been appointed junior councillor under Shogun Ieshige. This branch of the Ōoka family was of low rank and income, a mere three hundred *koku,* and had few hereditary retainers. But owing to Ieshige's favor, Ōoka Tadamitsu found himself the most powerful man in Edo, enjoying a 25,000-*koku* income. So he suddenly needed a large retinue of housemen appropriate to his new status.

It is unclear why Ōoka Tadamitsu employed Yamagata Daini. Some historians claim it was because he prized Daini's rich knowledge of court ceremonial. In 1754, the year of Tadamitsu's ascendance, Shogun Ieshige's heir apparent, known to us as Ieharu, married the daughter of a prominent court noble; so Tadamitsu was supposedly drawn to Daini's expertise in matters of court ritual.[4] But that explanation is not credible. Yamagata Daini hardly received grand treatment to begin with. His income of seven man-rations, or about 12.6 *koku,* was roughly one-sixth of what he had enjoyed as a police constable in Kōfu. Moreover, he received the post of intendant at Katsuura, far from Edo Castle where the ceremonies took place. One and a half years later, in mid-1756, Yamagata Daini was suddenly transferred to Ōoka Tadamitsu's Edo mansion in Tokiwabashi, where he served as physician and Confucian teacher until 1760. Again, we do not know why Tadamitsu chose him for this post.

Service under the Ōoka was of crucial importance for Daini. He gained further experience in local policing and administration at Katsuura, and Tadamitsu's salary supported him while he wrote the *Ryūshi shinron.* Daini also learned the sordid details of political corruption firsthand at Tokiwabashi, where Tadamitsu was known as "the court rank and title broker" whose underlings solicited bribes openly.[5] Thus Ōoka Tadamitsu no doubt was the model for the influence-peddling high officials described in Sections IV and XI of the *Ryūshi shinron.* Some prewar historians assert that Daini learned of the Hōreki Incident and communicated with Takenouchi Shikibu in Kyoto at this time.[6] But that claim cannot be substantiated by reference to the surviving sources.

In any case, Yamagata Daini's service with the Ōoka ended when Tadamitsu died in 1760, one year after the *Ryūshi shinron* was completed. Daini seems to have had few regrets about leave-taking. He wrote to a friend that it was "the mistake of my life to accept this trifling post" and that he was grieved for having prospered from it.[7] Daini then moved to Nagasawachō in Edo's Hatchōbori district, where licensed physicians had lived since Genroku times. There he rented a home that doubled as a clinic and private academy. By coincidence, this house stood on the same lot as Kurizaki Michiari's (1660–1716), the physician who tended the wounds inflicted on Kira Yoshinaka by Asano Naganori, the aggrieved daimyo of Akō, in 1702.

Like many scholars of brilliance, Yamagata Daini was a bit eccentric. He flouted social conventions in dress and lifestyle, and it appears that his brash nonconformity did nothing to endear him to the political authorities.[8] Yet Daini was no longer a destitute physician practicing among the poor. His scholarly reputation was at its height, and he easily attracted students. They included physicians, samurai from many domains, and the servants of court nobles. It is worth noting, however, that commoners seem to have been few in number. One source lists a figure of three thousand students, although that number is probably inflated.[9] In this way, Daini came to practice medicine at his private clinic and school in Hatchōbori-Nagasawachō, where he taught military science, the Chinese classics, and yin-yang divining. He might well have lived out his remaining days uneventfully as a physician, scholar, and teacher. But events in the winter of 1766–1767 conspired to implicate him in the so-called Meiwa Incident that led to his execution.

The Meiwa Incident

There are few primary documents from which to reconstruct this incident because the bakufu ordered most official records burnt, and persons involved with Daini seem to have destroyed private papers for fear of incrimination. As well, there are no extant records in Obata that relate to the affair. Transcripts of the bakufu verdicts survive and are reliable, but other sources must be used with extreme caution. The *Bengiroku* and *Kaien yawa*, for example, are hearsay accounts written in 1795, twenty-eight years after Daini's execution and some thirty or more years after the events they purport to describe. Their author, Gamō Kumpei (1768–1813), was a sometime student of Mitogaku who is famous for his pro-court sentiments, and that bias is reflected in his documents. Still, we cannot reject Gamō's accounts offhand. Flawed as these are, they are still the best primary sources available that deal specifically with the Meiwa Incident in detail. Fictional contemporaneous accounts of the Meiwa Incident—such as the anonymous *Meiwa fudoki* or its variant manuscripts—definitely should not be used. But, as historian Yokoyama Seiji shows, the Meiji-era writer Fukuchi Gen'ichirō (1841–1906) based his 1892 short story *Yamagata Daini* on such flawed sources; and many later historians, Ichii Saburō included, have followed Fukuchi uncritically on numerous key points.[10] As a result, the incident and Daini's role in it are often recounted in garbled form.

Although their true nature can never be fully ascertained, the events can be related in broad outline as follows.

The Meiwa Incident was actually two separate affairs that involved Yamagata Daini between late 1764 and 11/1767: a power struggle in Obata domain and a supposed *rōnin* plot to rebel against the Edo bakufu. In VII/1764, Oda Nobuhide was serving as a guardian for his son Nobukuni, whom he had installed as Obata's new daimyo. Nobukuni knew Daini from Tokiwabashi days and made the mistake of introducing him to domain officials stationed in Edo. Contrary to many accounts, Yamagata Daini never visited Obata domain itself, nor did he ever receive any kind of salary from it. But some of his Confucian political ideals did impress a reform-minded domain elder *(karō)* named Yoshida Gemba, who was stationed in Edo. Daini believed, for example, that one key to sociopolitical and economic reform was revealed in the *Book of Changes* passage: "Take away from the ruler above and add to the people below" by cutting taxes. It seems that Yoshida Gemba often petitioned Oda Nobukuni to implement this principle in domain government under Daini's influence. According to Gamō Kumpei: "Gemba was very earnest about administration and about caring for the people's needs. . . . He believed that Obata's twenty thousand *koku* revenue should be reduced so that peasants would retain ten thousand." Gamō's account of Yoshida's petition continues: "Use those savings to let the peasants study and practice military arts in their spare time. . . . That will make them identical to the samurai who lived on the land in olden times."[11]

Ichii Saburō cites this source, attributes Yoshida Gemba's idea about arming peasants to the *Ryūshi shinron,* and argues that it reveals the revolutionary character of Yamagata Daini's thought.[12] But nothing in the *Ryūshi shinron* suggests that Daini ever inspired such a proposal; and if Yoshida actually did advance it, Obata domain authorities were quite right to reject it as unworkable. In fact, Edo leaders would soon authorize the very opposite. Before 1769, the bakufu had always forbidden the use of "missiles," including firearms, to quash peasant uprisings. But in that year it expressly permitted daimyo throughout Japan to use this category of weapons against commoners when the need arose.[13]

By chance, nearby domains such as Takasaki witnessed large-scale peasant uprisings from XII/1764 to I/1765. Yamagata Daini had nothing to do with these revolts, sparked by commoner opposition to transport corvées.[14] But the coincidence must have worried Obata leaders and inclined them toward caution. Obata retainers on duty in Edo attended Daini's school; and that alarmed a high domain official named Makita Giemon, who sternly warned Yoshida Gemba to clamp down on such activities. Yoshida ignored the warning. Practical-minded domain leaders such as Makita knew it would be impossible to cut taxes by as much as fifty percent. They wished to shield Obata samurai, to say nothing of the new daimyo, from such vacuous political theorizing. Thus Obata domain administrators were deeply hostile toward both Yoshida Gemba's Confucian-inspired reforms and Yamagata Daini's attempts to influence domain government from Edo.

By IX/1766, political intrigue and a family feud had catalyzed that hostility into an "incident." On the one hand, Oda Nobuhide, father of the new daimyo, schemed to replace his rival Yoshida Gemba with a loyal minion in order to monopolize power in Obata. On the other hand, a petty official named Matsubara Gundayū nursed a grudge toward Gemba for having dismissed a relative on graft charges. Led by Oda Nobuhide and Matsubara Gundayū, high domain leaders placed Yoshida Gemba under arrest in IX/1766 and persuaded him to spurn any more overtures from Daini. Therefore, whatever influence Yamagata Daini may have had in Obata lasted two years at the very most— from late 1764 to IX/1766. The Meiwa Incident might have ended then and there as a matter strictly internal to Obata domain; and, in truth, bakufu leaders still knew nothing of it or Daini's part in it.

Sometime in 1764 or 1765, however, a garrulous character from Kyoto named Fujii Umon had arrived in Edo and asked to enroll at Yamagata Daini's school in Hatchōbori-Nagasawachō. Within a short span of one or two years, Fujii had become a trusted disciple. Gamō Kumpei depicts him as "a dissolute rogue. . . . He was neither a civil nor a military official, but claimed renown as a *waka* poet."[15] Fujii Umon does not seem to have been close to Takenouchi Shikibu, and his exact role, if any, in the 1758 Hōreki Incident is unknown.[16] In any case, Fujii came to worship his new mentor. He interpreted Daini's ideas all too freely and was none too careful about keeping these to himself.

Toward the end of 1766, while Yoshida Gemba was under arrest in Obata, the unruly Fujii picked a quarrel with a *rōnin* named Momonoi Kyūma ("Heima" in some sources) at a drinking establishment in the Ryōgoku district of Edo. After imbibing a bit too much at this party, Fujii apparently launched a tirade about revering the emperor and about the evils of Edo bakufu rule. These were views that Momonoi did not particularly cherish, and they were expressed in a rather loutish manner. Apart from such verbal abuse, it seems that Fujii quarreled with Momonoi over the affections of a lady named Komiyo and decidedly got the better of it.[17] So, with his samurai honor and male ego grievously hurt, Momonoi Kyūma vowed revenge in league with three disgruntled students from Daini's school. These four malcontents drew up a list of Daini's prominent confidants, including Obata retainers and officials, and informed the bakufu that Yamagata Daini and Fujii Umon were about to lead them all in an armed uprising.

Bakufu authorities proceeded to arraign a total of forty persons beginning in II/1767. Clearly this was a small-scale affair compared with either the Akō *(Chūshingura)* Incident of 1702–1703 or the Ōshio Heihachirō Rebellion of 1837 after which seven hundred and fifty men were punished.[18] Sixteen of the forty individuals were simple witnesses let go after questioning, and four others died or escaped before sentencing. The other twenty persons break down as follows: the four informers, the twelve Obata suspects, Yamagata Daini, his older brother Masaki (alias Ichirō-zaemon, the peasant), Fujii Umon, and Takenouchi Shikibu.[19] Verdicts were delivered six months later, in VIII/1767. Momonoi and the three other informers were found guilty of laying false and malicious charges. They were bound and put on public display for three days before being exiled to distant areas. Four of the twelve Obata suspects were pardoned; eight were ordered into exile or forced to retire under house arrest; and, as further punishment, the Oda lost their domain and suffered relocation to the remote and undeveloped province of Dewa. Yoshida Gemba was among the four pardoned, probably because he testified to having cut ties with Daini several months before the latter's arrest. Takenouchi

Shikibu and Daini's older brother Yamagata Masaki received sentences of remote exile; Shikibu died en route, perhaps from unnatural causes or owing to illness brought on by the rigorous journey.

Yamagata Daini and Fujii Umon both succumbed to the executioner's blade; and Umon suffered the further indignity of having his severed head placed on public display. However, the two men had *not* been found guilty as charged. To Umon the bakufu explicitly admitted: "Of course, this does not constitute rebellion."[20] And in a separate verdict to Takenouchi Shikibu, it expressly declared: "Neither Daini nor Umon was involved in treason *(hangyaku).*"[21] Instead, Yamagata Daini and Fujii Umon were pronounced guilty of "extreme disrespect and the utmost insolence" *(fukei no itari, futodoki shigoku),*[22] or what in modern Japanese is called "lese majesty" *(fukeizai).*

What did that mean specifically? In Yamagata Daini's case, the verdict read:

[1] You teach your disciples and comrades that, in making their way through life or pursuing their arts, they should always think of how to turn insurrections or other incidents to their advantage and so achieve success. This shows that you look with favor on revolt.

[2] You paraded your knowledge of the weaponry and number of defenders stationed at Kōfu Castle.

[3] You cited ancient sources [the *Shih chi*] to say that "a comet entering Scorpio is an omen of armed revolt." And later you said that "peasants in Kōzuke [Obata] created a disturbance [in late 1764]; this shows the omen to be true."

[4] You have said, among other things, that imperial tours of the provinces no longer take place today and that the emperor is a virtual prisoner.

[5] You wrote in a notebook *(sōshi)* that the condition of court nobles today is contrary to what it was in antiquity.

[6] On the pretext of clarifying topography in talks on military science, you mentioned specific areas of strategic importance in the realm such as Kōfu. All of this shows extreme disrespect and the utmost insolence. Hence you are sentenced to death.[23]

The bakufu's verdict to Fujii Umon read:

[1] You stated that Daini's lectures on military science, using Kōfu as an example, were lucid and penetrating.

[2] [Same as for Daini.]

[3] You stated that although Kōfu is well fortified, it would fall if attacked in the way Takeda Katsuyori did [at Takatenjin Castle in 1574].

[4] You said it is best to use flaming arrows with the wind at one's back, and that southwesterly winds warrant shooting these from the direction of Shinagawa [to attack Edo].

[5] Pretending to talk about Kōfu, you said the defenses of Edo Castle were weak on the west and that therefore you would attack its strongly fortified eastern side.

[6] Of course, this does *not* constitute revolt. But owing to your high regard for Yamagata Daini, you came to discuss military science and grew increasingly vehement in debating strategy. Thus you were transformed into a tactician yourself and came to say irreverent things. All of this shows extreme disrespect and the utmost insolence. Hence you are sentenced to death and your head will be placed on public display.[24]

A Rebel Pure and Simple

The Edo populace was barred from these secret bakufu trials, and news of their proceedings leaked out only piecemeal in vague terms. Therefore, at the time of the incident in 1767 and immediately after, the general population formed an image of Yamagata Daini based solely on rumor and hearsay. The public viewed him as a hateful and dangerous rebel leader, no different from similar figures in recent history. This early image of Daini, though egregiously wrong, nevertheless stuck; and the stigma attached to his name would not be shed until halfway through the next century.

From an early stage in the trial proceedings, Edo townsmen learned by word of mouth that charges of rebellion had been laid against Yamagata Daini and Fujii Umon, and knowledge of these allegations soon spread beyond the city's immediate environs. This fact is substantiated by a diary entry dated IV/1767. It was made by a wealthy peasant named Hosaka, who had just returned home to Akao village in Kai province, not far from Daini's native village of Shinohara, after a trip to Edo. Hosaka wrote: "Rumor there [Edo] has it that [Daini] is a rebel *(muhonnin)* who delivered lectures on how to attack Edo by disguising his plan as scholarly commentaries on the military classics."[25] Note, however, that

Hosaka did not mention the fourth and fifth points in the bakufu's verdict to Daini, points that can be construed as pro-court in nature. This shows that Hosaka probably was unaware of them.

As in the *Chūshingura* Incident involving the forty-seven Akō retainers six decades before, Edo leaders chose cruelty over clemency when their prestige and authority were on the line. This time the public showed little sympathy for those convicted. One trenchant contemporary account reads: "Yamagata's corpse was dumped in the street. He had friends and students, but no one showed any concern because he was now called a rebel and a traitor."[26] And the sardonic author of a little ditty that appeared at the time callously punned:

> Yamagata bungled his military science;
> and Daini had his precious *(daini, daiji)*
> little head lopped off.[27]

Yamagata Masaki and three faithful students bribed a bakufu guard into surrendering Daini's corpse. The four held a proper funeral and erected grave markers to Daini in cemeteries in Kai, Hitachi, and Edo; but they had to do so secretly owing to intense public hostility.[28]

It is in this context, then, that Yamagata Daini's famous last poem should be interpreted. Feared and detested as a menace to society for his alleged crime of rebellion, Daini likened himself to the bright moon on an overcast night, "waiting in earnest for the clouds [of slander] to clear away,"[29] so that his true intentions, whatever those might be, could shine through. Such exoneration of his maligned character was not soon coming. In 1768, Warashina Shōhaku, an official in far-off Yonezawa domain, condemned Daini as the ringleader of one in a series of the recent "uprisings and conspiracies" which threatened the peace and security that Tokugawa rule had conferred on the realm.[30]

Thus, several primary sources dated within one year of Daini's execution contain bitter denunciations of him. But none gives any indication that the general public identified him as being "loyalist" in the sense of wanting to restore the emperor and court to power. The bakufu physician and Dutch Studies expert Sugita Gempaku, who enjoyed privileged access to classified information two decades later, was still unable to uncover details about the Meiwa Incident. But in his *Nochimigusa* of 1787, Sugita was exceptional in citing Daini as having been acquitted:

> Another disturbance occurred in the spring of 1767. I note with fear and trembling toward the shogun that although the world enjoys peace and order, Yamagata Daini and Fujii Umon plotted revolt to eliminate the bakufu—or so it was divulged to shogunal authorities. . . . The bakufu arraigned all those involved, whether or not guilty of anything, but thorough investigations produced no incriminating evidence. Nevertheless, Daini was beheaded and Umon's head was put on public display. . . . Such an incident had been unheard of since Yui Shōsetsu and Marubashi Chūya [in 1651].[31]

Here, as well, we find no trace of "loyalist" leanings attributed to Daini.

Quite to the contrary, Motoori Norinaga displayed total revulsion for Yamagata Daini two years later in 1789. At that time, Hagiwara Motoe, a trusted disciple from Daini's native Kai province, asked his teacher to draft an inscription for the monument dedicated to Yamatotakeru—a monument that Daini and his followers had erected at Sakaori twenty-six years before. To this request Motoori retorted:

> You showed me a copy of the classical Chinese inscription to this monument, and I see that it was composed by a certain "Yamagata Masasada." Would that by any chance be Yamagata *Daini?* . . . If so, I would be horrified to have my own inscription placed next to his, and I would refuse to write one.[32]

In this way, the premier Kokugaku scholar in Tokugawa Japan vehemently distanced himself from Yamagata Daini. We can be sure that Motoori Norinaga would have felt more than a bit annoyed at those latter-day scholars—both Japanese and Western—who equated or associated Daini's "loyalism" with his own. But equally important, in this letter written within a quarter-century of the Meiwa Incident, Motoori shows that he did not imagine Daini to be harboring restorationist designs. Rather, Motoori found him loathsome for being a run-of-the-mill insurrectionist, nothing more, nothing less.

By way of summation, certain important inferences can be

drawn from these eighteenth-century primary sources. First, Yamagata Daini's contemporaries greeted news of his alleged plot with repugnance and derision, not the admiration shown to the forty-seven Akō retainers in 1703. Nor did Tokugawa commoners worship Daini as a "world savior" in the way they would deify Ōshio Heihachirō after his revolt on behalf of the Osaka poor in 1837. Second, Daini was instead likened to Yui Shōsetsu and Marubashi Chūya—those seventeenth-century archvillains who would plunge society back into the treachery, civil war, and mass suffering of medieval times. Third, none of these three detested rebel leaders was reputed to harbor pro-imperial, as opposed to just anti-Tokugawa, sentiments.

It is true that one anonymous eighteenth-century fictional account did ascribe pro-imperial sentiments to Yamagata Daini. The author of the 1774 *Meiwa fudoki* gave free rein to fancy by embellishing his saga with a scene in which Daini urged the emperor in Kyoto to "raise an imperial army, depose the eastern barbarians, and rule from the imperial court as in antiquity."[33] (In fact Daini never traveled to Kyoto at the time in question.) The *Meiwa fudoki* did not gain wide currency, however, even allowing for a few variant texts. Thus its image of Yamagata Daini never took hold among the general public. Instead, records left by Hosaka the Kai peasant, Warashina Shōhaku in Yonezawa, Sugita Gempaku in Edo, and Motoori Norinaga in Matsuzaka, as well as other contemporaneous sources cited above, all show otherwise. These documents clearly demonstrate that Yamagata Daini was popularly perceived in the eighteenth century to be a common, ordinary rebel—one who boasted no loyalist or restorationist aspirations.

Even that image was in truth unfounded. Bakufu prosecutors admitted to the defendants that no evidence had been found to sustain an indictment of treason or insurrection. The best that Edo authorities could do was pronounce that Yamagata and Fujii had "looked with favor on revolt" *(heiran)*. To borrow a collo-quial Japanese expression, the bakufu itself did not "poke the thicket to drive these snakes out into the open *(yabuhebi)*."[34] It would rather have left them alone—safely away from public pur-view—by turning a blind eye. And that passivity stands in marked contrast to Ii Naosuke's bakufu regime of the Ansei era ninety years later. But after Momonoi Kyūma and the informers did lay charges of plotting an insurrection—thus feeding rumor mills throughout Edo—the bakufu had to mete out maximum sentences as if the allegations were true. Otherwise its image of omnipotence and its awe-inspiring majesty *(go-ikō)* would be grievously impaired. Moreover, because detailed information on the Meiwa Incident was never declassifed and made publicly known, few contemporaries realized that the Edo bakufu had in truth acquitted Daini and Umon of treason and executed them for lese majesty.

Some historians hold that bakufu authorities purposely rendered a verdict of "not guilty" in order to skirt politically damaging implications. As this argument runs, it would be highly dangerous to admit that pro-imperial sentiment had developed to the point of launching an anti-bakufu insurrection as early as the Hōreki and Meiwa eras—even by a ragtag band of *rōnin* on this small scale. Therefore, Edo bakufu leaders wanted to declare its ringleaders innocent and play down the baleful significance of this whole affair. However, this hypothesis of a bakufu tactical cover-up is factually flawed, in addition to being contrived. First of all, it mistakenly assumes that people at the time commonly imputed restorationist aims to Daini and Umon. Second, it ignores the simple truth that their trials were held in secret. Therefore, the bakufu's calculated denial of their putative restorationist aims went unpublicized and so could not have the desired effect.

Viewed in the context of that era and from the standpoint of bakufu strategic interests, Momonoi Kyūma and his henchmen—not Yamagata Daini and Fujii Umon—were the real troublemakers. By laying an absurd charge that leaked out in highly problematic fashion, Momonoi forced Edo leaders to crack down in a case they would rather have dismissed. The general public miscast Daini and Umon in the role of villainous rebels—but not that of imperial loyalists—who flouted bakufu authority and endangered the social order. Bakufu leaders could not correct this misrepresentation, so they chose the only course available to minimize its damage.

But even if Momonoi's charge of plotting an armed insurrection had been grounded in fact, an important nonsequitur must be reiterated: to be anti-Tokugawa does not ipso facto mean one is also pro-emperor and restorationist. So, launching an insurrection against a certain bakufu—in this case the Tokugawa—is not necessarily the same as repudiating warrior rule and daimyo ownership of domains in order to restore imperial government. Therefore, Yamagata Daini's execution by itself does not make him—any more than Yui Shōsetsu—a successor to Kusunoki Masashige or a precursor of Yoshida Shōin. What is more, Daini's execution by itself does not even prove that his *Ryūshi shinron* called for violent revolution from below. The Tokugawa regime executed Daini for his "extreme disrespect and the utmost insolence"—a premodern Japanese expression connoting "sacrilege" or "lese majesty". There are no valid grounds for reading treason (which prosecutors flatly denied), or restorationism (as prewar historians did), or radical egalitarianism (as postwar humanists do) into the bakufu's verdict. Instead, we should accept that verdict at face value.

Bakumatsu Resurrection

Just before his execution in x/1859, Yoshida Shōin came to advocate destroying the Tokugawa bakufu; and during the following decade, his radical Chōshū disciples such as Kusaka Genzui found themselves invoking the name of emperor and court in order to achieve that goal. Yoshida Shōin and his militant followers gained access to some less-than-accurate accounts of Yamagata Daini and the Meiwa Incident, mainly through the itinerant monk Utsunomiya Mokurin. As a result, they traced the inspiration for their loyalist-restorationist program to Daini.

Yoshida Shōin did not obtain and read Daini's *Ryūshi shinron* until VIII/1856, during an ongoing debate about national politics conducted with Utsunomiya.[35] We cannot determine just how well Shōin understood Daini's treatise or how accurately Utsunomiya conveyed its contents to Shōin in their debate. But during that same month, Utsunomiya described Daini's life and work in another dialogue as follows:

> The *Ryūshi shinron* comprises thirteen sections. Its author, Master Yamagata, was from Kai province. He served the Tokudaiji [at court], but took leave of them in order to further his great aspira-

tion—only to be executed by Edo on trumped-up charges of treason. Without doubt, this was the worst mistake made by the Tokugawa in all of their shogunal reigns because it would certainly undergo scrutiny in later ages. Japanese Confucians have dismissed Daini's tract as being worthless, although not one in a million of them has written anything as good. Moreover, only the very rare scholar has ever seen this work.[36]

Utsunomiya seems to have believed that the bakufu's demise was imminent or at least a foregone conclusion. What is more, he identified the bakufu's handling of the Meiwa Incident as the decisive long-term cause of that downfall. Utsunomiya's sense of where the Edo regime was heading proved right, but his analysis of the reasons was clearly wrong. And he probably got his misinformation from Gamō Kumpei's post hoc hearsay accounts of the Meiwa Incident. For example, Utsunomiya's erroneous reference to the Tokudaiji court-noble family in Kyoto shows that he mistook Yamagata Daini for Takenouchi Shikibu—who did serve that family prior to the Hōreki Incident of 1758. And Utsunomiya wrongly asserts that bakufu prosecutors exploited "trumped-up charges of treason" to execute Daini in the Meiwa Incident of 1767—when in fact they acquitted him of that charge. But it was in the Bakumatsu era that this badly flawed historical account surfaced, and Kusaka Genzui was not one to treat it with the skepticism of a fine Cartesian mind.

Kusaka fumed in 1861: "Yamagata Daini died for righteous principles in VIII/1767. . . . He gathered students, lectured on strategy, and aspired to 'revere the imperial court and subdue the military hegemon.' Truly, we should grieve over his failed aspiration."[37] Then Kusaka vented his anger at men like Motoori Norinaga (though not by name) and the "Japanese Confucians" mentioned by Utsunomiya. Such eminent scholars had consigned Daini to virtual oblivion after his execution in 1767, and Kusaka snapped: "Why has the memory of Daini been snuffed out for close to a hundred years now? It is because most men of letters were all too eager to avoid incriminating association. They feared for their lives, and so dared not write or speak in connection with him."[38] Kusaka here implies that, unlike the maverick Gamō Kumpei, establishment scholars such as Motoori Norinaga and like-minded Confucian "men of letters" dissociated themselves

from Daini due to fear or perhaps jealousy—and not from loath-
ing. Kusaka then deduces that this conspiracy of silence alone
explains why Daini receded from popular consciousness "for
close to a hundred years." But this explanation is not credible. It
is quite true that the *Ryūshi shinron* was considered a dangerous
work and therefore did not circulate widely in Daini's time. But
we are on far safer ground assuming that people in later decades
just forgot about Daini as a matter of course with the passing of
time. In any case, he remained largely forgotten until resurrected
for political purposes by men like Utsunomiya Mokurin in the
Bakumatsu era.

Thereafter, revolutionaries such as Yoshida Shōin and Kusaka
Genzui all too readily ascribed restorationist ideals to Daini. They
credulously accepted inaccurate accounts of his life and letters
that they stumbled across in those bleak years before the Sat-Chō
Alliance was forged and prospects for their loyalist endeavor
began to improve. But these *shishi* never lived to see such hope-
filled days. The bakufu beheaded Yoshida Shōin during its 1859
Ansei Purge; and Satsuma troops killed Kusaka Genzui in 1864 at
a pitched battle outside the Kyoto imperial palace. Critical examination of sources and painstaking empirical inquiry were not big
concerns for these men. Instead, they derived meaning from
Daini's life and letters in accord with a presentist agenda: first,
to justify a loyalist-restorationist cause and so win desperately
needed support for it; and second, to gain solace amid despair by
seeking out spiritual forebears.

Thus careful and objective scrutiny of the available evidence
will conclusively show that the Meiwa Incident of 1767 did not
foreshadow, and should not be likened to, the Ansei Purge of
1859. In the late eighteenth century, Yamagata Daini was an
abhorred but conventional villain who reputedly plotted to rebel
against the Edo bakufu; during the first half of the nineteenth century, he was for the most part buried in oblivion. But either way,
Daini had yet to be idolized as a loyalist martyr to the restorationist cause. Bakumatsu *shishi* such as Yoshida Shōin and Kusaka
Genzui were the first to establish that delusion as an accepted historical fact; and many *kōkoku shikan* scholars would echo their
refrain in those heady patriotic days before August 1945.

An Erudite Scholar

Most latter-day biographical accounts of Yamagata Daini portray him as a man wholly committed to radical thoughts, if not radical deeds. But a close examination of his writings reveals a scholar of remarkable depth and diversity. Therefore, we can get a more balanced and accurate assessment of Daini's *Ryūshi shinron* by viewing this work in the context of his writings as a whole. Before his ignoble execution, Daini won renown for erudition, not extremism. In 1767 Hosaka, the wealthy peasant from Kai cited above, noted: "His knowledge of things ancient and modern is so vast that people call him the greatest scholar in Japan."[39] And one Bakumatsu source says: "Daini was extremely famous at the time. . . . It was the rare scholar indeed who did not visit his home."[40] This reputation for extraordinary learning explains why anxious students now visit his shrine to pray for help at examination time.

Daini began Shinto studies at the age of ten under Kagami Ōu (1710–1782), a follower of Yamazaki Ansai's Shinto-Confucian syncretism. At seventeen, Daini took up Confucianism under Gomi Fusen (1718–1754), a disciple of Dazai Shundai (1680–1747) in the Ogyū Sorai school of ancient learning. Historians have long disputed whether the Ansai or Sorai school was more important in forming Daini's ideas. I argue that he owed more to Sorai Learning.[41]

Before his fortuitous and tragic involvement in the Meiwa Incident of 1767, Yamagata Daini was best known for his expertise in military science, yin-yang divining, medicine, Sanskrit, archaic Chinese linguistics, astronomy, and Japanese mathematics. As noted earlier, he acquired the title "Governor-General of the Thirty-Three Eastern Provinces" from the Tsuchimikado court-noble family in the mid-1760s; and the name "Daini" accompanied that title. The Tsuchimikado patronized yin-yang diviners throughout Japan and were charged with conferring honorary court ranks and titles on them.[42] Hence Daini's chief claim to social prestige in his own day rested on this laurel bestowed by the imperial court in recognition of his expertise in traditional Chinese learning, specifically his mastery of the classic *Book of Changes.*

Daini produced two works on language: a tract on Sanskrit in 1755 titled *Shittan moji kō* and an introduction to archaic Chinese phonology in 1761 titled *Hatsuon ryaku*.[43] This second work reintroduced some of the ideas he had discussed earlier in the *Ryūshi shinron*. In *Hatsuon ryaku*, Daini showed unabashed contempt for Japanese who did not know the original pronunciation and meaning of Chinese characters. As well, he noted that Sanskrit, Japanese, Dutch, and Manchu were polysyllabic and polytonal as opposed to Chinese, which was monosyllabic and monotonal. He also argued that Sung tracts on phonology, available in Japan since Kamakura times, were inferior to more up-to-date Ming studies.

The converse was true for medicine, as Daini explained in his *Iji hatsuran* of 1765. In this work, he followed the yin-yang Five Elements theory revealed in the *Book of Changes*. A staunch follower of the Ancient Method school, Daini rebutted Sung, Yuan, and other latter-day medical texts and theories by arguing that Han-dynasty texts were superior because physicians then were closer in time to the Yellow Emperor. Daini had especially high regard for the *Shang-han lun* by Chang Chung-ching of the Later Han dynasty; and he favored *ch'i* monism over Sung-style *li-ch'i* dualism in medical theory. In the fields of cosmography, astronomy, and geography, Daini produced two major works: *Tenkei hatsumō* in 1762 and *Seikei tōta* in 1764. He accepted the Ptolemaic geocentric theory of the universe as introduced by Yu I in *T'ien-ching huo-wen* (circa 1675).[44] That notion, of course, was logically incompatible with the traditional Confucian "spherical-heaven, flat-earth" theory. As Daini noted: "Most of the ancients said, 'Heaven is round and the earth is flat.' But that view is not based on [observation of] their actual shapes; it is just inferred through Principle *(li)*."

Despite his contemptuous reference to "adherents of alien cults and barbarian learning" made in Section X of the *Ryūshi shinron*, Yamagata Daini was hardly culture-bound in scholarship. Unlike Sugita Gempaku, he could not read Dutch, and so cannot properly be called a Rangakusha, or Dutch Studies expert, in the strict sense. Nevertheless, Daini was fairly familiar with "Western Learning," or knowledge of Western subjects broadly conceived as derived from Chinese or Japanese sources. In cosmology and astronomy, for example, he praised Western theories as being more complete than the Chinese and acknowledged that the moon revolved around the earth, a fact that explains the occurrence of eclipses. Daini was ahead of his time in accepting the spherical-earth [*chikyū*] theory.[45] And he was indebted to Western Learning for his knowledge of world geography as well. He wrote about six continents: Asia, Europe, Africa, North and South America, and the newly discovered "Magellanica." Asia was made up of India, Tungusland, Japan, and China, designated as the "Middle Kingdom" *(Chung-hua, Chūka)*. Daini learned of "Magellanica" from Western cartographers, who conjectured that it was a large continent in the southern hemisphere.[46] In 1763 Daini completed a detailed treatise of Chinese and Japanese harps and harp music entitled *Kingaku hakki*. This musicology, too, had found its way into the *Ryūshi shinron* earlier. His study of Japanese-style mathematics, *Gachū-fu*, was completed in 1765; he also wrote several tracts on military science, but none of these survive.

It is well worth noting that all seven of Daini's extant dated manuscripts fall between 1754 and 1765, yet only two predate 1759, the year he completed the *Ryūshi shinron*. Thus four of his scholarly works, and they are major works, postdate it. The *Ryūshi shinron* was without doubt Daini's magnum opus in the area of sociopolitical thought. But that was not his sole, or even major, field of academic endeavor. If he had not been dragged into the Meiwa Incident—that is to say, if he had exercised more care in screening prospective students—his claim to historical significance would be quite different today.

Master Ryū

When analyzed in the context of Yamagata Daini's scholarly output as a whole, the *Ryūshi shinron* stands out for its highly politicized commentary on socioeconomic affairs. Master Ryū elucidates court-bakufu relations as these evolved through Japanese history, and he brings to light key problems plaguing Tokugawa society. However, he expounds his "new thesis" by contrasting lamentable Japanese realities against exemplary Chinese models. The tract comprises thirteen sections:

Sections VIII and XI clearly lend themselves to division into two parts each. So it seems that Daini adhered to the figure thirteen on purpose—probably to conform with the number of sections in the Chinese military classic, the *Sun Tzu,* which dates from the middle of the third century B.C.[47]

Yamagata Daini's debts to the Sorai school thinker Dazai Shundai are unmistakable in terms of content. Most of Daini's "Heaven-Mandated Peoples" section, for example, derives from chapter nine of Shundai's 1749 work, the *Sango,* titled "The Four Peoples."[48] About one-third of Daini's "Exhorting Officials" section is adapted from Dazai Shundai's *Keizai roku* of 1729.[49] Some passages in Daini's "Man and Adornment" section follow the *Keizai roku* so closely that he must have simply cribbed them from Shundai's Japanese text into classical Chinese.[50] Much the same can be said about parallels in form and style. Daini begins each section in his tract with the phrase "Master Ryū said: . . ." He also appends an afterword wherein he disguises the tract's authorship and date of composition. These literary devices are clearly taken from Dazai Shundai. In his afterword to the *Sango,* Shundai avers that: it is an anonymous Chinese eclectic work devoted to political economy, it was discovered in a Nara temple, it has been lost in the "Middle Kingdom" *(Chūgoku, Chung-kuo),* it survives only in Japan, and its contents should be kept secret.[51] In his afterword to the *Ryūshi shinron,* Daini contends that: Master Ryū cannot be identified, the book was unearthed in a box along with old Chinese coins, it probably dates from "the age of Oda Nobunaga" in the sixteenth century, and it is a family heirloom not to be disclosed except to a trusted few.[52]

Yamagata Daini was in fact secretive about the *Ryūshi shinron*. He neither published the work nor circulated it widely while alive, and one finds few references to it by name before Bakumatsu times. One notable exception was Matsumiya Kanzan (1686–1780), who made critical comments in the margins of Daini's manuscript and also wrote a postscript to it dated "early autumn 1763." This was some three and a half years after the *Ryūshi shinron* was completed and four years before Daini was executed in the Meiwa Incident. But Matsumiya Kanzan too observed the fiction of anonymous sixteenth-century authorship as laid down in Daini's afterword. Bakufu prosecutors probably never had access to the tract. One primary source states that Yamagata Daini was waiting to be captured by bakufu constables, and it goes on to explain: "When he was arrested, his room had nothing in it—just a spear and one copy each of the *Tso chuan* and *Hōken taiki*."[53] No mention is made of Daini's own writings here or in other documents that describe his capture. Japanese historians assert—and it is fair to assume—that he burned his original and hid other copies with family and trusted friends. Indeed, he explicitly left such instructions in his afterword. The bakufu's verdict to Daini read: "You wrote in a notebook *(sōshi)* that the condition of court nobles today is contrary to what it was in antiquity." For state prosecutors seeking evidence to justify the death sentence, this is a rather lame way to describe Master Ryū's invective; so this "notebook" probably was not the *Ryūshi shinron*. Therefore, we can be reasonably sure that, contrary to most accounts of the Meiwa Incident, Edo authorities never had access to the tract and could not use it as evidence against Daini.

As Tokutomi Sohō pointed out decades ago, even if bakufu officials had gained access to the *Ryūshi shinron,* they probably would not have been able to read the tract and comprehend all of its complex arguments.[54] Daini composed the work in an archaic form of classical Chinese replete with obscure quotations from Confucian, Legalist, and Taoist texts. Aside from difficulties posed by language, the tract is hard to understand because Daini was deliberately cryptic and ambiguous. Rather than state his

ideas explicitly, he conveyed these through obscure literary allusions and through passing references to events or persons in Chinese and Japanese history. Latter-day historians, especially in
Japan, have made our tasks of reading and comprehension even
harder. Their accounts usually ignore Daini's tract as a whole and
focus on Sections I, II, XII, and XIII: "Making Name and Actuality Conform," "Attaining Oneness," "Benefits and Evils," and
"Wealth and Strength." In these sections, Daini seems to be saying
that the current court-bakufu dyarchy must be abolished and
national unity recreated through a restoration of imperial rule to
be achieved by loyalists similar to Kusunoki Masashige and Nitta
Yoshisada. Above all, modern historians have misread and played
up Daini's use of the Mencian term "*hōbatsu*," which appears in
Sections XII and XIII. In its original classical Chinese context, the
term meant "to depose a ruler" through regicide and dynastic
overthrow.[55] Hence Yamagata Daini seems to be advocating a
popular uprising to destroy the Edo bakufu itself, if not the
bakufu form of government in general. Prewar *kōkoku shikan*
advocates claimed this rebellion was for the sake of the emperor;
postwar humanist scholars claim it was for the good of the
people.

Yet it must be admitted that Daini's pedantry and penchant for
indirect expression do leave Master Ryū open to different interpretations with varying degrees of plausibility on a number of
important points. Thus it is wise to adopt certain strategies for
deciphering the author's original meaning behind the text in a
holistic fashion. First, we should place Daini's polemics in proper
historical perspective by defining his scholarly filiations within the
intellectual milieu of his day. In this regard it is helpful to interpret
Master Ryū against the contemporary criticism provided by
Matsumiya Kanzan in his marginal notes to Daini's text. Second,
we should relate the *Ryūshi shinron* to Yamagata Daini's other
political writings—his monument inscriptions to Prince Yamatotakeru and Princess Ototachibana—which historians often cite
but rarely analyze. Third, we should examine Daini's literary and
historical allusions in order to identify the classical Chinese
sources of his thought; this strategy will disclose the meanings he
intended readers to infer. But in order to accomplish all this, we
must come to grips with the logic running through, and the pre-

suppositions underlying, Master Ryū's polemic as a whole. It will not do simply to pick out and explicate brief passages from selected parts of this work, as previous interpreters have generally done. For this reason I have translated and annotated the *Ryūshi shinron* in full. If nothing else, a complete English translation will encourage other Western scholars to pursue this topic by making their criticism, revision, or refutation of my arguments easier.

CHAPTER 3

Textual and Contextual Analysis

The Daini myth of "restorationism" or "revolutionary loyalism" stems from three related beliefs that we entertain about his views on Japanese history and Tokugawa sociopolitical realities. First, Daini assumed that the imperial court's decline vis-à-vis warrior houses was reversible; so future reversion to rule by the emperor, though difficult, was possible. Second, Daini empathized with Japanese commoners grievously exploited under warrior rule since 1185; that empathy led him to glorify high antiquity when the common people enjoyed the blessings of imperial virtue—the best form of government on earth. Third, this idealization of Japan's archaic past inspired him to devise radical reforms that would end discrimination predicated on bloodline and establish the merit principle for determining socioeconomic status under an ideal new order.

All three beliefs are delusory. The first—concerning revertibility to imperial rule—flies in the face of generally held notions, or what might be called the "common sense," that prevailed in Japan down to the last decades of the Edo period. The second and third assumptions—concerning Daini's empathy with the commoners' suffering, his idealization of Japanese antiquity, his repudiation of warrior rule, and his agenda for drastic social engineering—are betrayed by a careful reading of *Master Ryū's New Thesis*.

A Defunct Dynasty

Virtually all pre-Bakumatsu thinkers took it for granted that an irreversible transfer of power from imperial court to warrior houses was complete by the time of Godaigo—the hapless sovereign who reigned between 1318 and 1339 and was responsible for splitting the imperial court into Northern and Southern regimes from 1333 to 1392.[1] In effect, Yamagata Daini's contemporaries assumed that Japan's imperial house was a defunct regime. Even Shinto-inspired nativists who stressed the imperial dynasty's divine lineage and never-ending reign—core tenets in the latter-day *kōkoku shikan* dogma—concurred that actual imperial rule was a relic of the past. Before we can determine Daini's significance for the history of Japanese political thought, we must situate him in this key controversy about history and dynastic legitimacy as waged by Tokugawa Confucians and Shintoists.

In Chinese Confucian political thought, continuity of lineage or bloodline was one criterion used to measure a dynasty's legitimacy. But it was not all-important. According to Chu Hsi, for example, the state of Shu was the true hereditary successor to the Han royal house and thus could claim legitimacy in the Three Kingdoms era (220–280) based on lineage. Yet that claim was meaningful only because the Shu house still controlled a bit less than one-third of the lands and peoples in "the realm"—conceptualized as "all under heaven" by Confucians. After all, hereditary descendants who found themselves without a state to administer were just private individuals. No lands or peoples submitted to them; hence they no longer constituted a bona fide dynastic line, and much less could they claim to be retaining the mandate of heaven. In Confucian political terms, these once-legitimate descendants and their erstwhile regime were known as *"shō-koku"*—a "fallen dynasty."

Opposed to this criterion of lineage was that of virtue or benevolent government as "proven" by the unified rule that a dynastic house achieved or maintained in the realm. Thus Ssu-ma Kuang argued that Wei, not Shu, was legitimate in the Three Kingdoms period because continuity of bloodline counted for less than virtue. As this essentially circular reasoning went, the realm will always submit to virtuous rulers; hence whoever controls most of the realm must have superior virtue. Wei was larger and more populous than Shu. This showed that the Wei house was conducting benevolent rule on a vaster scale than the Shu and so had won allegiance from more lands and peoples under heaven. In this manner, Ssu-ma Kuang concluded that Wei possessed the Way, had won the heavenly mandate, and therefore was the legitimate ruling house.

In sum, the criterion of virtuous or benevolent rule, like that of lineage, was equated by Confucian political theorists with possession of the Way and heaven's mandate. After a period of disunity and civil war, the founder of a new dynasty would typically "depose" his erstwhile sovereign—who up to then had been "legitimate" in terms of lineage. And he would overcome other contenders for power—who all claimed to be dispensing benevolent government. But he had to achieve unified rule; that is, he had to win control over most, if not all, states under heaven. Then this new ruler could legitimize the triumph of his own regime and rationalize the destruction of his rivals, as described by Master Ryū in a passage that has been frequently misinterpreted:

> Manifest cases in point are T'ang's destruction of the Hsia, and Wu's of the Shang. If a deposer ends up as emperor, he is deemed to possess the Way; if he ends up at the level of a state head—or, indeed, anything lower—he is deemed to lack it.[2]

To repeat, widespread popular submission was the decisive factor in this Chinese debate over dynastic legitimacy because it putatively demonstrated that a ruling house—whether continuing or newly arisen—possessed virtue and therefore retained or had recently acquired the Confucian Way and heavenly mandate. A Chinese regime might choose to assert its legitimacy based on bloodline or on benevolent rule; either way, it had to exercise actual control of the realm.[3] This traditional Chinese Confucian concept of dynastic "legitimacy" comes close to denoting the modern political idea of "sovereignty," as claimed by a particular regime over and against contenders for power within a certain territory.[4] It is in this sense that I employ the terms "sovereign" or "sovereignty" when discussing disputes between Tokugawa Confucians and Shintoists.

What happens when we apply these Chinese Confucian arguments about "sovereignty" or dynastic "legitimacy" to Japan? After Godaigo's disastrous Kemmu Restoration of 1333 to 1336, the emperor and imperial court found themselves squeaking out a bare existence in one tiny corner of the land. At first the court was divided, with Godaigo's splinter regime operating in the Yoshino mountains, outside the capital of Kyoto. After 1392 the court was reunited, but it was stripped of power and limited in influence to

Kyoto, which, by Edo times, had become merely the administrative seat of Yamashiro province.[5] Thus Japan's emperor and court could not credibly advance Ssu-ma Kuang's logic to claim legitimacy based on virtuous government; for they were not governing at all. Worse still, neither could they cogently evoke Chu Hsi's criterion of lineage; for even that required them to enjoy submission from much, if not most, of the realm. By Confucian standards, the Kyoto imperial court resembled China's Eastern Chou dynasty (770–256 B.C.) in that figurehead emperors enjoyed a measure of respect but military hegemons commanded actual obedience. If Tokugawa Confucians were to remain true to their creed, they had to admit that the emperor in Kyoto was no longer a bona fide sovereign in the realm from at least the 1330s—if not from the 1180s or the 1150s, when warrior hegemony first emerged. Only then could they try to explain the anomaly of a defunct dynasty that had remained intact for so long.

Yamaga Sokō (1622–1685) held that Japan's polity began as centralized imperial rule *(gunken)* under civil bureaucrats and later evolved into feudal rule *(hōken)* under regional warrior chieftains—the converse of Chinese historical development. Thinkers in the Edo period generally accepted the historicity of emperors in the imperial line before Ōjin; and Yamaga Sokō was no exception. But he believed that Amaterasu's dynasty, begun by Jimmu, had caused its own demise. It had exemplified rule by "illustrious sovereigns and sagacious ministers" in antiquity, but it came to neglect government in favor of "poetry and dance, or excursions and banquets" later on. "Under Emperor Goshira-kawa, state administration decayed and the court became blind to the imperatives of the age *(jigi)* [to accommodate warrior power]; so rebellious subjects threw the realm into civil war."[6] The situation deteriorated beyond repair in the Northern and Southern Courts era: "After warrior-subjects [Kusunoki Masashige and Nitta Yoshisada] pacified the land and restored the ancient dynasty to power, [Godaigo's] imperial rule was unjust. Hence warriors assumed the reins of government in the realm." Even so, Yamaga Sokō unequivocally stated: "Rule by warrior dynasties did not come about because military chieftains forcibly seized power; emperors turned it over to them, which is to say that heaven itself sanctioned the transfer."[7]

Yamaga Sokō held fast to two essential Confucian concepts: the Way is an absolute measure of good government, and heaven is an impartial political arbiter. He declared: "Heaven backs anyone who follows the Way and ends warfare and disorder—whether he be a court noble or a warrior."[8] Elsewhere he maintained: "The mandate of heaven rests with warriors now because they have achieved the Way."[9] Diametrically opposed to Bakumatsu restorationists such as Yoshida Shōin—who argued for unconditional loyalty even to evil sovereigns—Yamaga Sokō staunchly affirmed the right of warriors to assume political power when "the king is not a true king and the imperial court does not rule as an imperial court should."[10] This is why Sokō readily acknowledged that "warriors have been governing in the emperor's stead for over five hundred years now."[11] And he deemed this transfer of power irreversible: "Even if we wanted to revive government by court nobles and the methods of imperial majesties, and even though we continue to honor the dynastic laws and statutes [the Ritsu-Ryō codes], a myriad oxen could not restore the imperial court to the power it enjoyed in antiquity."[12]

Like Yamaga Sokō, Kumazawa Banzan (1611–1691) saw Japanese history progressing more in linear than in cyclical fashion. It had gone through three stages: the "age of the gods" prior to 660 B.C.; the eighteen-hundred-year "dynastic age" from Jimmu to Goshirakawa lasting from 660 B.C. to A.D. 1192; and the five-hundred-year "warrior age" from Goshirakawa to the present.[13] To Banzan, the emperor and court had "lacked virtue"—in part since ex-Emperor Goshirakawa (1127–1192) and in toto since Emperor Godaigo. Thus Japan "more or less belonged to the warriors after Goshirakawa entrusted the realm to Minamoto no Yoritomo [in 1183]."[14] Still, the imperial court's power half-remained because "many people revered dynastic virtue up to Emperor Godaigo's time." Godaigo took advantage of that lingering reverence and staged a coup: the Kemmu Restoration. But his Southern Court "violated the Way, employed no wise ministers, and failed to cope with the changing times and with rising warrior power. So the resentful people yearned for warrior rule once more." In other words, Godaigo ignored historical inevitability by treating warriors with the same contempt shown to court underlings, and that behavior turned the realm against him. Thus, "after Ashikaga Takauji arose to conquer the realm [in the 1330s], it has belonged totally to the warrior houses."[15]

Kumazawa Banzan too believed that warrior rule was an incontestable and irreversible fact. Skeptics could point to the continued existence of the emperor and court in Kyoto and might conjecture: "After all, they were sovereign in Japan before; is it not possible for power to revert to them?" But Banzan quickly replied: "Control of the realm will never revert to imperial court nobles [for] even if we warriors restored it to them, their rule would not last long."[16] Kumazawa Banzan expounded two basic theses: "It is absurd for a warrior to ascend to the throne or for an emperor to take charge of the realm"; and the shogun "rules the realm as an imperial regent *(sesshō)*." The emperor and nobles had fully displayed their administrative incompetence during Godaigo's inept Kemmu Restoration: "So they lost all power over the realm that they had temporarily won back."[17]

By Tokugawa times, Kumazawa Banzan deemed, the emperor and court were even less fit to rule. But, he said, the all-powerful shogun still revered the emperor for shrewd political reasons:

> When people in the realm see their overlord, the shogun, venerating an impotent emperor as Japan's sovereign, they realize that the shogun truly follows the Way. Then they would say: "How can we, who receive territories from him, be disloyal?" Those who harbored treachery in their hearts would become as loyal as hereditary retainers, and all under heaven will be at peace.[18]

Muro Kyūsō (1658–1734), a Chu Hsi Confucian, and Yusa Bokusai (1658–1734), a Shinto scholar and disciple of Yamazaki Ansai, introduced other important points in this debate over the imperial court's lost legitimacy and forfeiture of power to warrior regimes. Although there was a strong Confucian component in Ansai's school, it often lost out to Shinto when the two conflicted.[19] So, as might be expected, Yusa Bokusai argued that Japan's divine unbroken imperial line evinced moral excellence throughout the world.

Muro Kyūsō, who sought to purge all Shinto traces from Japanese Confucianism, retorted that Confucian moral laws of nature were universally valid: "All things that begin must end. That is a constant law of heaven and earth. One founds a dynasty in the hope of having successors. But the absence of a dynasty's demise has never signified exaltation." Likewise: "Men watch their health in order to avoid illness and to prolong life. But the lack of death has never signified honor." Muro's main point was this: "To hope for long life or a long-lived dynasty stands to reason. But to desire eternal life or a never-ending dynasty does not. . . . [For] no one given life has ever escaped death, and no dynasty that rose to power ever avoided falling from it." Thus Muro Kyūsō poignantly argued that "Confucians cherish the Three Dynasties [2205–249 B.C.] as much as Shintoists cherish Japan's imperial house. But even those venerable [Chinese] regimes lost vigor and fell."[20] Japan's dynasty could not be any different. He called the Edo bakufu "the imperial court" (chōtei), thus implying that the dynastic regime in Kyoto was no longer a sovereign, legitimate government in the realm as a whole.[21]

Yusa Bokusai conceded that Japan's ruling house had seen better days: "Imperial reigns have been recorded for twenty-three hundred years since the first manifest emperor [Jimmu]; yet emperors have not actually ruled for the last five hundred. . . . Nevertheless, we revere them now no less than we did at the outset," even after warrior rule became established. Yusa assailed Muro Kyūsō for applying foreign concepts of dynastic "rise and fall" to Japan. Dynasties rose to power and fell from it only in China. The imperial house did not "rise" to power in the sense of overthrowing and usurping sovereign authority from a previous regime. As revealed in the Kojiki and Nihon shoki, Sun Goddess Amaterasu had established Japan's imperial house by divine decree (shinchoku). And it could never "fall" from power because Amaterasu stipulated that its sway should remain "coeval with heaven and earth."[22] Yusa grudgingly admitted some degree of analogy to Chou—the last of ancient China's Three Dynasties—whose Western and Eastern regimes totaled eighteen hundred years: "But no one ever slighted them in decline toward the end of their reign. How much truer this is of our own kingly house. The realm reveres it even though it does not actually administer political affairs." For Yusa Bokusai, Japan's imperial house was unique: "It bestows honors by granting noble ranks and by regulating court dress. Therefore we should not consider it to be just another Chou regime on the wane."[23] These functions, centered on court rank and costume, were imperial prerogatives of cardinal importance to Shinto nativists.

To stretch an analogy, Muro Kyūsō was somewhat like prewar Japanese Marxists who were hard put to account for the lack of a bourgeois revolution in Japan; in his day, he had to explain why a dynastic revolution had never taken place. And, much like the latter-day Marxists, he came up with a plausible answer in the idea of Japanese historical atavism. To lack a dynastic revolution, he said, did not connote eminence or uniqueness relative to other peoples in the world; to the contrary, it proved cultural backwardness and tardy social development. Japan was "a tiny country full of people with absurd customs, such as not daring to show disrespect to an emperor descended from a goddess." Shinto scholars like Yusa Bokusai, who gloried in their unbroken dynastic line and hoped it would last forever, were no better than ignorant Chinese commoners who sought out Taoist adepts in a vain quest to find the elixir of never-ending life.[24]

Thus, although agreeing that Japan's imperial dynasty reigned but no longer ruled, the Confucian Muro Kyūsō and the Shinto-inspired nativist Yusa Bokusai clashed on at least two basic and irreconcilable points. First, Muro believed that the dynasty's divorce from political and military power directly stemmed from its lost virtue, as manifested in its forfeiture of the realm. By contrast, Yusa stressed that the dynasty's spiritual qualities and its *non*-administrative ceremonial functions induced popular reverence precisely because it lacked political and military power. Second, Muro Kyūsō contended that certain Chinese political dicta held true everywhere. He believed, for example, that "the Way is impartial for all [lands] under heaven. It is not biased in Japan's favor."[25] And he maintained that "the constant law of heaven and earth"—that "all things which begin must end"—was binding for ruling houses everywhere. Opposed to Muro, Yusa Bokusai insisted that any such Confucian moral laws lacked universal validity and should not be forcibly applied to Japan. Japan had its own unique criteria to measure sovereignty and dynastic legitimacy—and these were found in Amaterasu's divine decree, not the Confucian classics.

Yamagata Daini's understanding of how bakufu-court relations had evolved through Japanese history must be examined in the context of this Tokugawa-era controversy. Many modern scholars place Daini in a tradition of imperial loyalism going back to Yusa Bokusai's mentor, Yamazaki Ansai. But Daini and Master Ryū owed far more to Ogyū Sorai's Ancient Learning school of Confucianism than to the Shinto-inspired nativism in Ansai's thought. And, in particular, Daini adhered closely to the ideas of Sorai's disciple, Dazai Shundai.

Ogyū Sorai argued that "the realm passed into warrior hands three hundred years after Fujiwara no Fuhito [659–720] created the Ritsu-Ryō codes based on T'ang models [in 701]."[26] Here Sorai too equated the imperial dynasty's fall from power with its loss of unified control over the realm; and he dated that watershed as taking place even before the Hōgen Uprising of 1156, the earliest benchmark of warrior ascendancy. As Sorai put it, "the imperial house barely managed to stay intact—like a thread" *(ito no gotoku)*.[27] Like Arai Hakuseki (1657–1725), Ogyū Sorai believed that the Tokugawa shogun had in truth become "King of Japan" by Edo times and ought to use that title in diplomatic correspondence.[28] Both Arai Hakuseki and Ogyū Sorai called the emperor in Kyoto "the other sovereign" *(kyōshu),* and both clearly considered him to be the less important one.[29] Dazai Shundai was even more blunt. He labeled Japan's imperial house a "fallen dynasty" *(shōkoku),* and Daini used that term three times in his *Ryūshi shinron* to refer to the court.[30] It may be that Daini felt a certain nostalgia for Japan's ancien régime; but he still took its political demise for granted as a fait accompli.

Yamagata Daini's reading of Japanese political history followed earlier Tokugawa thinkers on other points, too, such as the five-hundred-year period of warrior rule. Master Ryū notes: "Five hundred years have elapsed since government has moved to the Eastern Plain."[31] And he asserts that present-day rulers could not "restore things to what these were in antiquity."[32] Furthermore, he reckons that Japan's dynasty began with the sage-emperor Jimmu's accession in 660 B.C. and lasted "two thousand years." In other words, the dynasty had ended with Godaigo's fourteenth-century Kemmu Restoration.[33] Daini subdivided this two-thousand-year imperial reign into three stages: 660 B.C. to A.D. 603, 603 to 1156, and 1156 to the present. And, of course, Master Ryū purports his "present" to be the late-sixteenth-century Warring States age of Oda Nobunaga.[34]

The first stage, lasting over twelve hundred years, saw Jimmu's "radiant virtue." Daini wrote very little about this era—by far the longest of his three stages. In the second stage, from 603 to about 1156, Shōtoku Taishi (574–622) set up court ranks, ritual, music, and dress codes. Thus he instituted *bun,* or cultured civil rule, in Japan. On this point Daini differed from Ogyū Sorai, who attributed that role to Fujiwara no Fuhito. Daini also claims that the ninth-century Fujiwara regents Mototsune and Yoshifusa were counterparts to Yi Yin, Fu Yueh, the Dukes Chou and Shao, Shusun T'ung, and other sagacious chief ministers to the Chinese imperial throne throughout history. In this way, Daini echoes the Confucian classic, the *Book of Documents,* which stresses that meritorious service rendered by the first four of these Chinese ministerial exemplars—their "assistance" to the sovereign— accounts for the ideal government of high antiquity. Also in Daini's second stage, Sakanoue no Tamuramaro and Fujiwara no Hidesato placed *bu*—the military power to enforce laws and punish offenders—under imperial aegis.[35] So the second stage, not the first, was Japan's golden age because the civil predominated over the military and both remained firmly under unified control. Daini's third stage lasted from 1156 to the late-sixteenth-century age of Master Ryū. Imperial rule began to decline with the Hōgen and Heiji wars of the 1150s. Decentralization of political power— the opposite of Ssu-ma Kuang's ideal of unified administrative control—became acute throughout the realm. And deterioration reached crisis proportions in the Juei-Bunji eras (1182– 1189), when "barbarian" warrior rule began, as demonstrated by the establishment of the Minamoto military regime in 1185. The imperial dynasty's fall was complete by the 1330s. Emperor Godaigo and his Southern Court could make no pretension to sovereignty or dynastic legitimacy in the realm as a whole because they ruled "only a small provincial state."[36] And even that claim smacked of hyperbole.

The logic behind this last expression follows Dazai Shundai. He disparaged contemporary emperors by calling them "Emperor of Yamashiro Province," which contained Kyoto. Thus both Shundai and Daini stress that Yamashiro—one of Japan's sixty-six provinces—marked the limits of imperial sway. We should also note that Dazai Shundai, like Ogyū Sorai, held that Shogun Ienobu (r. 1709–1712) was justified in following Arai Hakuseki's advice to use the title "King of Japan" for diplomatic correspondence.[37] In other words, Yamagata Daini follows Sorai and Shundai in admitting that Japan's imperial dynasty had lost unified control over the realm and popular allegiance from it. Logically speaking, this meant the emperor and court in Kyoto were no longer legitimate or sovereign in Japan by Confucian standards.

Such considerations explain why Master Ryū does not place supreme emphasis on the continued existence of the imperial house. He does say: "It has survived over four-hundred years [from Godaigo] to the present." But elsewhere in the *Ryūshi shinron,* he quotes Ogyū Sorai to state: "The dynastic line survived like a thread" *(ito no gotoku).*[38] Daini also concedes that the granting of Ritsu-Ryō court ranks and titles such as "provincial governor" to daimyo, samurai, and commoners—a practice known as *zuryō*—had lost all meaning and admits that these court titles were merely honorific. Like Ssu-ma Kuang and Muro Kyūsō, Yamagata Daini considered the biological continuity of any dynastic house to be less important than the ideal of virtuous rule:

> Wicked sovereigns like Chieh of Hsia and Chou of Shang lived in bygone eras. If those ruling houses had remained intact and their descendants had remained kings during later generations, should they have clung to the customs set down by Chieh and Chou? If so, this means that good government requires lewd music in state ceremonies, night-long naked orgies amid pools of wine and forests of meat, and law codes calling for fire-pit executions by amused rulers.[39]

Moreover, like Yamaga Sokō, Yamagata Daini perceived popular loyalty for Japan's ancient dynasty to be lingering from the Hōgen and Heiji wars of the 1150s until Godaigo's reign of 1318 to 1339. But after that, he argued, cultured civil rule *(bun)* totally succumbed to military might *(bu).* Japan then plunged into an era of Warring States, which for Daini meant regressing to a primeval condition of violent disorder. In sum, then, Daini contended that the realm of Japan belonged solely to warrior houses after Godaigo's abortive Kemmu Restoration of 1333 to 1336: "Our dynastic rituals were devised over a thousand years ago [in 603]. Today we live in a different world *under a different state.*"[40]

Yamagata Daini's critic, the Shinto-inspired nativist Matsumiya Kanzan, retorted by appealing to Yusa Bokusai's arguments. Matsumiya insisted that Japan's imperial court retained sovereign authority despite no longer exercising it—and the beauty of that fact was "something you Confucian scholars cannot appreciate."[41] Like Yusa, Matsumiya denied universal validity to Chinese moral and political standards. Dynastic legitimacy and sovereignty in Japan did not depend on practicing "virtue," "benevolence," or the "Way"—all of which was supposedly proven by unified political and military control over the realm, which in turn was rationalized as possessing the "mandate of heaven." Instead, Japan had its own criteria to determine legitimacy and sovereignty. First, the court in Kyoto continued to guard the sacred imperial regalia; second, it issued ranks, titles, and the calendar recognized all over Japan.[42] Judged against either of these nativist criteria, the imperial court's impotence and inability to govern were irrelevant.

Earlier, Kuriyama Sempō (1671–1706) had foreshadowed Matsumiya's first criterion by writing Hōken taiki in 1689. Kuriyama found that Confucian theories of legitimation could not be adjusted to fit Japanese political realities in certain key respects. Thus he contended that: "He who possesses the regalia on His Person is our legitimate sovereign"; for "no subject is plagued by doubts when pledging loyalty to a divinity." But as Hayashi Razan (1583–1657) had argued even earlier, religio-mystical qualities attached to the imperial regalia made this argument logically incompatible with the basic tenets of Confucian rationalism. Hayashi insisted: "It turns things upside-down to say that possessing the regalia, and not dispensing virtue," determines legitimacy.[43]

According to Matsumiya Kanzan's second criterion of dynastic legitimacy, evidence of popular allegiance to the imperial house did not lie in submitting to the emperor's political and military power—which was nil. Rather, it lay in affirming the emperor's spiritual authority by employing only those era names (nengō) that he promulgated and by accepting only those court ranks and titles that he bestowed—even though these honors were purely formal in nature. By Matsumiya's logic, the Kyoto imperial court was legitimate and sovereign because peoples (in the plural) in daimyo domains all over Japan reckoned time by eras such as "Hōreki" or "Meiwa" and incorporated honorific ranks and titles such as "junior fourth rank lower level" or "Provincial Governor of Chikugo" in their names. In this nativist sense, Ssu-ma Kuang's ideal of unified control over the realm applied to spiritual rather than political affairs.

Sinophilia and Caste Boundaries

Thus Yamagata Daini was thoroughly Confucian in his views on political legitimation and Japanese historical development, and he mainly followed the Sorai school on both counts. The nativist rebukes that Master Ryū received from Matsumiya Kanzan indicate that Daini cherished many of the sinocentric conceits inherent in Sorai's Confucianism. Daini worshiped antiquarian Chinese culture and never hid contempt for those less versed in it than himself. So it comes as no surprise that his haughtiness provoked a sharp backlash from Matsumiya. But on top of that, Daini insisted on strengthening and perpetuating current forms of class discrimination based on residence and family occupation. By pursuing these lines of analysis—that is, by flushing out the sinophilic and hierarchy-affirming elements in Master Ryū's "new thesis"—we can gain important insights into Daini's sociopolitical thought.

Yamagata Daini subscribed to the Sorai school's paradigm of monolithic cultural evolution, which presupposed concepts of sagely discrimination and categories of progressive historical development defined by Chinese moral culture. For example, Dazai Shundai argued: "When heaven and earth first separated," humans were created through spontaneous generation "like maggots spawn in rotting matter." In that original state, "there was no discrimination of the high from the low or the exalted from the despised; all were 'commoners' of equal status." For Daini too the primeval state of human existence everywhere was: "Men are equal, with no distinctions of noble or base."[44] Both Dazai Shundai and Yamagata Daini identified this original human condition as one of violent anarchy in which men behaved like "birds and beasts." This stock Confucian metaphor implied the absence of moral imperatives—such as ritual, music, and social hierarchy—without which "the strong overpower the weak, and the resolute despise the infirm. Men harm and wound, oppress and kill, rob and pillage."[45]

On the surface, this Confucian primeval condition of violent anarchy resembles the "state of nature" idea expounded by early-modern political thinkers in the West as diverse as Hobbes, Locke, and Rousseau. But the key difference lay in how humans purportedly left that aboriginal condition and went on to form the political order and sovereign authority. According to the social contract theory of Hobbes, Locke, and Rousseau, humans did so voluntarily and from self-serving motives: to obtain certain benefits not available in the state of nature, such as greater security or happiness. Since humans had purposely created the sovereign authority and sociopolitical order for their own benefit, they reserved the right to overthrow these if they suffered thereunder. In sum, as the autonomous creators of their own government institutions, they claimed to retain certain inalienable natural rights; and these rights included that of revolution as a first step to establishing a better or more just ruling order. Here was a key theoretical component of liberal democracy as it evolved in the West.[46]

Postwar historians such as Ichii have likened Daini's Confucianism to Western political theory based on certain superficial affinities. That comparison is mistaken, for the differences outweigh the similarities. To Confucians such as Dazai Shundai and Yamagata Daini, the masses had not created their own sovereign authority and sociopolitical order in autonomous fashion; the sage-kings of antiquity had created these from on high. Civilized social life *(bun)* was deemed possible only after those sage-kings had established normative social classes and other distinctive "marks of culture" *(bun)* that "adorned and differentiated" humans much as fur and feathers adorned and differentiated members of the beastly kingdom. Moreover, it was only owing to this *bun* that the ignorant masses were enabled to leave their original state of violent *dis*-order for one of hierarchic order in Confucian civilized society.

As culture heroes, the sage-kings also taught vital skills such as farming and spinning to ensure the peoples' livelihood. Thus Daini cited one key criterion of sagehood from the *Book of Documents:* "to nourish peoples and eliminate hardship from their lives."[47] Above all, the sages created a social hierarchy on which each of the "four peoples" *(shimin)* had a heaven-prescribed call-ing, or socioeconomic function, defined by its "name." For Dazai Shundai and Yamagata Daini, there were four "good" peoples, or classes. In descending order of rank and esteem, these were gov-ernment officials, peasants, artisans, and merchants.

Confucians in general, and the Sorai school in particular, equated civilized life with what they termed "implementing the Way," or "morally transforming customs," which in effect meant sinifying native Japanese folkways. Ogyū Sorai argued that ancient Japanese had been hopelessly barbaric until Wang Jen, known in Japan as Wani, brought the Confucian classics during Emperor Ōjin's reign in the fourth century A.D.[48] Dazai Shundai minced no words on this point:

> The Way did not exist in Japan to begin with. . . . This can be seen from the lack of native Japanese readings for Chinese ideographs signifying [Confucian virtues of] "benevolence, righteousness, rit-ual decorum, music, filial submission, and respect for elders." There are native Japanese readings for all things originally found in Japan. To lack these readings means that those virtues were missing here.[49]

According to the Sorai school the Japanese people became civi-lized only after their indigenous customs were transformed and uplifted by the coming of Chinese moral culture as embodied in Confucianism. And that civilizing process required forty impe-rial reigns—from 660 B.C. through the Taika Reform, which began in A.D. 645.[50]

Daini's Master Ryū generally agreed with this time frame. For him, the Chinese civilizing of Japan began with Sage-Emperor Jimmu in 660 B.C., who met the key criterion of sagely kingship: "to nourish peoples and eliminate hardship from their lives."[51] The sinification and civilization of Japan begun by Jimmu reached culmination under the sage-regent Shōtoku Taishi (574–622), who "assisted" Suiko, the seventh-century female sovereign *(jotei)*.[52] Shōtoku's meritorious achievements were to institute rit-ual and music in government and create court-dress regulations for differentiating noble ranks. But this cultured form of life in Japan gave way to mean and vulgar folkways over time, and civil government succumbed to warrior rule totally by the mid-fourteenth century. So, Japan was long-steeped in barbarism by Master Ryū's sixteenth century. In stark contrast, Daini argued, Chinese emperors upheld regulations for court dress even after their land was overrun by Jurchen and Mongol steppe invaders from the twelfth through mid-fourteenth centuries. What is more, enlightened Ming rulers restored civilized ancient Chinese ways in toto upon coming to power in 1368.[53]

This contrast between Chinese civilization and Japanese barbarism is best illustrated by Master Ryū's harsh criticism of forehead-shaving. According to historian Mitamura Taisuke, East Asian peoples from the thirteenth century onward saw themselves engaged in a recurring clash between two main ethnocultural groups: those who grew their forelocks long and those who shaved the top-front portion of their heads. The "long-locks" were mainly Chinese and Koreans, who esteemed civil virtues.[54] The "head-shavers" included Mongols, Manchus, and Japanese, who prized martial exploits.[55]

During the Edo period, and to a lesser extent in the previous Muromachi (or Ashikaga) period, certain nonmilitary status groups in Japan let all the hair on their heads grow long in what came to be called the *sōhatsu* fashion with or without a topknot folded forward—a hairstyle similar to that of sumo wrestlers today. In general, these Tokugawa nonwarrior groups included physicians, court nobles, Confucian scholars, Shinto priests, and itinerant mountain priests who belonged to Buddhist or shaman sects. For warriors in the Edo period, a half-shaven head with a topknot signified an office-holding, salary-receiving samurai; the *sōhatsu* style, by contrast, was the mark of a *rōnin*. Thus portraits of the mature Yamagata Daini, who held no official bakufu or domain posts after 1751, show him without a topknot sporting the *sōhatsu* characteristic of physicians and samurai who served no liege lord.

On the East Asian continent, forcing conquered peoples to shave the top-front portion of their heads became a way to make them acknowledge their subject status. That is why Han Chinese had to shave their heads under the Mongol Yuan dynasty, established in the late thirteenth century.[56] But as Master Ryū notes, Ming rulers abolished such "barbaric" ways after attaining power in 1368. In Japan, as Master Ryū bewailed, "cropped hair was common in the realm by Ashikaga times, but only among base fighting men whose calling required short hair." After the Ōnin War of 1467 to 1477, however, "even state officials such as court nobles and generals-in-chief cropped their hair and shaved their foreheads."[57] In other words, Yamagata Daini contended that long forelocks on the Chinese showed that their land had maintained its advanced status as Middle Kingdom civilization *(Chung-kuo)* despite having suffered barbarian conquest and occupation. By contrast, clean-shaven heads on samurai-officials proved that the Japanese ruling classes had plunged headlong into barbarity even though their land had never succumbed to foreign military domination.[58] Not surprisingly, Master Ryū makes no reference to the queue that Chinese officials and commoners were forced to adopt under the contemporary Manchu Ch'ing dynasty.[59] Of course, his studied silence was to avoid giving away the actual period in which he wrote.

Daini's scholarly treatises on archaic Chinese phonology and linguistics show that he was no less a sinological purist than Ogyū Sorai or Dazai Shundai. All three openly sneered at Japanese scholars—even those literate in classical Chinese—for not knowing the proper meaning and pronunciation of Chinese ideographs.[60] Sorai deemed the Japanese language vulgar; classical Chinese was elegant.[61] Shundai and Daini disparaged countrymen for ignorantly misusing the ideograph *"gyo."* It properly connoted "chariot driving"; when used to denote the honorific prefix *"go"* or *"on,"* it should refer only to the emperor.[62] Sinocentric affectation and high-brow linguistic quibbling of this sort earned biting rebukes from Matsumiya Kanzan: "Did the sages intend to standardize all languages when they insisted that 'name and actuality conform'?" Matsumiya and other Shinto-inspired nativists denounced the Sorai scholars for calling Japan "a land of eastern barbarians."[63] To Matsumiya, Master Ryū was a conceited "follower of alien doctrines" who demeaned his native tongue and folkways.[64] Matsumiya adhered to the conventional nativist line advanced by Shinto-Confucian syncretists—namely, that Japan's Way of the Gods and China's Way of the Sages were separate and distinct but "coincided by chance" *(myōkei)* in all truly important moral and cultural matters. As Matsumiya snorted, "even by [purely] Confucian standards," the Way is "being more or less practiced in Japan without our having altered traditional customs."[65]

For Master Ryū, a ruler assumed several heaven-appointed duties in upholding the adornments of cultured rule *(bun)*. One was to maintain the class-specific dress codes created by the sages, the most important of which differentiated noble ranks among state officials at court. Shōtoku Taishi instituted these dress codes, beginning with a system of graded court caps and garments in 603. But these regulations could not be enforced for long because economic advancement fostered conspicuous consumption among the lower orders in Japan. Master Ryū fiercely opposes any blurring of status lines because that would further debase values and standards: "True discrimination of high from low is lost so that the canons of behavior integral to civilized life are destroyed."[66] Such had been true even in Confucius' day, when disciple Tzu-lu's rectitude was exceptional: "In tattered cotton-padded garments, he felt no embarrassment next to men wearing fox-fur or badger-skin coats."[67] In Master Ryū's degenerate era, Japanese rulers and commoners alike keenly desired to ape their social betters. Shōtoku Taishi's court caps and garments had long ago given way to the dress of barbarians who "donned neither cap nor headcloth" and whose "garments lacked collar and sleeves."[68] In short, Japanese emperors had failed to discharge this key heaven-appointed duty of upholding dress codes to discriminate the esteemed from the base.

But "rectifying names" had been their most important duty. And for Master Ryū, this meant upholding the hierarchy created by the sages comprising "four peoples," or hereditary social classes, that had found ideal embodiment in China during Western Chou times. Remove that normative order, and society perforce reverted to a primitive state of violent disorder. Japan's imperial dynasty had failed in this task, too; and the proof was clear for all to see. Proper music, rituals, court-dress regulations, and the other adornments of cultured rule *(bun)* had atrophied long ago owing to neglect or misuse. These came to be eclipsed by the penal codes and coercive force of martial rule *(bu)*. So Japan reverted to a primeval condition of Warring States wherein "men harm and wound, oppress and kill, rob and pillage." The key to "rectifying names" was for the ruler to ensure that each people, or socioeconomic class, adhered strictly to the heaven-mandated line of work expressed in its status name. But this task had proved impossible because Japanese commoners were "wholly undiscriminating and incapable of reason." They would "seek profit and shrink from loss by nature," so they "strove to garner ill-gotten gains in mercantile activities" like "ants racing to putrid meat." Seeing that they had nothing to gain by staying and nothing to lose by leaving, commoners deserted farming in their native abodes and fled en masse to urban areas. Motivated by such selfish instincts, they bore no comparison to the "superior men"— would-be state officials such as Daini himself—who wished nothing more than to "offer up their lives to perfect their virtue."[69]

The problem had become most acute in Master Ryū's Warring States era. He defined the Way of government: "Civil rule *(bun)* maintains order under normal conditions; martial rule *(bu)* deals with emergencies."[70] This definition, usually hailed as unique to Yamagata Daini, echoes an injunction found in Ogyū Sorai's *Mondō sho* of 1724: "Employ *bun* in times of order, and *bu* in times of disorder."[71] When Master Ryū asserts that "conditions, then, are *not* normal,"[72] he means they were so bad that civil rule alone would not suffice. The severe laws and punishments of martial rule were absolutely needed to "rectify names" at all levels of society, but especially at the bottom. Commoners refused to perform their class-specific socioeconomic functions as mandated by heaven. They changed occupations, assumed aliases, and fled their native abodes to become renegades or city-dwellers. Yamagata Daini could have been describing his fugitive brother Bumon, or even himself, when he had Master Ryū observe:

> Cities teem with vagrants; and each year thousands more flee the countryside.... Once a man has begun life anew elsewhere, his past will never catch up with him. Many live out their lives in secure anonymity, escaping arrest forever in the city.[73]

For these reasons, coercive laws and harsh measures were needed to keep commoners living and working where they belonged. In line with Ogyū Sorai and Dazai Shundai, Yamagata Daini argued for compiling detailed records to list the name, address, and occupation of each person in every household. As well, Daini advocated creating mutual surveillance groups, comprised of several households each, in order to force popular compliance with the law.

Bakufu officials had always turned a deaf ear to such reform proposals for being unenforceable; indeed, Daini's own family violated these repeatedly. They had gone by four different sur-names—Yamagata, Sakatomi, Nozawa, and Murase—and they had changed lines of work several times: from warrior chieftain, to wealthy peasant, to bakufu police constable, to freelance physician and scholar, to lowly peasant, and, finally, to Shinto priest. During his own lifetime as well, members of Daini's family assumed numerous different aliases. Daini himself started out as Murase Gunji, changed his name to Yamagata Masasada, and adopted the sobriquet Dōsai in 1745 after he moved to Edo and began to practice medicine. Indeed, by becoming a physician, Daini took up one of the "base" occupations that Master Ryū derides in his "new thesis." The name "Daini" itself is an imperial office title: "senior assistant governor-general" in Kyushu government headquarters. Daini's elder brother Masaki began as Murase Kiyozaemon Tamekiyo, but he later assumed peasant status and went by the name Ichirōzaemon.[74] After being exiled in the Meiwa Incident, Masaki changed his surname again, this time to Nozawa, when he became a shrine priest. And if all that were not enough, Masaki adopted the imperial office title "Provincial Governor of Bungo," thus calling himself "Nozawa Bungo no kami."[75]

Such practices were not out of the ordinary. The mid-Tokugawa thinker Nishikawa Joken (1648–1724) explained how the custom of incorporating imperial office titles in personal names had come about:

> In olden days, townsmen and peasants did not have names suffixed with "emon" or "bei." But ever since the era of upheaval and civil war, many samurai who fell on hard times concealed their lineages and lived among nonaristocrats. As a result, their custom of naming gradually spread to commoners. "Emon" [gate guard] and "bei" [middle palace guard] are office titles and thus should not be suffixed to the names of townsmen or peasants.[76]

Whether historically accurate or not, Nishikawa's explanation shows that the practice of incorporating lower-ranking imperial court titles in personal names was common by the early Edo period.

In sum, then, Yamagata family members reflected prevailing trends in Tokugawa society by repudiating several key measures that Master Ryū advocates. They violated with impunity the Ritsu-Ryō law codes that prohibited changes in abode, the desertion of one's inherited family occupation, and the use of imperial office titles in personal names. In the *Ryūshi shinron*, Daini complains: "If we enforced those codes strictly, who in the realm today would *not* be guilty?" He should have asked that of himself.

Master Ryū posits an immutable moral hierarchy composed of four "good" classes: state officials, peasants, artisans, and merchants. Of course, he insists that rigid status barriers be upheld between these four peoples. But even more important, these four peoples, or "good classes," had to be permanently segregated from, and kept from intermarrying with, the so-called despised classes: performers, prostitutes, monkey trainers, blind persons, fortune-tellers, outcastes, and menial servants in merchant establishments. Here again Daini follows Ogyū Sorai faithfully. Master Ryū differentiates these "despised" classes—whom he calls "putrid incense" and "foul water"—from merely "base" persons such as diviners, physicians, craftsmen, and merchants. This distinction is based on the rationale that "base" persons perform needed services for the realm despite their mean status.

As intellectual historian Kinugasa Yasuki shows, Japanese Confucians before Ogyū Sorai generally supported what we today would call "liberation" for stigmatized groups; but the Sorai school revised certain key tenets in Confucian ethical thought and thereby decisively redefined conceptions of prejudice in early modern Japan.[77] For example, there had never been any taboos against eating the meat of four-legged animals in China. Quite to the contrary, references to meat eating by commoners in the Chinese Confucian classics signified proof of popular welfare under benevolent government. Nothing in Chinese Confucianism sanctioned discrimination against persons who killed animals, handled corpses, or tanned hides for a living. If pre-Sorai Japanese Confucians affirmed these stigmas, it was only from a need to "naturalize" or gain acceptance for their alien creed by accommodating native beliefs and values derived from Shinto or Buddhism.[78] But they fully believed such backward indigenous ways would die out after their Confucian-style civilization and enlightenment took root in Japan.

Pre-Sorai Tokugawa Confucians did place certain groups of people below merchants in the four-class social hierarchy. These groups were termed *yūmin,* or "idlers," and they included beggars, entertainers, prostitutes, blind persons, fortune-tellers, and the like. But their status was not seen as hereditary in nature, and their supposed fall from respectability was blamed partly on bad government. There had never been any counterparts to Master Ryū's irredeemably "despised" classes. As the pre-Sorai Confucian argument in Japan went, these stigmatized groups could rejoin the good classes if rulers would just practice the Way and govern benevolently; then any basis for discrimination would disappear. Succoring these lower classes, then, was both possible and desirable as a political goal.

As Kinugasa argues, the Sorai school changed all that by Kyōhō times (1716–1735); and its ideas became pervasive among Japanese thinkers from the Tanuma era (1767–1786) onward. Ogyū Sorai argued that certain "despised" classes in Japan descended from alien races termed "different species." And, he insisted, bakufu rulers should actively foster discrimination against them as a moral imperative, not help them to rejoin the good classes. In the *Seidan,* Sorai maintained:

> Despised persons such as prostitutes and performers are . . . descended from different species. That is why they come under the jurisdiction of Danzaemon [head of the outcastes]. But old laws have broken down recently. Thus, for example, performers become merchants or [conversely] commoners sell their daughters as prostitutes.[79]

Ogyū Sorai was adamant about the need to revive what he believed had been the laws of antiquity by which the infallible sage-kings had compiled separate domicile registers for such despised classes. That policy enabled the sages to uphold permanent segregation of those outcaste groups in apartheid fashion.

Yamagata Daini followed these views wholeheartedly. He argues that the mingling of good and despised classes had begun when performers and entertainers came to receive official stipends, thereby gaining wealth without achievement and honor without virtue. These toadies would change occupations outright—to become state officials—because they came to win the ruler's favor."[80]

This passage may refer to Shogun Tsunayoshi's employment of No actors in his administration. But given the context in which it is found, it more likely indicates the practice of conferring imperial court ranks and titles *(zuryō)* on performers in the theater arts.[81] The practice began with an act of grave misgovernment by Emperor Goyōzei (r. 1586–1611). He was the first emperor to grant imperial court titles such as *jō,* or "provincial ministerial secretary," to *jōruri* chanters and *kabuki* players. Goyōzei's precedent-setting act violated Ritsu-Ryō "imperial law codes [which] stipulate that false or unauthorized use of government titles warrants the harshest of punishments." As a result, Master Ryū laments that

peasants, artisans, merchants, menials, indentured servants, even the meanest, most despised classes—actors, outcastes, beggars, and untouchables—all suffix their names with imperial office titles such as "bei" (middle palace guard), "suke" (sssistant), or "jō" (provincial ministerial secretary).[82]

Now, Master Ryū charges, even the vilest classes in society are adopting imperial titles in their names. "Courtesans" in the gay quarters or traveling performers received honorific titles such as "Tayū," a general designation for holders of court ranks one through five; and they began to incorporate imperial titles such as "secretary in the provincial government of Harima" *(Harima no jō)* in their names. Thus they called themselves, for example, "Takemoto Harima no jō Gi-*dayū*," or "Tajima-*dayū*."

As the Genroku thinker Nishikawa Joken had noted, such practices were commonplace early in the Edo period. In fact, they were so commonplace that bakufu attempts at prohibition were bound to fail. The imperial court conferred, or was seen to confer, honorific ranks and titles not only on courtesans and entertainers, but also on artisans or craft-masters *(shokunin)* in scores of professions: yin-yang diviners, hunters, physicians, tub and barrel makers, blind usurers, metalsmiths, carpenters, confectioners, mirror-casters, sumo wrestlers, tea-whisk makers, and hairdressers, to mention but a few.[83]

In 1611, the bakufu had decreed that it alone could petition the imperial court for ranks and titles granted to warriors. That decree stopped potentially hostile daimyo from claiming these honors without authorization or from receiving them directly from the court as they had in earlier centuries. So, in effect, the Edo bakufu established a system whereby it determined which daimyo received what ranks and titles.[84]

The situation with commoners differed. In order to acquire a court rank or office title legitimately, commoners first needed a formal letter of introduction from a bona fide court noble addressed to the appropriate imperial officials. Thus Yamagata Masasada applied to the Tsuchimikado because they granted honors to yin-yang diviners. But that was just the start. Then commoner applicants had to get certified seals from official guarantors, go through more elaborate procedures, and pay stiff "thank you" fees.[85] Because this process was so difficult and costly, few commoners obtained rank and title through legitimate channels. Instead, they laid spurious claim to these honors—much as the daimyo and warriors had done in pre-Tokugawa days. The Edo regime had seized control over imperial honors granted to daimyo and samurai in 1611. And it tried to end the use of fraudulent ranks and titles by commoners as well by issuing regulatory edicts beginning in 1707. By the early nineteenth century, however, Edo bakufu authorities had to concede that their efforts were futile.[86]

The desire of commoners to acquire court rank and title can be surmised from *Yōmei tennō shokunin kagami,* one of the thirty-three works in Chikamatsu Monzaemon's (1653–1724) genre of "*tennō* dramas."[87] This play, cast in the late sixth century, begins with craft-masters in various professions mourning the death of Emperor Bidatsu (r. 572–585), who had granted many of them imperial office titles. Led by a valiant tub maker, they go on to repay Bidatsu's august virtue by backing his chosen heir in a violent succession struggle. Armed with the tools of their trades, they form politicized militia-like bands—clearly outlawed under Tokugawa law—to fight in this "loyalist" cause. Due to their heroism, Emperor Yōmei's succession is ensured despite the evil machinations of his rival.[88]

Thus Tokugawa commoners and even some groups of "despised" persons received (or claimed to have received) court ranks and titles similar to those conferred on the shogun, daimyo, and samurai. To some extent, this commoner craving for imperial honors may be construed as an aspiration for social advancement, or even liberation, on the part of those classes that suffered discrimination in early-modern Japanese society. Kobayashi Shinsuke, a puppeteer who endured discrimination for his "despised" occupation, proclaimed in 1707 that

> a man named Jirōbei was the first *jōruri* chanter to acquire an imperial provincial-government title *(zuryō)*, that of *sakan*, or "senior clerk" in the provincial government of Kawachi.... So puppet play chanters are not of the despised classes. Proof for this is that they are summoned to the imperial court and awarded imperial provincial governorships.[89]

Clearly, Kobayashi's desire to overcome discrimination and win respect in Tokugawa society is here linked with the acquiring of imperial honors—whether genuine or spurious. By contrast, Yamagata Daini was bent on denying such honors to all commoners, especially the stigmatized classes. Daini's sinocentrism and contempt for the masses—like his understanding of political legitimation and bakufu-court relations in Japanese history—were solidly Confucian in nature and mainly inspired by the Ogyū Sorai school.

Prewar Japanese nationalist scholars conveniently ignored criticisms of the type lodged by Matsumiya Kanzan, who lambasted Daini's snobbish sinophilia. On the other hand, postwar humanist scholars and Yamanashi schoolchildren have praised Daini as a revolutionary advocate of populism or as a democratic leveler who called for eradicating discrimination based on hereditary social class.

Any close reading of the *Ryūshi shinron* will show that Master Ryū was no friend of the toiling masses—those "stupid, unlettered masses,"[90] as he calls them. He graphically depicts how working men and women "clamor like swine and bicker like dogs."[91] He employs unflattering metaphors such as "more repulsive than a peasant clod sweating in the summer sun."[92] He takes pains to note: "But commoners are stupid. If they stray from the

Way which must be followed—and so create harmful disorder—they must be punished to eliminate evils" in the realm.[93] Indeed, Daini opposed rather than encouraged direct action by the oppressed classes to gain redress for grievances: "Desperadoes now employ the occult to lead stupid commoners down evil paths; and those commoners plunder the homes of local leaders, or they appeal directly to provincial lords."[94] This statement shows that he disapproved of their violent uprisings directed against local officials and that he supported current bakufu and domain laws to block appeals lodged directly with higher officials (jikiso) even by peaceful means.

Above all, Yamagata Daini followed the Sorai school in claiming that the Chinese sage-kings of antiquity based their policies of segregation and discrimination on theories of bloodline and race. Sorai and Daini applied that claim—whatever its historical validity—to contemporary Tokugawa society. By so doing, they helped perpetuate prejudice in Japan by making its determining factor biological and hence unalterable. Later Tokugawa-era thinkers such as Kaiho Seiryō (1755–1817), Hoashi Banri (1778–1852), and Buyō Inshi (dates unknown) reiterated Ogyū Sorai's claim that these outcaste or despised classes were of foreign descent by arbitrarily ascribing Korean or Okinawan origins to them.[95] In this way, the egalitarian elements found in pre-Sorai Confucianism—which stressed the ruler's duty to lead "base" classes back to "respectability"—were largely forgotten. And the myth of Japanese superiority to other East Asian ethnic groups was made that much easier to foster.

Sagely Reforms

Master Ryū's whole critique of problems in Tokugawa society—and all his proposals to solve these—were directed at those social orders from which worthy government officials were to be drawn: the daimyo and samurai. The lower orders would just follow enlightened leadership from above. In Daini's mind, two types of problems plagued the existing order: specific socioeconomic ills and structural-institutional flaws. But neither was life-threatening; both could be solved if rulers followed certain sagely tenets of reform outlined in the Confucian classics and practiced by exemplary Chinese emperors. For Master Ryū, those sagely tenets amounted to "immutable laws governing heaven and earth" that serve as "main guidelines" for rulership. Get these right to start with, and "details will work themselves out later on."[96] Thus, for example, the Confucian classic, the *Doctrine of the Mean,* said: "When equilibrium and harmony *(chūwa)* reach their apogee, heaven is high, earth is low, and the myriad things are nurtured."[97] Following Dazai Shundai, Daini believed that "equilibrium and harmony" were achieved when each social class adhered to its designated status name and did its proper work. Another Confucian classic, the *Book of Changes,* conveyed still other guidelines: "Neither yin nor yang, security nor stagnation, remain constant. There can be no increase and benefit in one place without a decrease and loss elsewhere."[98] In other words, to cure current socioeconomic woes, Master Ryū proposes reform policies that were revealed in cryptic passages taken from the classical Chinese sources. Hence we must decipher and elaborate on those here.

Each hexagram in the *Book of Changes* contains two trigrams, an upper and a lower; and each trigram consists of three broken and/or unbroken lines. For example, the hexagram for "security" *(t'ai)* ䷊ is made up of the upper trigram ☷ and the lower trigram ☰. The hexagram for "stagnation" *(p'i)* ䷋ is made up of the upper trigram ☰ and the lower trigram ☷. Daini's expertise in the *Changes* earned him the imperial title "Governor-General of the Thirty-Three Eastern Provinces." Long years spent studying that classic told him that the hexagram for "security" ䷊ turns into that for "decrease" *(sun)* ䷨ when we "add to the ruler above and take away from the people below."[99] This is symbolized by one unbroken line removed from the lower trigram in "security" and added to the upper trigram in "decrease." It represents a "loss" for the people at the bottom of society and a "gain" for the ruler at the top. Therefore, security in the realm disappears when the ruler benefits at the people's expense. Conversely, the hexagram for "stagnation" ䷋ turns into that for "increase" *(i)* ䷩ 当 when we "take away from the ruler above and add to the people below."[100] This is symbolized by one unbroken line removed from the upper trigram in "stagnation" and added to the lower trigram in "increase." It represents a gain for the people at the bottom of society and a loss for the ruler at the top. Therefore, stagnation in the realm disappears when the people benefit at the ruler's expense. These two "main guidelines" had also been expounded by Dazai Shundai.[101]

Daini found another tenet of sagely reform in the *Book of Documents:* "The Kingly Way is level. . . . Leveling must be the aim of those in government today." And "to level means for the ruler to distribute benefits impartially. . . . Only then could commoners enjoy a secure livelihood and devote themselves to their callings in their native abodes." As well, he said, "the Way for ensuring enough food is . . . to promote farming; and the policy for distributing wealth is to level prices."[102]

Master Ryū's reform proposals may be summed up as follows. Commoners had certain physical and emotional needs—for economic well-being and a sense of "repose." But because they were undiscriminating and hopelessly lost to reason, the masses fulfilled these needs without a thought to virtue or to the implications of their behavior for society as a whole. The ruler's task was to meet their needs in ways that would increase political stability and equalize the distribution of wealth throughout the realm. Then "the four peoples will find their proper places in society and all under heaven will be at peace."[103] And the sagely ideal of "equilibrium and harmony" would be restored as well. In more down-to-earth terms, Master Ryū's program was this. Taxes were far too high, causing peasants to abandon farming and flee from their native abodes to pursue commerce in urban areas. As a result, the realm's food supply dwindled and people starved everywhere. Meanwhile, profiteering merchants hoarded scarce grain and goods, hoping to drive prices even higher. Thus it was time to follow the sages' advice: "Level" (cut) both grain taxes and commodity prices by government fiat. That measure would "take away from the ruler above and add to the people below."[104]

Such, no doubt, was the message that domain elder Yoshida Gemba took from Daini to Obata leaders in 1766. Master Ryū argues that grain taxes should be cut from current rates of fifty or sixty percent to ten percent as in ancient China. Then commoners would gain a sense of repose and confidence in their ability to sustain a livelihood on the land. If the ruler made farming profitable again, the urban masses would gladly return to their native

abodes and grow vast quantities of grain in the countryside—
boosting the amount in circulation and depressing prices throughout the realm. But before any of that could happen, the ruler had
to adopt coercive measures of martial rule *(bu)* in order to curb
greedy merchant princes: "Create agencies and issue edicts to
make them eat the same food as farmers and live on a par with
artisans. . . . Prohibit them their luxury playthings and stately
mansions; [and] punish any who refuses to mend his ways and
obey." If the ruler implemented martial law to make merchants
slash prices and stop hoarding, the number of goods up for sale
would increase; and with more commodities thus circulating in
the realm, their prices would level off still further.[105]

But far from adopting these sagely reforms, Japanese rulers did
just the opposite. They "took away from those below and added
to themselves above," thereby creating "decrease" and destroying
"stability" in the realm. To tide himself over each new fiscal crisis,
the typical ruler of a state took away from his officials and retainers above by reducing salaries and took away from the people
below by raising grain taxes. Hence "day by day his state's officials become more destitute and its people more rebellious.
Resentment and anger explode." And, of course, "with hatred
comes revolt, and with revolts, chaos. Then disaster is bound to
occur."[106]

In Master Ryū's last analysis, the inability to "ensure that food
and currency circulate in the realm"—or to do anything else right
for that matter—stemmed from the unwillingness of state rulers
to purge bad officials and promote good ones. The average ruler
was not very discerning when it came to choosing ministers:

> Toadies ingratiate themselves and make him their stooge. The clev-
> erest liken his government to that of Yao, Shun, and the Three
> Dynasties. . . . They make him gloat in his wisdom and virtue,
> while keeping him ignorant of conditions in his realm and of the
> changing times. A benighted fool by nature, he becomes even more
> of one—until he fails to see the demise lying just ahead.[107]

Master Ryū argues that this problem could be solved if state
rulers adopted the right mental attitude until it became habitual.
They should make up their minds to seek out, employ, and promote worthy officials:

A ruler's best course of study is not to master the refinements of the Six Arts, not to recite the doctrines of the Hundred Schools. He should just accept the need to believe in the Way. Then those who have mastered it will come forth to serve him. If he but places his trust in them, how could villainous rebels ever arise in his state? All troubles in the realm would then cease.[108]

In effect, a ruler did not need to know very much. He himself did not have to read the Chinese classics in order to discover their "immutable laws governing heaven and earth" that constituted the Way of kingly government. What he needed was the humility to know his own limitations and the good sense to seek ministerial assistance in overcoming these: "When the ruler shows a desire to obtain worthy officials, they appear as quickly as shadow follows form, or echo follows sound."[109]

Daini's Master Ryū mentions but two Japanese emperors, Jimmu and Godaigo, and only Jimmu rates as a sage-king. Instead, Daini praises Chinese sovereigns: Shang-dynasty Kings T'ang and T'ai Chia, King Chao of Yen, and Han-dynasty founder Kao-tsu (formerly Liu Pang). King T'ang promoted Yi Yin to the post of grand minister, or *a-heng,* and King T'ai Chia accepted Yi Yin's advice and punishment. Liu Pang followed remonstrations from his chief minister Shu-sun T'ung to institute Confucian ritual in government. Only then, as Daini quotes Ssu-ma Ch'ien, did Liu Pang "come to know imperial majesty" as the first Han emperor, Kao-tsu.[110] As to precisely how an ideal ruler attracted ministers like Yi Yin or Shu-sun T'ung, Master Ryū asserts: "That is very easy; what is very hard is for men to make themselves known." To support this claim, he cites examples from the *Han Fei Tzu:* "King Ling of Ch'u liked slim-hipped consorts, so women starved to death trying to become slender; the King of Yueh liked brave troops, so men did not flinch from leaping aboard burning ships at the beat of a battle drum." Then Daini explains: "Nothing could be more painful than starving to death by trying to become slender or than leaping aboard a burning ship. But if that is what the ruler likes, people will do it without being ordered." After all, "it is very hard for men to make themselves known to a ruler, and so they eagerly perform the most painful acts to catch his notice. . . . If he but wants something done, endless streams of men will come forth to do it."[111]

Master Ryū supplies another example by alluding to the well-known story of Kuo Wei and King Chao. This episode is found in a Han-dynasty work, the *Chan kuo ts'e,* which describes interstate intrigues during China's Warring States period (403–222 B.C.). The youthful Chao came to the throne in the state of Yen and realized that he had to create national strength and unity if he hoped to avenge an earlier defeat suffered at the hands of arch-rival Ch'i. The first step was to recruit talented men for his government, and King Chao asked Master Kuo Wei how to proceed. Kuo Wei replied, "He who knows imperial majesty lives with his teachers," and then he related the famous tale about a thousand-mile steed. It went like this. A king in antiquity offered one thousand gold pieces to buy a steed able to run one thousand miles, and for three years he had no luck. Then a palace steward offered to find one and paid five hundred gold pieces for a dead horse. The king was enraged when he found out. But the steward explained his rationale as follows. If the king publicized his desire to pay this much for a dead steed of such caliber, people would see that he was a keen judge of horses, that he highly prized the best, and that he would offer even more money for a qualified living steed. Once that became widely known, he could obtain as many good horses as he wanted. And indeed, three were acquired within a year.

The moral of the tale was this: King Chao had to make people see that he greatly valued worthy ministers and that he could tell the able from the inept. If he wished to attract talented men to serve, he should "start with Kuo Wei." Offer a mediocre man like Kuo Wei an honored post with a generous stipend, and then truly superior officials would be attracted to Yen. King Chao took this advice, built Master Kuo Wei a palace, and went to live there under his tutelage. Word of this spread all over the realm, and three eminent ministers from other states soon came to serve Yen. King Chao lived with them and studied under them for twenty-eight years; as a result, Yen became so wealthy and strong that it easily avenged the earlier defeat inflicted by Ch'i.[112]

Yamagata Daini believed that Japanese rulers should follow King Chao's lead and "start with Master Ryū." Many teacher-advisors of Kuo Wei's caliber were available. "But they chafe in silence like the horses of northern Chi waiting in vain for Po Lo's

coming"—all because no one cared to search for them.[113] Thus
Daini's proposed cure for current socioeconomic problems hinged
on finding rulers endowed with King Chao's humility and judgment. They would realize that the Chinese classics contained eternal truths and guiding principles of rulership absolutely needed to
govern. And, though unable to comprehend these truths and principles themselves, they would employ wise ministers and teacher-
advisors who did.

Daini's proposal to attract and promote worthy men to officialdom was status-bound. He did not want to scrap the existing
hereditary-class order in favor of promotion by merit alone.[114]
The daimyo and samurai were not government officials as such;
they were the social orders from which capable officials were to
be drawn. Postwar humanist scholars often cite Master Ryū's
observation: "There is nothing wrong with elevating lesser officials to ministerial posts or with making foot soldiers into generals."[115] But we must not misconstrue the intent behind it. By
this comment, Daini meant that low-ranking worthy men—from
among the daimyo and samurai—should be promoted to office.
Totally different rules held for commoners. They were to stay in
their heaven-mandated hereditary callings no matter what. And
the "despised" classes were to be permanently segregated from,
and kept from intermarrying with, their betters. For Daini, Sorai-
style discrimination based on bloodline was an unqualified good.
Commoners would be elevated only in the realm of spirit. This is
why Master Ryū declares: "Cultivate benevolence and filial submission so that 'all are morally uplifted to the level of their
overlords.'"[116]

We can discern Daini's conception of the ideal government official by citing those whom Master Ryū lauded by name. They were
numerous, but three stand out: Yi Yin, Hou Kuang, and Fujiwara
no Mototsune. Yi Yin was the grand minister (a-heng) under King
T'ang of the Shang dynasty. King T'ang died in 1766 B.C. after
naming Yi Yin regent in charge of the crown prince who would
become King T'ai Chia in 1753 B.C. But T'ai Chia turned out to
be immoral and did not rule as a true king should. So Yi Yin
"deposed" him by banishing him from court to an area near his
father's grave. Yi Yin then became a critical mentor to the unruly
T'ai Chia for three years and harshly admonished him to mend his

ways. When T'ai Chia finally agreed to obey, Yi Yin restored him to the throne; T'ai Chia then implored Yi Yin to continue his remonstrative counsels. According to ministerial autonomy of this type, a grand minister or regent upbraided a wayward sovereign and, in an extreme case, might force that sovereign to abdicate in favor of a more worthy successor. But the minister did not kill his sovereign or terminate the dynastic line.

In China, this method of "deposing" evil monarchs evolved into a lesser-known secondary tradition behind Mencius' "regicide and dynastic overthrow," or *hōbatsu*. Yi Yin's form of deposing was also practiced by Hou Kuang, another Chinese exemplar cited by Master Ryū. Chief Minister Hou Kuang, who held the Han-dynasty post transliterated into Japanese as "Taishōgun," emulated Yi Yin by forcing his emperor off the throne in 74 B.C; and classical historian Pan Ku praised him as "an *a-heng* of Han times."[117]

This secondary Chinese tradition of "deposing"—in the sense of forcing a morally flawed sovereign to relinquish the throne to a worthy heir—became the major tradition in Japan. In fact, it was the only acceptable way to chasten evil or irresponsible descendants of the Sun Goddess Amaterasu. Ministers followed it to "depose" violent or corrupt emperors while keeping the inviolable imperial family line intact. Daini's model minister, Fujiwara no Mototsune, *sesshō* and *kampaku* from 872 to 891, was called an "*a-heng*" in the Heian era.[118] Mototsune was regent to the imperial prince who later became the violent Emperor Yōzei. After acceding, Yōzei went about killing people for no good reason. So, in 884, Fujiwara no Mototsune emulated Yi Yin and Hou Kuang. He banished Yōzei from court, forced him into retirement as a cloistered ex-emperor, and replaced him with the crown prince known to history as Emperor Kōkō. Like Daini, the late-Tokugawa historians Rai Sanyō (1780–1832) and Date Chihiro (1802–1877) placed Fujiwara no Mototsune in this Chinese *a-heng* tradition by comparing him explicitly to Yi Yin and Hou Kuang.[119] As we shall see in Chapter 4, that view carried on the appraisal of Fujiwara regents as "loyalist" in the sense construed by medieval thinkers such as Jien (1155–1225) and Kitabatake Chikafusa (1293–1354). Yamagata Daini too must be placed within this "other" loyalist tradition of imperial assistance rendered by devoted ministers who knew what was good for the sovereign and were never coy about letting it be known.

Thus, Master Ryū's proposals to cure specific socioeconomic ills under the current Tokugawa order required an ideal ruler who searched out able men of humble birth from among the daimyo and samurai classes and promoted them to ministerial posts. Then that ruler would accept abusively critical advice, or even punishment, from these faithful ministers. Daini did not call for an imperial restoration; nor did he tender proposals for drastic institutional change. His sought to make the Tokugawa shogun and regional daimyo into *a-heng* who would assist the emperor on the advice of astute teacher-remonstrators.

Civil and Martial

Yamagata Daini never championed the virtues of civil over martial rule in an unconditional fashion. To the contrary, Master Ryū was adamant that "neither the civil nor the martial can be done away with"[120] because both kinds of officials were indispensable for proper administration in Japan's current Warring States era: "In this they are comparable to horses and oxen. By nature, horses can run far and oxen can pull heavy loads. But if we made either do the opposite, neither could bear the task."[121] Hence, Daini did not argue that the bakufu should be eliminated in favor of reviving civil rule by the emperor and imperial court as in antiquity. For him, contemporary government in Japan was not bad because it was warrior government; it was bad because the military predominated over the civil when both ought to come under unified control. A strange emperor-shogun dyarchy had emerged whereby "[Kyoto] bestows honors without riches and [Edo] bestows riches without honor."[122]

Master Ryū describes these basic structural flaws in his typically indirect way—this time, by alluding to imaginary creatures found in the *Erh-ya,* a third-century B.C. primer that glossed difficult classical Chinese terms:

There is a beast called "Half-Flanks." To run, each of the pair must align with a mate of the opposite flank. There is a bird called "Single-Wings." To fly, each of the pair must align with a mate of the opposite wing. In each case, the two halves must form a whole in order to function; if either half went its own way, running or flying could not occur.[123]

Single-Wings *(pi-yi-niao)* was a symmetrically paired set of birds supposedly found on China's southern frontier. Each had a head, one eye, and one wing. To fly, the two had to form a whole by lining up side-by-side. Half-Flanks *(pi-chien-shou)*, supposedly found to the west of China, was a matched set of animals too. One of the pair had short front legs and long hind legs; so it was good at gathering and eating food but could not run without toppling over headfirst. The other had short hind legs and long front legs; so it ran well but could not gather and eat food. Hence both halves of the pair cooperated in symbiotic fashion.[124]

Daini argued that this type of symmetrical bifurcation and functional duplicity was fine in the world of beasts, but not in the realm's government. "Oneness," or unified command, had to be attained. Arai Hakuseki and Ogyū Sorai had pointed out decades earlier that such duality in Japan's government structure stemmed from the imperial court's continued existence and its hollow vestiges of sovereign authority. These remnants included the conferring of Ritsu-Ryō court ranks and office titles and the promulgating of era names—all of which were highly prized by nativists such as Matsumiya Kanzan, Yusa Bokusai, and Kuriyama Sempō. Imperial ranks and titles were purely nominal; and that was precisely the problem. Name did not conform to reality because the shogun and his military government were sovereign in fact but not in title. As Ogyū Sorai had put it: "All daimyo in the realm are retainers of the shogun, but some may think that the imperial court is their true sovereign because they receive court ranks on the order of Kyoto."[125] Arai Hakuseki was a case in point, even though his view of the "other sovereign" *(kyōshu)* in Kyoto closely resembled Sorai's.[126] Though not a daimyo, Hakuseki was a direct bakufu retainer who owed his livelihood to Edo. But he also boasted junior fifth rank lower level and the Ritsu-Ryō office title "Provincial Governor of Chikugo." So he received honor and social status from Kyoto.

Sorai believed that this side of the Japanese Half-Flanks posed a danger because it presented an alternate source of moral legitimacy around which Tokugawa enemies might rally: "Right now they are submissive because they fear bakufu power. . . . Who knows what may happen if the times turn against us?"[127] By contrast, Matsumiya Kanzan was sanguine about any potential danger stemming from this Kyoto-Edo bifurcation: "Obedience or disobedience was an issue in ancient times, when there were two kings and two imperial courts in the land: the Northern and Southern. But now one is sovereign and the other is its subject. So what is the problem?"[128] In fact, Matsumiya lauded the present court-bakufu dyarchy as a "beautiful Japanese custom without parallel anywhere."[129] From a more Machiavellian perspective, Kumazawa Banzan believed that the spectacle of an all-powerful shogun deferring to a powerless emperor and his remnants of imperial sovereignty would awe daimyo into respectful submission. By contrast, the Sorai school contended that any shogunal self-abasement toward Kyoto invited the daimyo to flout bakufu authority.

Daini's view was in-between Kumazawa Banzan and Ogyū Sorai, but closer to Banzan. Though admitting that the imperial court was a fallen dynasty, Daini did not call for the shogun to proclaim himself King of Japan as Sorai and Shundai did. Still, Daini stressed the contradictions, if not the possible danger, that arose from Japan's dual locus of sovereignty: "Which side should we follow? One must be sovereign; the other, subject."[130] Referring to warriors in liege to the bakufu while holding rank and office granted by the imperial court, Master Ryū sardonically muses: "Today we revile as 'lewd' any woman who gives herself over to two men, but we think nothing of a subject who serves two masters. So there must be many chaste wives and no faithful officials."[131] The imperial court's granting of ranks and titles caused a serious mix-up in civil and military government functions. *Fudai* and *tozama* daimyo, bakufu bannermen, and other direct retainers were military officials. But they also received civil appointments such as provincial governorships from the court. If that were not confusing enough, few had ever been to the provinces they were charged with administering. Thus Arai Hakuseki had never set foot in Chikugo, and Daini held no executive writ over the Thirty-Three Eastern Provinces where he nominally served as "governor-general." Like Kumazawa Banzan, Daini believed that the shogun, who represented military might, or *bu*, should submit to the court's cultured civil authority, or *bun*. Yet, unlike Banzan, he called for more than just a cynically calculated display of shogunal reverence for the emperor.

Master Ryū arrives at no clear-cut solution to this basic structural problem. So we must resist any temptation to view Yamagata Daini as a pivotal transitional figure leading away from probakufu thinkers of the early Tokugawa period toward loyalists who called for an imperial restoration at the end of the period. Historians must be on guard against finding neat patterns of logic where none exist. In this case, the best we can do is clarify as much as possible Master Ryū's essentially muddled conception of the proper relationship between *bu* and *bun* in government. Yet that exercise is rewarding because the dead end he arrives at brings to light a key contradiction in Tokugawa (indeed, in all of Japanese) political thought. In short, Daini raised but never solved the perennial problem for Japan's titular head of state—the fact that "name" and "reality" did not conform.[132]

Daini held that government in Japan had to incorporate both the civil and martial, both the court and bakufu, both the emperor and shogun. A ruler must "promote great benefits and eliminate great evils in the realm." He promoted benefits through cultured civil rule *(bun)* and eliminated evils through laws and military power *(bu)*. The coercive quality of *bu* was indispensable for putting an end to merchant profiteering as well as for compiling domicile registers to make commoners continue farming in their native abodes. As Master Ryū insists: "There are civil *and* military officials in the state because neither can perform both functions."[133] Once again, his ideal prototypes are found in Chinese antiquity: King Wen and his son, King Wu, whose very names express the virtues of *bun* and *bu* (Ch. *wen, wu*):

> The Chou dynasty would not have enjoyed so flowery a civilization given Wu's martial prowess *(bu)* alone, without Wen's cultural refinement *(bun)*; nor would it have enjoyed such glorious exploits given Wen's cultural refinement alone, without Wu's martial prowess.[134]

Daini argued that "civil rule is the norm *(jun)*; martial rule, a last resort *(gyaku)*."[135] Japan's government "carried on the evils of an era of warring states."[136] Because the imperial dynasty's cultured civil rule had atrophied permanently, reliance on military power was now unavoidable. But the issue was one of degree. Current methods of martial law went far beyond what was called for. This was partly because some bakufu leaders believed that restoring samurai virtues would solve the realm's ills—as proclaimed in the Kyōhō Reform slogan, "Esteem the Martial" (shōbu). Daini thought that was a delusion. How, then, did he plan to bring both the civil and military Single-Wings of state under unified command so that the civil predominated?

His answer was to have the military component, the shogun and daimyo, place their services under civil control by assuming a deferential attitude toward the imperial court. This is clear from the three military figures Daini idealized in Japanese history: Prince Yamatotakeru, who conquered the Kumaso and Emishi in the mythic Age of the Gods; Sakanoue no Tamuramaro (758–811), who supposedly vanquished (the nonhistorical) Akuro no Takamaru in the late eighth to early ninth centuries; and Fujiwara no Hidesato, who led imperial forces to quash Taira no Masakado's tenth-century insurrection.

Daini and his cohorts erected a monument to Yamatotakeru at Sakaori outside Kōfu city in IV/1763—the monument that Motoori Norinaga found so repugnant twenty-six years later. Daini's followers at the time included Takenouchi Shikibu, who visited Kōfu in 1763, but not Fujii Umon, who had yet to appear at Daini's school.[137] The inscription to that monument read:

> The gods founded this land, and imperial majesties have established its moral precepts. But wild men on our frontiers gave free rein to their violent ways and refused to submit. Brandishing his imperial sword, the great prince subdued the four quarters in accord with the people's wishes. He submitted the Kumaso leaders' heads to the court and induced Emishi chieftains to accept the imperial aegis; that is why his power and virtue met welcome everywhere. On his triumphant return, he composed an ode, the "Niibari," whose lyrical strains have retained their fragrance for over a thousand years. This is truly the cultured [bun]; this is truly the martial [bu]. The world enjoys peace because of his lasting achievements.[138]

Three years later, in IV/1766, Daini erected a monument dedicated to Princess Ototachibana, Prince Yamatotakeru's faithful consort, located at Azuma Woods in Katsushika county, Shi-mōsa province, just outside the Edo city limits. Daini prefaced his inscription by paraphrasing the *Nihon shoki* account of how she threw herself into the "Sea of Running Waters," the Uraga Strait. This act of self-sacrifice calmed wind and wave and let Yamatotakeru proceed safely to conquer the Emishi. On his return, he stopped at Usui Peak to grieve over her sacrifice: "My wife, alas" *(azuma haya)*. And from then on, "people called the provinces east of Usui 'Azuma.'" Daini's inscription reads: "Her heroism and purity are that of Mencius' 'Great Man.' But a far different image emerges after hearing this tale. ... The prince and princess will be worshiped eternally; their spirits will never sink into obscurity as long as the heavens remain in place."[139]

The inscriptions on these two monuments eulogized loyal servants of the imperial court who protected it against rebels. We should note that Daini's understanding of these supposedly historical accounts was based on the *Nihon shoki*, not the *Kojiki*; for the prince and his campaigns are depicted quite differently in the two works. To explain why Yamatotakeru conquered the Kumaso in the west, for example, the *Kojiki* has Emperor Keikō dispatching him out of fear: the prince's ferocity might pose a threat. In the *Nihon shoki*, Keikō sends him because the Kumaso had cut off tribute and planned to rebel. Much the same holds for Prince Yamatotakeru's campaign against the Emishi in the east. In the *Kojiki*, he is distraught because Keikō has ordered him into combat alone, right after an exhausting war against the Kumaso; but in the *Nihon shoki*, he volunteers to demonstrate his martial prowess.[140]

Generally speaking, personalities and emotions figure prominently in the more literary *Kojiki* accounts; by contrast, the *Nihon shoki* annals focus on state affairs. In the *Kojiki*, the prince is depicted as a tragic figure who performs dangerous tasks on the order of a capricious despot eager to see him die; the Kumaso and Emishi are simple instruments of harm devoid of political motives. In the *Nihon shoki*, the prince is a trusted general who loyally obeys central government orders, not the emperor's whimsical commands; the Kumaso and Emishi are subversive elements in the state who "refuse to accept civilizing imperial powers of transformation." In commanding Yamatotakeru, the *Nihon shoki* has Keikō echo King Wen by quoting from ancient Chinese sources: "Display power and tame them with virtue, so that I induce them to submit voluntarily without recourse to war." And the prince too displays classical erudition by parroting King Wu: "I will manifest virtuous teachings; and if any refuse to submit, I will smite them with my army."[141] This is why Daini wrote of Yamatotakeru: "This is truly the cultured; this is truly the martial."

Daini's ideal of *bu,* the legal and military component of government, was exemplified as well by generals who served the imperial court and dutifully obeyed commands issued by civil officials. In the halcyon days of Sakanoue no Tamuramaro and Fujiwara no Hidesato, "generals commanding the nation's far-flung militia reported to the Ministry of War in the capital and took orders from local civil officials." As the legendary rebel Akuro no Takamaru discovered to his great misfortune, these heroes "exemplified military prowess in antiquity—long before anyone had heard of 'esteeming the martial.' "[142]

But all of this begs Master Ryū's original question. Under the current Tokugawa form of government, military officials exercised power as they saw fit; and this simple fact logically contradicted Daini's ideal of a unified command under civil control, which would require the shogun and daimyo to submit to imperial government orders. To repeat: Daini incisively raised, but refused to tackle, this all-important issue—except to stress the need for unity. Rather than devise institutional solutions to an institutional problem, he resorted to Confucian moral exhortation to produce that unity in the hearts of ruler and minister. Indeed, Daini himself—as opposed to his modern interpreters—probably never saw the problem as mainly institutional in nature.

All of Master Ryū's proposed reforms call for a self-effacing ruler who accepts remonstration from high-ranking civil or military officials; and they in turn seek frank advice from sagacious Confucian teachers. Daini himself hoped to play this role of loyal teacher-remonstrator after the example of Master Kuo Wei. But there was no King Chao in the Ōoka household or in Obata domain to heed his wise counsels. When interrogated by bakufu officials in 1767, Daini dejectedly confessed:

To foment rebellion under august bakufu rule fills me with awe and trembling. Such is beyond my imagination. . . . The people below suffer and the world totters on the brink of disorder and rebellion because bakufu rule has violated proper law so often in recent eras. I desperately want to remonstrate with the authorities. But there are no channels for me to do so because I hold no government post. So I schemed to get arrested on the contorted charge of plotting rebellion. Then I could admonish the bakufu point by point at my interrogation. That is the whole extent of my "conspiracy."[143]

Such were the sentiments of bitter vexation that inspired Daini's famous last poem wherein he deplores the false allegations of insurrection and treason that cloud the moonlike purity of his true aspirations. After being spurned by Yoshida Gemba during the Meiwa Incident, Daini lost his conduit into Obata domain. At that point, he must have realized: "It is very hard for men to make themselves known to [the ruler]." So, in desperation, he did something akin to the women of Ch'u "who starved themselves to death trying to become slender" and thereby catch King Ling's eye.

As numerous prewar and postwar historians note, Yamagata Daini bitingly denounced warrior government by having Master Ryū proclaim: "I see nothing of value in our nation's rule since Juei and Bunji times [1182–1189]."[144] This remark exudes "extreme disrespect and the utmost insolence." But nothing in Daini's actions and little in the *Ryūshi shinron* attests to, or even strongly indicates, a desire to destroy the Tokugawa bakufu through violence from below. Quite to the contrary, Sections XII and XIII of his tract should be construed as an earnest remonstration to provoke bakufu reform. Daini observes:

When a tall tree falls over, it is because termites have eaten through its trunk; when a large dike collapses, it is because cracks have penetrated its wall. Although the tree will not fall and the dike will not collapse unless struck by fierce rains or strong winds, only a fool would ignore termites in the tree's trunk or cracks in the dike's wall just because the weather is fair and winds are gentle.[145]

Daini took these dike, insect, and crack metaphors from a well-known passage in the *Han Fei Tzu*: "A dike one thousand *chang* long will dissolve due to the hole bored by a tiny ant; a mansion one hundred *ch'ih* high will burn due to the smoke blown through a slight crack." That original passage is prefaced by the injunction: "Cope with difficult matters while they are still simple; take care of grave matters while they are still trivial."[146] And the *Ryūshi shinron* ends with a final admonition from ancient Chinese history for Edo leaders to dwell on:

> In antiquity, the Duke [I] of Wei liked cranes; so his ministers perched them on their carriages. But when faced with an invasion [in 660 B.C.], his people refused to follow him, saying instead, "Make use of your cranes."[147]

Daini took this anecdote from the *Tso chuan* annals reputedly compiled by Confucius. Under "the second year of Duke I," it is recounted:

> Winter, 12th month. The barbarians invaded Wei. Duke I had always liked cranes, so some of his ministers perched them on their carriages. But now, when it came time to fight the invaders, the people to whom he had given weapons all said, "Use your cranes. They are the ones who enjoy state ranks and salaries. Why should we fight?"[148]

From these examples we can conclude that Yamagata Daini did not borrow Mencius' term *"hōbatsu"* to advocate killing the shogun and launching a revolution from below. Master Ryū does not argue that Edo bakufu leaders *should* be overthrown; he is urgently warning that they *would* be overthrown if they failed to cultivate popular support through moral reform.

CHAPTER 4
A New Appraisal

Popular perceptions of Yamagata Daini began to diverge from fact right after his execution in 1767, when he was improperly likened to Yui Shōsetsu and Marubashi Chūya—those vicious *rōnin* desperadoes who schemed to rebel after Shogun Iemitsu's death in 1651. Daini lapsed into relative obscurity in the first half of the nineteenth century as time passed and memories faded. But he reemerged to be miscast as an early martyr in the *tōbaku* ("destroy the bakufu") cause during Bakumatsu times—when Chō-shū revolutionaries such as Kusaka Genzui arbitrarily imputed their own ideals and aspirations to him after uncritically accept-ing flawed accounts of the Meiwa Incident conveyed by Utsuno-miya Mokurin. Later still, this divergence between man and myth became even more acute because scholarly and popular interpret-ers anachronistically imputed to Daini the social and political values prevailing in their own day. Thus during the 1930s and early 1940s, he won renown as the Japanese spirit incarnate. And after 1945, he emerged as an incipient democrat, a populist leveler of discriminatory status barriers, or the patron deity of nervous exam-takers hoping to enter a good university and thereby find lifetime employment with a government ministry or a first-rate business firm.

There is a little something in Yamagata Daini, his thought, and his role in the Meiwa Incident that can be twisted to support all these views. But my interpretation differs. I have repeatedly stressed that Daini was neither a *tōbaku* advocate nor a demo-cratic populist. Above all, it is misleading to label his brand of loyalism "revolutionary" or "restorationist" because he never looked beyond the existing order to envision creating a drastically different state structure in which the emperor and court would exercise power once more. However, the ministerial autonomy that he advanced should be construed as "loyalist" in a different, yet arguably more important sense; for it fits within a tradition of imperial "assistance" *(hohitsu)* rendered by high-ranking officials from behind the scenes at court. These principles of ministerial autonomy and imperial assistance bolstered Japan's emperor system from its beginnings down to 1947, when a new constitution based on democratic principles took effect.

Daini in Edo Times

Yamagata Daini affirmed what postwar intellectual historian Uete Michiari terms "the irreversibility of history,"[1] an assumption that more or less universally prevailed among early- to mid-Tokugawa thinkers and scholars. They simply took it for granted that, after the debacle of Emperor Godaigo's Kemmu Restoration between 1333 and 1336, the transfer of land ownership and ruling power from imperial court to warrior houses was absolute and final in Japan. This is not to say that restoring power and land rights to the emperor and court was inconceivable in the literal sense of being wholly unimaginable. The fourteenth-century classic, the *Taiheiki,* grew in popularity during the Edo period and helped create widespread sympathy for Kusunoki Masashige, Nitta Yoshisada, and other loyalists to the cause of Godaigo's Southern Court.[2] Beyond that, the eighteenth-century playwright Chikamatsu Monzaemon produced a series of "*tennō* dramas" that lauded imperial rule in antiquity and hinted that commoners might have been happier back then. Chikamatsu Hanji, his adopted son and heir, went even further in extolling the virtues of bygone imperial rule.[3] Indeed, a fictional account of the Meiwa Incident—the 1774 *Meiwa fudoki* and variant texts—portrayed Takenouchi Shikibu, Yamagata Daini, and Fujii Umon hatching plots to destroy the Edo bakufu in league with nobles at the imperial court.

A historian should not dismiss such works of imaginative literature offhand. Not only do they help us to gauge the limits of popular cognition about the imperial court, but the relative popularity of their reception helps indicate how far commoners may have envisaged an imperial restoration possible or desirable. Thus, for example, the unknown author of the *Meiwa fudoki* and his narrow circle of readers did in fact imagine that Yamagata Daini might be scheming with imperial court nobles to overthrow the Edo bakufu and restore power to the emperor—although Daini did not travel to Kyoto at the time in question and so could not have plotted this type of rebellion. However, two factors should caution us against exaggerating the significance of the *Meiwa fudoki* and similar literary sources. First, that document attributed supernatural or occult powers to Fujii Umon—such as flying through thin air or knocking out enemies located miles away. Hence we must treat it as a highly fanciful, not a histori-cally credible, account of the Meiwa Incident and Yamagata Daini's role in it.[4] Second, and more to the point, the *Meiwa fudoki* was never published: it remained in manuscript form with an extremely limited readership. Therefore its image of "Daini the restorationist" was exceptional, not commonplace.

This contention is substantiated by testimony from clearly iden-tified eighteenth-century figures in widely different parts of Japan: Hosaka the peasant in Kai, Warashina Shōhaku in Yonezawa, Sugita Gempaku in Edo, and Motoori Norinaga in Matsuzaka. They considered Daini to be a conventional rebel and an ordinary knave—one who boasted no restorationist pretensions. They wrongly judged that he wanted to overthrow the bakufu, but did not take the next step of wrongly purporting that he wanted to revive imperial rule. Yamagata Daini did not become miscast in that role of loyalist-restorationist martyr until well into the 1850s and 1860s.

In realistic commonsense terms, early to mid-Tokugawa con-temporaries assumed that the emperor and court in Kyoto had demonstrated irredeemable political incompetence by the 1330s. It was totally absurd to propose that they should ever again be entrusted with ruling power—as Kumazawa Banzan explicitly asserted. Moreover, we might add, even if some semblance of an imperial restoration were to take place, the court held virtually no land or wealth outside of Kyoto. Hence any new imperial govern-ment would have little more than honorary ranks and titles with which to reward those warriors who had achieved the restora-tion—and as Godaigo's experience had shown, that was not enough. More important, any new imperial regime would lack the fiscal and military resources needed to govern. So unless it were willing and able to overcome entrenched warrior interests and create a whole new land- and tax-system, it would more or less have to rely on the existing organs of bakufu and daimyo rule. Like other eighteenth-century Japanese thinkers—with the possible exception of Andō Shōeki—Yamagata Daini subscribed to these tenets of conventional wisdom and common sense. It is possible that Daini lamented the emperor's loss of power in ancient times. But he nevertheless assumed that loss to be permanent—as shown by Master Ryū's three references to the imperial court as a "fallen dynasty" (shōkoku). If we examine Daini's criticism of post-1185 warrior governments in the light of such prevailing Tokugawa assumptions, we cannot portray him as "revolutionary" or "restorationist" in thought or deed.

Before we can grasp the meaning of imperial restoration in Japan as a truly revolutionary movement, we must sort out four distinct concepts that would converge only at the end of the Tokugawa and in the first half of the Meiji periods.[5] Those four concepts are: conventional loyalism (kinnō, sonnō) as simple reverence for the emperor and court devoid of political implications; ordinary rebellion (muhon) against a particular warrior regime that still affirms warrior rule in principle; restoration as a replication of imperial rule as it supposedly existed in antiquity; and finally restoration reconceived as a Western-style constitutional monarchy.

There was a long tradition of apolitical imperial loyalism that went back at least to seventeenth-century Shinto-Confucian syncretists such as Yamazaki Ansai. That strain of "conventional" loyalism stressed the shogun's ritual obeisance to the emperor and the bakufu's fiscal support of the court. In the minds of Kokugaku scholars such as Kamo no Mabuchi, such loyalism might include a nostalgic yearning for antiquity when imperial rule truly obtained.[6] But none of that was anti-Tokugawa in nature; much less did it call for overthrowing the Edo regime; and it never questioned the right of warrior governments to rule Japan. Postwar Japanese scholarship on Kokugaku and Mitogaku has conclusively shown that loyalist doctrines of this conventional type were expressly designed to bolster Edo bakufu authority. And in fact they did just that until Perry and Harris spoiled things after 1853.

Armed uprisings might topple the Edo bakufu at any time. This is why its leaders were alert to the threat of revolts by disaffected daimyo, *rōnin*, or peasants. But contemporaries knew that reverence for the emperor did little or nothing to motivate such "ordinary" rebellions—as the Shimabara, Yui Shōsetsu, and Ōshio Heihachirō rebellions show. Moreover, small-scale revolts led by ne'er-do-well *rōnin*—such as that mistakenly ascribed to Yamagata Daini and Fujii Umon—were seen as acts of desperation, symbolic protest, or madness. Daini and Umon neither served nor sought aid from Obata domain, which in any case had resources of but twenty thousand *koku*. Ringleaders of such mini-revolts could not dream of success without powerful backing—as when loyalist *rōnin* persuaded the Chōshū and Satsuma domains to join their life-or-death *tōbaku* struggle in the mid-1860s. Even then they needed sophisticated modern weaponry smuggled by foreigners in order to win. On the other hand, it was generally assumed that large-scale daimyo insurrections would plunge Japan right back into the treacherous warfare and mass suffering of medieval times. And even if successful, these daimyo revolts envisioned little more than replacing the Tokugawa with an essentially similar warrior regime, such as a Date, or a Mōri, or a Shimazu bakufu. This limited political vision expanded only in the mid-nineteenth century, and only under the threat of foreign colonization.

In other words, the radical idea of having the emperor and court govern Japan once again entailed far more than just harnessing conventional imperial reverence to an ordinary armed revolt aimed at toppling this or that bakufu. The acid test of imperial restoration as a truly "revolutionary" act lay in repudiating warrior government based on domain ownership—categorical imperatives entrenched for seven centuries—and replacing that form of rule and system of land tenure with a drastically different state polity.

It would be unhistorical to expect Bakumatsu figures to envisage creating a republican or socialist form of government. The only realistic alternatives to Tokugawa rule were either a modified aristocracy of the sword or a revival of imperial rule in some fashion. Imperial rule was chosen, and it assumed two forms over time: first, direct rule by the emperor *(tennō shinsei)* to replicate government in Japanese antiquity *(ōsei fukko)*; and later, constitutional monarchy in a centralized nation-state as inspired by European political models and provoked by Western gunboats. During the mid to late 1850s, Yoshida Shōin espoused restoration as a literal revival of direct rule by the emperor as it supposedly existed in antiquity. By the time he died in 1859, Shōin came to advocate destroying "feudalism" *(hōken)* and implementing "centralized empire" *(gunken)* according to classical Chinese usage as applied to Japanese historical experience. He wanted to uproot the existing Tokugawa order and restore two sociopolitical ideals that putatively had obtained in Japanese antiquity: "all lands are imperial territory, all peoples are imperial subjects" *(ōdo, ōmin)*; and "all peoples under one sovereign's command" *(ikkun banmin).*[7] Yoshida Shōin's first ideal would terminate private fief-holding by warrior houses in order to bring all daimyo domains in Japan under imperial ownership, tax collection, and political administration. His second ideal would eliminate hereditary social classes by making all Japanese subjects direct retainers of the emperor. All this, of course, meant abolishing the existing hierarchy of warrior intermediaries: the shogun, daimyo, and samurai classes.

These "revolutionary" ideals in Yoshida Shōin's thought did not grow out of concepts enunciated in the *Ryūshi shinron* of 1759; in fact, his ideals flatly contradict the main arguments that Daini advanced there. Master Ryū staunchly affirms the existing "feudal" order as manifested in the form of "peoples" and "states" *in the plural.* First, Master Ryū conceptualizes Japanese society from top to bottom as a heaven-mandated hierarchy comprising "four peoples" *(shimin),* or hereditary classes: government officials (recruited from the daimyo and samurai), peasants, artisans, and merchants. Below these are "despised" or outcaste classes, also hereditary in nature, to be kept segregated forever. Second, Master Ryū conceptualizes Japanese territory as a Confucian-style "realm," or "all under heaven," comprising some 260-odd "states" *(kokka)* owned and administered by the shogun and regional daimyo. In other words, Yamagata Daini lacked Yoshida Shōin's overriding consciousness of Japan as one geopolitical unit inhabited by a single race whose members should all enjoy equality of status as direct imperial retainers. Indeed, Master Ryū's model government administrators are shogunal regents or ministers—precisely those baleful intermediaries between emperor and subjects that Shōin wished to get rid of.

Yoshida Shōin's idea lay in fostering "restoration as replication" to revive direct rule by the emperor exactly as in antiquity. It proved anachronistic and ill suited to Japan's efforts at national consolidation and strengthening in the second half of the nineteenth century. So, at that point, it gave way to restoration reconceived as constitutional monarchy in a centralized nation-state. This thoroughly alien conception of imperial rule gained ascendance from the early 1870s and found legal grounding in the Meiji Constitution of 1889. But "restoration as constitutional monarchy" assumed a detailed knowledge of Western political forms that Daini never had. And, what is more, its wholesale implementation in Japan could be justified only under a specter of foreign colonization that never loomed while Daini was alive.

Thus we may define the concept of imperial restoration in a revolutionary sense as follows: reverence for the emperor consciously espoused to destroy both the Edo bakufu and all similar forms of warrior government based on domain ownership, for the express purpose of reinstating direct imperial rule over all Japanese territory and subjects—either exactly as in antiquity or under a constitutional monarchy. This concept, so defined, did not emerge in Japan until the end of the Edo period at the very earliest. As such, it should not be applied to a mid-Tokugawa thinker such as Yamagata Daini.

There are perhaps two decisive events in late Tokugawa history in which "conventional" pro-bakufu loyalism took on "restorationist" hues so that "ordinary" rebellions might acquire "revolutionary" significance. One turning point came in 1825, when the Mitogaku scholar Aizawa Seishisai (1781–1863) composed his *Shinron* (New Theses). This tract asserted that, in order to govern Japan effectively, the shogun had to borrow religio-spiritual authority from the court by manipulating the emperor as a pope-like symbol to instill loyalty in all Japanese whatever their social status or domain affiliation; and that it was tactically astute for the Tokugawa shogun to redefine "conventional" imperial loyalism *(sonnō)* by equating it with a solemn pledge to expel foreign barbarians militarily *(jōi)* if the need should ever arise. This redefined form of loyalism made bakufu political legitimacy hinge on the shogun's eagerness and ability to uphold "national isolation" *(sakoku)*, which was deemed to accord with the imperial will.[8] The second turning point came in the years 1853 to 1858, when Perry and Harris forced the Edo bakufu to let Western nationals other than the Dutch trade with Japan and live there. After that, pro-Tokugawa loyalists had to decide whether to obey the emperor and court, who ordered these new foreigners expelled on the spot, or the shogun, who let them stay despite earlier and continuing pledges to the contrary. These two events were decisive because they provided explosive political content that had been lacking in "conventional" loyalist notions up to then. And, coupled as they were with new and detailed knowledge of Western political forms assimilated under crisis conditions, these events provided a compelling alternative to the principles of bakufu rule and warrior landownership that had gone unquestioned up to then. Both of these turning points, however, came in the nineteenth century, well after Yamagata Daini's death.

All of Daini's model sovereigns in the *Ryūshi shinron* were Chinese except for Jimmu. One would expect far more praise of imperial rule in Japan's antiquity from a thinker bent on restoring power to the emperor and court. Ōshio Heihachirō is almost never portrayed as advocating an imperial restoration. Even so, his war banner was inscribed "Amaterasu, the Sun Goddess" and his "Call to Arms" proclaimed: "We cannot bring back the eras of Yao, Shun, and Amaterasu, but we can restore *(chūkō)* the good government of Emperor Jimmu."[9] By contrast, Daini's proposed reforms would have done much to bolster shogunal prestige and authority in relation to the imperial court.

Yamagata Daini's thought owed far more to Ogyū Sorai than to Yamazaki Ansai. As a snobbish sinophile, Master Ryū despises Japanese intellectuals and commoners who do not share his erudition in antiquarian Chinese learning. His legitimation of the existing order, his identification of the socioeconomic problems plaguing it, and his theoretical and practical proposals to solve these—all find revelation and sanction in the sacred Chinese classics. Daini also carried on Ogyū Sorai's rationale for perpetuating discrimination against the so-called despised or outcaste classes in Japan. Earlier in the Edo period, their purportedly despicable nature had been viewed as temporary and salvageable by virtuous government. But after Sorai and Daini, that nature became linked to bloodline and construed as ineradicable. Indeed, the Ogyū Sorai school deemed it virtuous to uphold stigmas against these groups. That is why Master Ryū cites the sage-kings' insistence that beggars, prostitutes, entertainers, and the like be permanently banned from marrying or even living with the "good" classes. This is quite close to apartheid.

It is highly unlikely that Tokugawa officials actually read Daini's *Ryūshi shinron*. If they had, they certainly would have found grounds for executing him on the charge of sacrilege or lese majesty. Master Ryū clearly berates warrior regimes after 1185 for creating popular misery through misrule and also for assuming certain prerogatives that had belonged to the emperor and court. But the ills that Master Ryū brings to light stemmed far more from faulty mental attitudes than from defective government structures. So, most of those ills could be cured by instilling proper Confucian character traits in bakufu and domain leaders. Master Ryū has surprisingly little new to say about institutional reform. His program to combat specific socioeconomic ills consists largely of warmed-over ideas taken from Ogyū Sorai, Dazai Shundai, and, to a lesser extent, Kumazawa Banzan and Arai Hakuseki. For decades bakufu and domain leaders had ignored or rejected these Confucian proposals for being impractical; perhaps most telling of all, Daini and his family violated these with impunity in their daily lives.

Master Ryū does see the need for some institutional fine tuning—to undo the harp strings and stretch them taut again, as he puts it. Someone would have to emulate Shōtoku Taishi and Shu-sun T'ung by creating dynastic ritual and music so that the shogun and daimyo could foster "equilibrium and harmony," though under imperial aegis. But the ideal political system that Daini really favored was de facto rule by a grand minister *(a-heng)* who also had the martial virtues needed to uphold law and order. Such a shogunal *a-heng* in Edo and his regional daimyo deputies would actively seek out critical advice from astute teacher-remonstrators in order to "assist" a figurehead emperor in Kyoto. This shogun, as an imperial minister or regent, might "depose" an emperor through forced abdication in favor of an heir; but he might never kill that divine descendant of Amaterasu in a Mencian-style act of *hōbatsu*. Such a polity for the realm accorded both with the Way of the ancient Chinese sages and with Daini's ideal of cultured civil rule *(bun)* that subsumed martial prowess *(bu)*.

How, then, did Daini's Sorai Learning relate to the actual conduct of government administration in the Tokugawa period? As intellectual historian Watanabe Hiroshi persuasively argues, social mores in early Tokugawa Japan differed vastly from those in Ming- or Ch'ing-dynasty China. Because Confucianism ill suited Japanese sociopolitical realities in the seventeenth century, it could not serve as a bakufu orthodoxy.[10] In fact, Confucianism and Christianity were equally alien to Japan and most Japanese early in the period could not tell the two apart. Few Japanese could read classical Chinese, much less grasp difficult Confucian concepts or dispute the primacy of *li* over *ch'i*. Both the ruling warrior class and the general populace prized loyalty and valor over book learning and benevolence. No self-respecting man of the sword cried at funerals, although that behavior was stipulated in the *Book of Rites*. The grisly samurai custom of self-immolation on the death of one's lord *(junshi)* lasted until 1680—although it had been banned earlier. And in 1703 Edo townsmen lionized the forty-seven retainers of Akō for obeying their master's will to conduct what amounted to a gangland-style killing worthy of today's Yamaguchi-gumi syndicate.

Hence it is not surprising that Confucian rites and music received scant attention in warrior government. Unlike the *shih* scholar-official class in China from Sung times onward, early Tokugawa Confucians enjoyed little social esteem and held no posts of true political responsibility. The right to govern in Japan was determined by birth, not alien ideals of virtue, merit, or benevolence. As Matsudaira Nobutsuna (1596–1662), a thirty-year veteran of bakufu councils, declared: "What Confucian scholars say should never be implemented in state administration. They expound all sorts of things harmful to government." Or, as the Okayama daimyo Ikeda Mitsumasa remarked about his Confucian advisor, Kumazawa Banzan: "His arguments sound reasonable enough. But if we really did what he said, it would be disastrous for the domain."[11]

According to Watanabe Hiroshi, this warrior anti-intellectualism and distrust of Confucian scholars prevailed until about Genroku times (1688–1710), when the caliber of Japanese Confucians improved and a few rulers such as Shogun Ienobu began to lend them an ear. Domain schools were built and the social prestige of Confucian teachers rose. But the most important lesson they taught came from the classic *Great Learning:* personal cultivation and proper regulation of family members made for order in the state and peace under heaven. Tokugawa Confucians could not be truly Confucian, at least in their own eyes, unless they translated this dictum into state policy—and that required sustained access to political power. Arai Hakuseki and Kumazawa Banzan therefore implored warrior rulers to admit that Confucianism was essential for good government. But both of these scholar-reformers were thwarted by warrior officials jealously bent on protecting their monopoly over the administration of socioeconomic affairs.

Then Ogyū Sorai appeared. Having devoted his life to creating a workable Confucian political philosophy suited to Tokugawa realities, he radically and systematically reinterpreted (some would say "distorted") the Chinese classics with one aim in mind: to convince skeptical warrior-rulers once and for all that they really did need Confucianism to govern properly. As Watanabe emphasizes, Sorai's greatest theoretical innovation was to claim that the ancient sage-kings had invented rites and music as the Way itself—an indispensable technique for ruling the realm. They had invented it for public and political ends, not private or didactic purposes of moral cultivation as Chu Hsi mistakenly claimed. The founder of each new Chinese dynasty was a sage-king who established its rituals and music; and the Edo bakufu, having received heaven's mandate in Japan, should set up new dynastic rites apart from those of the defunct imperial court. Arai Hakuseki had urged Edo leaders to do precisely that, but the *fudai* daimyo in charge of bakufu administration detested him as "a devil" and spited him at every turn. Now Ogyū Sorai provided authoritative textual "evidence" to back up the same claim. He warned that bakufu control over the realm would soon lapse if Edo leaders refused to implement his Confucian reform proposals and create a new set of dynastic rites and music.

Shogun Yoshimune chose to ignore that dire admonition. But, to the supreme vexation of Sorai and his followers, the realm remained at peace and even seemed to prosper over the next few decades—exposing Ogyū Sorai's lifework to be false and useless in government. In general, his disciples did not stress personal morality to start with. Now, with their raison d'etre called into question, many indulged to the hilt in dissolute ways and thereby besmirched their teacher's name. The school broke into two wings after Sorai's death in 1728. One, led by Hattori Nankaku (1683–1759), devoted itself to philology, poetry, and belletristic pursuits. The other, led by Dazai Shundai, kept pleading for bakufu and daimyo leaders to adopt Sorai-style Confucian political reforms.

Dazai Shundai commanded respect as a scholar and teacher, but high government posts somehow kept eluding him. Like his mentor, he persuaded no warrior ruler to apply Confucian political principles in state administration. Shundai expressed life's bitter frustration by relating this Taoist parable: "Once in ancient times, a man expended his whole fortune mastering the art of dragon slaying, only to live out his days in despair when he learned there are no dragons in the world to slay. He is just like me."[12] Yamagata Daini fared much worse. He first hoped that bakufu Junior Councillor Ōoka Tadamitsu would develop into an *a-heng* of Fujiwara no Mototsune's caliber but was dismayed by the bribery and corruption he encountered at Tokiwabashi. Next Daini pinned his hopes on the Obata domain elder Yoshida Gemba, and this time his endeavors seemed likely to bear fruit. But under pressure from hostile domain leaders, Yoshida Gemba betrayed Daini's hopes by disavowing his Confucian reform proposals. Then the crestfallen Daini reckoned that only a spectacular act of defiant insolence would earn a hearing for his political ideals. So he allowed himself to be arrested on false charges of plotting rebellion so that he could remonstrate with bakufu officials during his arraignment.

Sorai Learning enjoyed incontestable prestige in scholarly, though not political, circles from the 1710s to the 1740s. But people began to challenge it in the 1750s and 1760s, and it declined rapidly thereafter so that few avowed it openly from the 1800s onward.[13] This means that Daini embraced Sorai's teachings just as their popularity peaked and began to wane. He was the school's third and last ardent teacher-remonstrator. But, like Sorai and Shundai before him, Daini too learned the sad futility of searching the world for dragons to slay.

Another Loyalist Tradition

Yamagata Daini is not, however, a trivial figure unworthy of study. His importance for the overall history of Japanese political thought—as opposed to just Tokugawa political thought—lay in carrying on a nonrevolutionary tradition of imperial loyalism that was extremely conservative and hierarchy-affirming in nature. It was conceived and justified in terms of ministerial autonomy for a regent, chief minister, or some other imperial surrogate to "assist" *(hohitsu)* state administration in the name of a figurehead sovereign. This other brand of imperial loyalism suffered neglect at the hands of *kōkoku shikan* ideologues. But it was perhaps the more powerful—and surely the more adaptable and durable—tradition of loyalism throughout Japanese history as a whole. And Daini occupied an important place in it.

Ever since Tsuda Sōkichi's pioneering textual scholarship on the eighth-century *Kojiki* and *Nihon shoki*, the earliest formal writings in Japan, we have accepted his thesis about how and why these official court annals were compiled. According to Tsuda, the Yamato rulers of ancient Japan—forebears of the imperial family—placed mythical accounts in these two histories that attributed divine origins to themselves in order to bolster their religious prestige and ruling authority against rival contenders for power. Thus they had Sun Goddess Amaterasu bequeath the three imperial regalia and establish their ruling house through a divine decree *(shinchoku)* issued to Ninigi no mikoto. It stipulated: "Japan is the land over which my descendants shall be sovereign. Go to rule it, my imperial grandson. Your dynastic line shall flourish coeval with heaven and earth."[14] And Ninigi's great-grandson duly acceded as the first emperor Jimmu on 11 February 660 B.C. In this way, Yamato court chroniclers fabricated evidence cited by latter-day patriots to support nativist claims that Japan's imperial line did not "rise or fall" and therefore was morally superior to royal houses in foreign lands.

But Tsuda missed a key point. In the same passage that contained this divine decree, Sun Goddess Amaterasu also orders "Amenokoyane no mikoto, ancestor of the Nakatomi," and "Amenofutotama no mikoto, ancestor of the Imbe," to accompany and loyally serve her grandson Ninigi no mikoto on his descent to earth.[15] Elsewhere in the two chronicles, Amaterasu charges these two deities with guard duty and priestly functions at the Yamato court while her divine offspring reign supreme over Japan.[16] In other words, these *Kojiki* and *Nihon shoki* myths were not designed to benefit the Yamato ruling house alone. Amaterasu also gave divine sanction for the Imbe and Nakatomi—quite undistinguished clans at that time—to "assist" the imperial dynasty govern forever. The Imbe fell into obscurity rather soon. But the Nakatomi flourished as de facto rulers of state at the imperial court under the lineage name of Fujiwara after A.D. 669.

These considerations lend credence to a provocative thesis tendered by cultural historian Ueyama Shumpei.[17] In the seventh and eighth centuries, he suggests, the Fujiwara and the Yamato court schemed to overcome powerful regional magnates in central Japan such as the Ōtomo, Mononobe, Soga, and Kose. To achieve that end, the political authority held by those magnates had to be undercut by the Taika Reform and their religious authority had to be displaced by Sun Goddess Amaterasu, the putative progenitrix of the imperial house. The chief Fujiwara schemer in this complex conspiracy was Fuhito (659–720). Under his leadership, the Yamato court built the nation's first permanent capital at Nara, imported Chinese bureaucratic institutions to conduct state affairs, and established T'ang-style law codes to serve as a legal basis for the new imperial state. These reforms, together known as the Ritsu-Ryō system, transformed the rebellion-prone regional magnates into docile court nobles and civil servants who were tied to central government salaries far from their local power bases. Thus they lost all ability and any desire to revolt against the newly consolidated imperial regime.

Perhaps most important of all, the imperial court and Fujiwara family had to abolish the brother-to-brother succession method native to Japan in favor of the father-to-son method imported from China. In this regard too their creative writing of history proved crucial. Actual, as opposed to mythical, emperors began with Ōjin who reigned roughly from 270 to 310. Although early emperors tended to favor the native over the Chinese method of succession, there was no fixed rule. Thus bloody succession disputes broke out—as between Princes Ōtomo and Ōama, the son and brother of Emperor Tenji, in 672. Feuds of this type caused immense political turmoil and decimated many branches of the imperial house. Fuhito solved this problem after Emperor Temmu (former Prince Ōama) died in 686. But Fuhito did so in a way that later established Fujiwara control over the imperial line through maternal relatives. Temmu's principal wife Jitō (r. 690–697) did not want his son, whom she had not borne, to become the new emperor.[18] Instead she wanted the throne passed on to her grandson, Mommu, who married Fuhito's daughter Miyako. So Fuhito arranged to have Jitō stand in as a temporary female sovereign (jotei) until his seven-year-old son-in-law Mommu could mature and accede in 697. Mommu then fathered Shōmu by Miyako in 701 and reigned until his death in 707. Next Fuhito got Gemmei and Genshō to stand in as female sovereigns until his seven-year-old grandson Shōmu could mature and accede in 724. Fuhito then married his daughter Kōmyō to Shōmu, who reigned until 749. Their daughter, Fuhito's great-granddaughter, would reign twice: as Kōken from 749 to 758 and as Shōtoku from 764 to 770.

Fuhito's palace intrigues ended the brother-to-brother form of succession in Japan, and that change had two significant results. First, it meant stability for the imperial house. Succession disputes now might occur only between an emperor's sons, not his brothers as well, and the court began to regularize procedures for declaring heirs apparent. Second, this change opened the door to Fujiwara domination at court through marriage politics and the institution of regency (sesshō or kampaku).[19] The native practice of succession assumed that each newly installed emperor had to be mature enough to bear the duties of rulership; this is why an adult brother took precedence over a very young son. With that practice and assumption gone, emperors could become figureheads valued merely as links in Amaterasu's divine bloodline—not for any real ability to govern. And if the imperial successor were a small child, that would be all the better; then he would be unfit to rule and would require "assistance" from a willing Fujiwara regent. The first regent was Fujiwara no Yoshifusa, who began to assist the nine-year-old Emperor Seiwa in 858.

The Kojiki and Nihon shoki historical records—compiled on Fuhito's orders—played a key role in this change of succession methods. These court annals placed a mythical line of fifteen emperors, from Jimmu through Chūai, at the head of Amaterasu's dynastic line before Ōjin, the first truly historical emperor.[20] Thus these imperial chronicles "proved" that the first fifteen emperors—closest in time and bloodline to Amaterasu—had acceded to the throne in father-to-son fashion. In other words, this spurious imperial genealogy, when strategically placed in the

Kojiki and *Nihon shoki,* helped turn a convenient Chinese political practice into a venerable and divinely sanctioned Japanese tradition.

Fujiwara hegemony in the Nara and Heian periods rested mainly on marriage politics and control over landholdings throughout Japan. When these institutional and fiscal bases of support broke down in Kamakura and Ashikaga times, the Fujiwara and related high-ranking court families began to exploit Amaterasu's divine decree in a more assertive and purposeful way. This is shown in Jien's *Gukanshō* of 1219 and Kitabatake Chikafusa's *Jinnō shōtōki* of 1339.

Fujiwara scion and Tendai chief abbot Jien (1155–1225) was a direct descendant of Nakatomi no Kamatari and Fujiwara no Fuhito through Morosuke (908–960), who had founded the Fujiwara-Kujō house. Jien was not famous for writing the *Gukanshō* during his own lifetime; indeed, he was definitely confirmed as its author only in 1920. Rather, he was Japan's most honored lyricist at the time and had ninety-one verses chosen for the *Shinkokinshū*—no other living poet could boast as many in a single imperial anthology.[21] Fujiwara fortunes were slipping badly owing to the steady rise of warrior power; as clan scion, Tendai chief abbot, and master poet, Jien embodied all the interests of a ruling class in steep decline, desperately clinging to the status quo.

For our present purposes of contextualizing Yamagata Daini's brand of imperial loyalism, the *Gukanshō's* complex philosophy of history may be distilled as follows.[22] Moral Reason *(dōri)*—a term appearing seventy-five times in chapter seven alone—determines all past, present, and future events. According to Jien's karmic chiliasm, the world was heading toward ultimate destruction; his aim in writing the *Gukanshō* was to show precisely how Moral Reason operated from era to era. This would teach rulers how to adjust state policies so that society's inexorable decline would be arrested, if but temporarily.

Only direct descendants of Amaterasu could reign as sovereigns in Japan; but equally important, their methods of rule varied from age to age. Ancient emperors from Jimmu through Seimu, roughly 660 B.C. to A.D. 190, ruled in the age of Buddha's True Law when Moral Reason was fully understood. This is why these thirteen emperors enjoyed long reigns (of up to 101 years) and administered affairs by themselves, with little need of assistance from Fujiwara ministers. The next era, roughly 192 to 1027, corresponded to the age of Buddha's Imitation Law when Moral Reason became obscured. Emperors came to the throne as children, suffered brief reigns, and fully relied on the assistance of Fujiwara regents in strict accordance with Amaterasu's divine decree. Thus Emperor Seiwa assiduously followed the wise counsel advanced by Fujiwara no Yoshifusa beginning in 858.[23] Of course, state ministers in this second era had to be drawn from the Fujiwara-Kujō, who were direct descendants of Amenokoyane, and Jien likened this emperor-regent relationship to that of "a fish in water."[24]

It is imperative to note that Jien idealized the Fujiwara regency of this second era, not the direct imperial rule of the first. But he insisted that neither form of rule would work in his contemporary third era, that of the Buddha's Final Law. Degeneration in the form of rising warrior power was now so acute that the assistance provided by civil officials at court no longer sufficed. Emperors now required "a ruling state minister who coupled civil with martial functions in unified fashion."[25] Jien thus revised the thrust of Amaterasu's divine decree in keeping with contemporary needs to accommodate warrior power. Moral Reason now dictated that both the imperial regent and the Kamakura shogun must be Fujiwara-Kujō descendants. And if that admonition were not compelling enough, he further contended that Amaterasu and Hachiman Bosatsu had concluded a karmic covenant stipulating that Kujō Yoritsune, Jien's two-year-old nephew, would become the new shogun in 1219. This supposedly fortuitous event took place just before Jien completed the *Gukanshō*.

Jien composed this history mainly to dissuade ex-Emperor Gotoba and his attendants from revolting against the new Kujō shogun and Kamakura regime. (As historian Akamatsu Toshihide notes, this is why prewar and wartime *kōkoku shikan* ideologues deemed the *Gukanshō* unfit for educational purposes.)[26] Jien reasoned that any attempt to destroy warrior power would prove futile and disastrous. Direct imperial rule in the current age was both anachronistic and contrary to Amaterasu's divine decree.[27] If any of her offspring should dare to rule in the despotic fashion suited to ancient times, disorder would result, degeneration would speed up, and final devastation would come sooner rather than later.[28] And if any of Amaterasu's offspring resented or disobeyed the Kujō regent-shogun, divine forces would ordain the same fate that had befallen Emperor Yōzei—that is, the offending sovereign would be deposed through forced abdication and retirement into Buddhist vows.[29]

The Jōkyū War of 1221 seemed to bear out Jien's harsh prophecies of imperial woe. Emperors Juntoku and Chūkyō were in fact forced off the throne; and, later, ex-Emperors Gotoba, Tsuchimikado, and Juntoku suffered banishment to remote islands. Worse still, as history went on to show, warrior power became even more firmly entrenched owing to this botched restorationist coup. Emperor Godaigo's effort in 1333 proved somewhat more successful, but it too met defeat by 1336. Thus two major attempts to crush warrior power and reinstate imperial rule had failed miserably by the time that Kitabatake Chikafusa (1293–1354) had completed his magnum opus *Jinnō shōtōki* in 1339 and revised it in 1342.

In Kitabatake's day, the mere survival of Godaigo's Southern imperial line seemed dubious. Its fate hinged largely on Kitabatake's ability to win warrior support, which he solicited most importunately. Kitabatake, like Jien, was the scion of a high-ranking court family, the Murakami-Genji. He composed *Jinnō shōtōki* with two readerships in mind: one was Emperor Gomurakami, who acceded at age twelve after his father Godaigo died in 1339; the other was warrior bands in the Kantō and Tōhoku regions headed by men of low birth such as Yūki Chikatomo. Kitabatake's ideas—as these directly relate to Yamagata Daini's loyalist thought—are summarized here.[30]

To Emperor Gomurakami, Kitabatake repeated the argument that only Amaterasu's descendants might reign over Japan; but, he added, not all of them warranted that privilege. Heaven's will *(ten'i)* and Right Reason *(shōri)* dictated that only sovereigns in the "legitimate" branch of the imperial house might accede. The Southern branch headed by Godaigo and Gomurakami was legitimate now. But if Gomurakami ignored "virtue," it would die out. Then succession would pass to another imperial branch—just as Buretsu's vicious reign had spelled the end for Ōjin's branch and restored legitimacy to Chūai's in A.D. 506. In this way, divine retribution might require a few generations to take force. But virtue would find ultimate reward; and evil, ultimate punishment.[31] According to Kitabatake, Godaigo had ignored virtue in two key respects despite his many achievements. First, Godaigo flaunted despotic power in a hopelessly outdated manner; second, he flouted Amaterasu's decree about governing with the "assistance" of Fujiwara offspring or related high-ranking ministerial families such as the Murakami-Genji. Quite to the contrary, Godaigo willfully conferred high rank and office on court nobles of mediocre pedigree or, worse still, on riffraff warriors such as Nawa Nagatoshi and Kusunoki Masashige. Such high-handedness showed contempt for time-honored, divinely sanctioned stipulations that promotion at court must accord with lineage.[32]

On the other hand, Kitabatake warned warriors such as Yūki Chikatomo that Godaigo's Southern branch of the imperial house was legitimate now; so it, not the Northern branch, retained the sovereign authority to grant rewards of court rank, office title, and fief confirmation. Owing to their mean birth, provincial warriors such as Yūki normally had no right to acquire high imperial honors. But Kitabatake could not stem the historical tide, which clearly had crested in the warriors' favor. So, perhaps quoting from the *Shih chi*, he presaged Sorai and Daini by begrudging that "when society suffers violent disorder, the martial takes precedence over the civil; when states enjoy peace, the civil takes precedence over the martial."[33] After its final victory, the Southern Court would reward warriors such as Yūki Chikatomo for rendering meritorious service—but only in line with their genealogy. They invited certain disaster for their offspring by seeking more. Heaven snuffed out the Minamoto in the second generation beyond Yoritomo after a mere thirty-seven years in power; but it had allowed the Hōjō to rule for seven generations, more than a hundred years. This was because Minamoto no Yoritomo had been insolent and greedy, whereas Hōjō Yoshitoki and Yasutoki knew the humble limits of their pedigree and declined high court honors as a reward for their services.[34] Thus, Hōjō Yoshitoki and Yasutoki—not "restorationist" heroes such as Kusunoki Masashige or Nitta Yoshisada—were ideal warriors for Kitabatake.

Jien and Kitabatake Chikafusa failed in the realm of political action. Neither won a hearing for his views; indeed, the course of history ran directly counter to their main proposals. Nevertheless, we should note elements in their political thought that they shared with Tokugawa Confucians. First, both medieval thinkers agreed on the need for Fujiwara regents to assist imperial government. As Kitabatake reconfirmed: "There has been a covenant in our land ever since the age of the gods that Amaterasu's offspring will reign in the land and that ministers descended from Amenokoyane are qualified to assist those sovereigns."[35] Second, both men agreed on the stages of Japanese history and on the form of imperial government suited to each. Direct rule by the emperor was right and proper only in the high antiquity of stage one. Fujiwara regency took effect in stage two, which began in the ninth century A.D. The Hōgen and Heiji wars of the 1150s marked the onset of stage three, when Fujiwara regency broke down owing to ineluctable historical forces—namely, the rise of warrior houses to power in the realm. Warrior "assistance" in government, however repugnant in principle, had to be tolerated and rewarded from that point on. Ideally the Fujiwara-Kujō regent at court would also serve as a shogun; but in any case, these civil and military wings of government had to be unified so that the civil predominated. Third, Jien and Kitabatake lauded Fujiwara regents for the ministerial autonomy they exercised vis-à-vis wayward emperors. Both praised the first Fujiwara regent Yoshifusa by comparing him explicitly to minister Yi Yin of the Shang dynasty, and both glorified Fujiwara no Mototsune for having "deposed" the evil Emperor Yōzei in 884—an act they lauded through allusions to Hou Kuang, the exemplary Han-dynasty a-heng. Kitabatake acclaimed Seiwa's reign, and Jien acclaimed Kōkō's reign, as epoch-making in Japanese political history. But the credit went to the ruling Fujiwara grand minister—Yoshifusa or Mototsune—not to the reigning emperor.[36]

Jien took special pains to defend Fujiwara no Mototsune against charges of imperial irreverence. In fact, he extolled Mototsune's deposing of Emperor Yōzei as one of "the three meritorious acts by Fujiwara regents."[37] Jien's rationale was that a grand minister might dethrone a sovereign from two possible motives. Taira no Kiyomori ousted Goshirakawa on a personal whim; that constituted rebellion (muhon), plunged the realm into chaos, and could not but fail. By contrast, Fujiwara no Mototsune deposed

Yōzei in accordance with Moral Reason, which stipulated that "when an emperor is clearly evil, he must be replaced both for his own good and for that of the world at large."[38]

Tokugawa Confucians adopted this patently nonrevolutionary form of imperial loyalism and further adjusted it to suit conditions in their own era. Bakufu and warrior supremacy over the imperial court and civil aristocracy was self-evident and overwhelming by the seventeenth century; it required little explicit justification. Simply to suggest a revival of direct imperial rule or Fujiwara regency would have seemed ludicrous. Even Emperor Gomizuno-o (r. 1611–1629) resigned himself to warrior landownership and government "in this degenerate age"—though reluctantly and resentfully.[39] Edo was being commonsensical, not punitive, when it decreed in 1615 that the emperor and court must confine themselves to cultural, ceremonial, and religious pursuits; for, by universal agreement, these were the only affairs they were competent to handle.[40]

Pragmatic shogunal and daimyo rulers generally turned a deaf ear to ideologically inspired reform proposals—at least until Matsudaira Sadanobu's Kansei Reforms near the end of the eighteenth century. Therefore, Confucian political ideals could not be implemented in government administration on a consistent and sustained basis during the early to mid-Edo period. So, like Jien and Kitabatake Chikafusa centuries before, Tokugawa Confucian advisors were largely ignored in the realm of political action. But their links to these forebears in the realm of political thought are of prime importance and warrant close attention here.

Kumazawa Banzan, for example, held that Tokugawa shoguns were imperial regents (sesshō)—the same title that the Fujiwara had flaunted in their prime. Virtually all Tokugawa thinkers, Kumazawa Banzan and Yamagata Daini included, agreed that Japan's imperial house would reign forever in accordance with Amaterasu's divine decree. But equally important, they assumed that the imperial house was unfit to rule. Reflecting the self-evident warrior hegemony of Edo times, Daini and Banzan argued that a purely military shogun-regent deserved to wield imperial power—not a Fujiwara-Kujō courtier-regent who secondarily assumed military functions. Even so, this Tokugawa shogun-regent would subordinate his military to his civil functions in respect of the emperor's exalted position. Such a view clearly adumbrated Fujita Yūkoku's in his "Seimeiron" of 1791. According to Fujita, the Tokugawa shogun in Edo enjoyed unquestioned political and military supremacy over the realm, yet displayed impeccable virtue by revering the imperial house in Kyoto. That is, the all-mighty shogun deferred to an impotent emperor by acting as a loyally remonstrative "regent" *(sesshō)*.[41] Moreover, this shogun-regent would accept sagely advice from Confucian scholars below, especially those espousing the Mitogaku tenets that Fujita Yūkoku and his son Tōko would go on to establish.

"Loyalist" reasoning of this sort meant that Edo reserved all political rights vis-à-vis the Kyoto court, even that of deposing emperors. This "deposing" owed nothing to Kiyomori-style caprice or to Mencius' regicide and dynastic overthrow *(hōbatsu)*. Consistent with the ideal of ministerial autonomy inspired by Fujiwara regents and articulated by Jien and Kitabatake, Yamagata Daini construed *hōbatsu* to mean that the shogun-regent might force an emperor to retire and then proctor him about the need to accept harshly critical advice—the kind that T'ai Chia got from Yi Yin, or that Emperor Yōzei got from Fujiwara no Mototsune. This logic helps explain why Matsudaira Sadanobu's firm treatment of Emperor Kōkaku and punishment of court nobles in the 1791 Songō Incident did not constitute imperial irreverence by the standards of that day. (Modern ultranationalist historians would render a different judgment, though.) Indeed, Matsudaira Sadanobu relished the "loyalist" reputation that he had won by restoring the imperial palace to glorious ancient models and raising allowances to the court despite fiscal difficulties in Edo.

The prewar and wartime *kōkoku shikan* ideology stressed that Japan's sacred national essence was rooted in its imperial family line "unbroken throughout the ages eternal" *(bansei ikkei)*. This national polity, it was held, had been prescribed in Amaterasu's divine decree at the dawn of time as revealed in the *Kojiki* and *Nihon shoki*. Her divine decree—and the *kokutai* myths it later spawned—did not benefit the imperial house alone, however. That decree and those myths also justified a tradition of de facto control exercised by ministerial surrogates who claimed to "assist" *(hohitsu)* divine sovereigns in Japan's everlasting dynastic line.

Yamagata Daini's brand of loyalism should be placed in this nonrevolutionary tradition stretching back to Fujiwara rule. Ministerial autonomy and imperial assistance, Master Ryū's main new theses, assumed that sovereign emperors were not fit to rule and so could not be entrusted with politically significant state functions. Instead, emperors needed help from regents or grand ministers, who in turn sought advice from scholar-advisors able to fathom the cosmic principles that regulated sociopolitical affairs—whether revealed in Moral Reason, heaven's will, or the *Book of Changes*. There was nothing at all subversive in this form of loyalism; quite to the contrary, its centuries-long staying power derived from a capacity to meet the needs of imperial surrogates in all historical eras.

After the Edo bakufu fell in 1867–1868, this "other" loyalist tradition won adherents among Meiji leaders seeking to reinforce their newly-created status quo. Moreover, this tradition lent a peculiarly Japanese slant to Western theories of constitutional monarchy. While stipulating imperial absolutism in theory, this other form of loyalism granted significant power to civil and military officials who served the emperor. Their power was manifested in two forms of ministerial autonomy. The first was the legal type enshrined in Articles 55 and 56 of the 1889 Meiji Constitution which defined the prerogatives of cabinet ministers and privy councillors. The second was an informal type exercised by nonconstitutional bodies such as the *genrō*, army and navy chiefs of staff, palace officials in the Imperial Household Ministry, and ex-premiers *(jūshin)* of the early Shōwa era. Such advisors at court wielded immense behind-the-scenes influence over the emperor's nominally unlimited sovereign authority.

The Meiji Constitution's preamble *(kokubun)* stipulated that Amaterasu's descendants would always be heads of state in Japan by virtue of her divine decree. Article 4 made the emperor the locus of all sovereign power, and Article 3 made him "sacred and inviolable." This latter article did prohibit Japanese subjects from impairing imperial majesty through sacrilege, but it was not originally meant to deify emperors.[42] Instead, "sacred and inviolable" expressed the principle of legal immunity granted to monarchs worldwide. Thus Japan's emperor, like his European royal counterparts, could not be held culpable under domestic law for actions that his government took.[43] But this stipulation of legal and political non-culpability was based in part on the "other" loyalist assumption; that emperors were not competent to rule and so did not need to bear responsibility for politically significant acts of state, or for misrule.

Articles 5 and 6 seemed to grant the emperor absolute legislative and judicial power in performing these acts of state as specified in Articles 7 through 16. Some of the more important of these state acts were to command the armed forces and determine their peacetime size and organization, to appoint premiers and other state ministers, to conclude diplomatic treaties, to declare war, and to make peace. Article 55, however, expressly prevented the emperor from doing these things on his own—without "assistance" *(hohitsu)* from cabinet ministers.[44] Their official countersignatures were required before any imperial edict or proposed legislation could take force because they were the ones responsible for actually executing the emperor's acts of state and exercising his sovereign powers. Furthermore, it became virtually a binding custom for emperors not to veto any matter officially passed by these cabinet ministers—though he might choose to ignore it and thereby withhold the needed approval.

The Meiji Constitution placed no limits on whom the emperor might appoint as his premier or other ministers of state in the cabinet. But in actuality, he made these appointments on the recommendation of nonconstitutional, extralegal groups charged with assisting him—mainly the *genrō*, ex-premiers *(jūshin)*, lords keeper of the privy seal, and presidents of the privy council. Only at their sufferance, then, could parliamentary rule and the principle of party cabinets be maintained in prewar and wartime Japan. Moreover, cabinet ministers were not responsible as a group to the premier or to the Diet; each was directly accountable to the emperor alone. This sort of ministerial autonomy ultimately allowed the military to make or break cabinets by virtue of their control over the army and navy portfolios.

Many historians judge that such characteristics in the Japanese political system precluded the development of parliamentary democracy and constitutional monarchy in their "true" forms. That judgment may or may not be valid. My point here is that the "other" loyalist tradition of imperial assistance and ministerial autonomy—as represented by Yamagata Daini—helps explain certain features of modern Japan's imperial state structure and ideology that may seem puzzling from a Western political perspective.

Those forms of ministerial autonomy and imperial assistance best fit Japan's emperor system and constitutional order in middle to late Meiji times when the *genrō* combined civil with military functions but ensured that the civil predominated. In the Taishō era, popular demands for meaningful political participation created a semblance of parliamentary rule through party cabinets. Later, in the early Shōwa era, the service ministries, the military general staffs, and even field-grade officers claimed independence of the emperor's supreme command. What is more, these military officials arbitrarily expanded the scope of that concept to include acts of state normally handled by the cabinet.

But these party politicians, palace officials, and young officers availed themselves of the second, or informal, type of loyalist ministerial autonomy as it evolved under the Meiji constitutional order. They fully, and sometimes consciously, exploited that Fujiwara-inspired rhetoric by which officials charged with "assisting" the imperial house claimed wide discretionary prerogatives—even to the point of violating Emperor Shōwa's sovereign authority and supposedly unlimited powers. In fact, their self-ascribed discretion included a plot to force him off the throne and into a Kyoto monastery.

Ex-Premier Konoe Fumimaro—a direct descendant of Fujiwara no Mototsune—desperately groped for a way to end the war early in 1945. But his categorical imperative was to do so without endangering Amaterasu's family line or harming Japan's "twenty-six-hundred-year *kokutai*."[45] Konoe's bold scheme, as related to his son-in-law and trusted aide Hosokawa Morisada, called for making Emperor Shōwa retire and take holy vows under the priestly name "ex-Emperor Yūnin" (another reading of "Hirohito"). In Konoe's eyes, it was absolutely essential for Japan's head of state and the commander-in-chief of its armed forces to make a convincing public display of penitence for having brought total war and devastation to his people. Such penitence would entail "not just abdicating, but also entering Ninnaji or Daikakuji temple to pray for the souls of the war dead." Then Konoe added in fitting *a-heng* fashion: "Of course I will accompany him at that time."[46]

In sum, Konoe sought to defuse widespread popular enmity toward the imperial house at home. He reckoned that Emperor Shōwa's twelve-year-old heir apparent, Crown Prince Akihito, was clearly untainted by war guilt and so could be used to mollify anti-imperial sentiment after acceding. Thus, by "deposing" one bad emperor, Konoe's act of *hōbatsu* in the traditional Japanese sense would strengthen the imperial line as a whole. Through this act, he would forestall both a violent revolution and more moderate demands to replace the monarchy with a republican form of government—since either of those measures from below would destroy the *kokutai*.

Konoe's ploy was not designed for domestic use alone. Later that month, he met secretly with two other ex-premiers, Admirals Okada Keisuke and Yonai Mitsumasa. These imperial advisors calculated that, by dethroning Emperor Shōwa, they could thwart suspected Allied plans to execute him as a war criminal and eradicate the imperial house. No doubt reflecting on the exploits of his illustrious regent-forebears, Konoe asserted:

> If we want peace, we must be fully prepared to surrender unconditionally; and the Allies are likely to demand that the emperor be held responsible for [starting] this war. In that event, maybe we should *follow precedents* by having His Majesty take the tonsure and enter Ninnaji temple. Even the Allies would not think of doing anything to a cloistered emperor.[47]

CHAPTER 5

About the Original Texts

As we have seen, Yamagata Daini was widely misperceived as a villainous menace to society in the second half of the eighteenth century. He largely receded from popular consciousness in the first half of the nineteenth century. He emerged from that obscurity to be eulogized as an early martyr in the *tōbaku* cause during Bakumatsu and early Meiji times. He was hailed as an emperor-loving incarnation of the Japanese spirit in the 1930s and 1940s. And in the postwar era, he was transmogrified into a revolutionary friend of the people who helps nervous students pass their examinations. Not surprisingly, these drastic changes in Daini's image affected the way his *Ryūshi shinron* text has been circulated, published, and explicated since its composition in 1759.

Early Versions

Daini was understandably secretive about how he handled the *Ryūshi shinron*. This was not because it called for destroying the Edo regime or for restoring imperial government, but rather because it contained passages that bitingly indicted warrior rule —especially under the current Tokugawa house. That criticism explains why he never published the work, why he circulated it only among his family and closest friends, and why bakufu prosecutors never gained access to the tract and so could not explicitly cite it as evidence to justify his death sentence. Daini's original manuscript does not come down to us today. But one hand-copied text dating from the late eighteenth century—probably made by a close associate—does survive and is now housed in Tokyo's National Diet Library.

By mid-Meiji times, Daini's "dangerous rebel" image had lost its earlier opprobrium and the "loyalist martyr" image that had emerged in Bakumatsu times now qualified him for beatification by the new emperor state. Amid these favorable circumstances, the first *Ryūshi shinron* manuscript surfaced in 1883. It was owned by Miyazaki Sachimaro, a former samurai from Shimane prefecture, who submitted this hand-copied text and other related documents to the Meiji government. As well, Miyazaki petitioned that the government honor Daini's memory by duly rewarding his descendants for his imperial loyalism of the previous century.[1] As Japanese historians hold, Daini no doubt burned his original manuscript. But it appears that relatives did retain one copy as "a family heirloom"—just as Daini instructed in his afterword to the document. Apparently the loyalist zeitgeist prevailing in mid-Meiji times persuaded Daini's great-grandson to take this family keepsake out of hiding; in 1884, he produced the earliest published edition of the *Ryūshi shinron*. One copy of this rare volume is currently housed in the Tokyo University Library.

Although other variant manuscripts exist, modern Japanese scholars judge these three to be the most reliable: the National Diet manuscript dating from the eighteenth century, the Miyazaki manuscript that first came to light in 1883, and the Yamagata family manuscript published in 1884. Hence Japanese historians have compiled and published modern recensions based on these three documents.

Early published editions of the *Ryūshi shinron* appeared in two formats: either the classical Chinese in which Daini originally composed the work or transliterations into literary Japanese *(kakikudashibun)* that combine Chinese characters with *kana* syllabary according to the word order and inflections dictated by Japanese syntax. No critical edition of the *Ryūshi shinron* text has yet been produced in Japan. But modern Japanese scholars have published at least thirteen different printed editions, and I have consulted six of these—four prewar and two postwar—in producing this English translation.

First, there are two classical Chinese editions that date from the late Meiji and Taishō eras. One is edited by Inoue Tetsujirō and Kanie Yoshimaru in Volume 7 of the 1902 Ikuseisha *Nihon rinri ihen* series; the other, based on the Miyazaki manuscript, is edited by Takimoto Seiichi in Volume 26 of the 1915 *Nihon keizai sōsho* series. Both of these editions are punctuated and include the 1763 postscript composed by Daini's critic, Matsumiya Kanzan, plus letters exchanged between the two men. In addition, Takimoto's *Keizai sōsho* edition of the Miyazaki manuscript scrupulously reproduces critical comments on the *Ryūshi shinron* originally written by Matsumiya Kanzan in the margins of the text.

The *Rinri ihen* and *Keizai sōsho* compendia of Tokugawa-era political and socioeconomic treatises set high standards for scholarly and editorial competence in their day, and even now they are quite valuable for presenting variant manuscripts and unabridged sources not readily available elsewhere in print. Matsumiya Kanzan's critical comments in the margins of the *Ryūshi shinron* text, for example, were of crucial importance in shaping my analysis of Daini's thought; and these marginal comments can be found only in the Miyazaki *Keizai sōsho* text as edited by Takimoto. But these early-twentieth-century texts lack introductions and substantive commentaries. On the plus side, this means they allow the reader to frame interpretations and reach conclusions independently, without being misled by ultranationalistic *kōkoku shikan* polemics. On the other hand, these classical Chinese texts do not provide annotation or transliterations into literary Japanese—and that presents awesome language barriers to modern, and especially Western, readers such as myself. As well, these two texts contain misprints and other errors that compound such difficulties. So the general rule is: when a more recent edition of a text exists, consult it rather than the *Rinri ihen* or the *Keizai sōsho*.

Later Versions

All things considered, perhaps the most useful *Ryūshi shinron* text is the 1943 paperback Iwanami Library *(bunko)* volume edited by Kawaura Genchi. It is based on the 1884 printed text published by the Yamagata family. Kawaura includes both the classical Chinese original and its transliteration into literary Japanese, plus Matsumiya Kanzan's postscript and the Yamagata–Matsumiya correspondence in both formats. Kawaura omits Matsumiya's marginal notes, however, which were found only in the Miyazaki manuscript. Iwanami reissued this wartime *bunko* edition with a new introduction by the editor dated 1968, but it presents no new insights. And this reprint edition too has gone out of print, so it is no longer readily available. Of all existing printed editions, Kawaura's probably provides the most careful and scholarly annotation to the text. But serious flaws nevertheless remain both in his notes and in his introduction. Like some scholars who were once active in the 1930s and 1940s, Kawaura continued to advance elements of the nationalist *kōkoku shikan* view of Japanese history even in the postwar period. Thus his notes and commentary ignore, obscure, or even distort the meaning of key phrases or terms such as *"shōkoku"* in places where the text betrays his idealized image of Daini fostering revolutionary imperial loyalism.

Iizuka Shigetake's 1942 *Yamagata Daini seiden* (The True Life of Yamagata Daini) at times displays wartime nationalism to an even greater degree. Iizuka's work comprises two sections, biographical and textual. The latter includes Daini's *Ryūshi shinron* in the classical Chinese original, a Japanese literary transliteration, a modern Japanese translation, and lengthy commentaries to the work. But Iizuka's translation is often loose and his commentaries are at times marred by panegyrics and propaganda. For example, he portrays Daini heralding wartime government movements to cleanse Japanese culture of "enemy elements" by banning jazz and romanized street signs.[2] In all fairness, Iizuka's commentary to the text does shed light on certain important issues overlooked by other scholars; still, it must be used with caution. The biography portion of Iizuka's work is definitely worthwhile for acquiring general information on Daini's life, some of which is hard to find elsewhere. For example, Iizuka provides texts of the inscriptions that Daini prepared for the monuments he dedicated to Prince Yamatotakeru and Princess Ototachibana. These are important primary sources that most historians have ignored in analyzing Daini's thought. Yet Iizuka's information is dated and must be corrected on certain key points with respect to biographical and historical fact, especially those related to the Meiwa Incident and to Daini's service under Ōoka Tadamitsu. Much of this up-to-date biographical information can be found in Yokoyama Seiji's excellent essay, "Meiwa jiken kō."[3]

Japan's defeat and surrender in 1945 created an atmosphere of free critical inquiry that ended any need to propagate the old emperor-centered *kōkoku shikan* thesis as applied to Daini. The

Ryūshi shinron text edited by Nishida Ta'ichirō as part of Volume 17 in Chikuma Shobō's 1970 *Nihon no shisō* series is a fine example of postwar textual scholarship. Nishida's notes to the text, though sparse, correct those of Kawaura and Iizuka on several key points. Nishida supplements his literary Japanese transliteration of the text with a useful and generally reliable modern Japanese translation, but he omits Daini's classical Chinese original and excludes all the crucially important Yamagata–Matsumiya source materials. Nishida's introduction to the Chikuma Shobō volume traces the reception of Confucianism in Tokugawa Japan. It is scholarly and informative but says virtually nothing specifically related to Daini's thought. And Nishida's one-page prefatory comments to Daini's text and modern translation show that even the best postwar scholars may remain captive to the orthodox *kōkoku shikan* line. Thus he states: "Fujii Umon and Takenouchi Shikibu—whom the bakufu had banished from Kyoto on criminal charges of preaching 'reverence for the emperor'—came to Edo and linked up with Daini. . . . In 1767, he was executed for expressing doctrines inimical to the existing order." These doctrines included "ideas of revolution."[4]

The most recently published *Ryūshi shinron* edition is the most disappointing, especially because it comes from Iwanami Shoten, arguably Japan's most prestigious commercial publisher of academic and scholarly titles. This text is in Volume 38 of the normally authoritative *Nihon shisō taikei,* a sixty-three-volume compendium of source materials for premodern Japanese thought published in the 1970s. The editor of this particular volume, which appeared in 1976, is Naramoto Tatsuya, a respected Tokugawa historian; but in fact, his graduate students prepared Daini's text. This *shisō taikei* edition contains only a transliteration into literary Japanese. It lacks annotation, substantial commentaries, the classical Chinese original, and the all-important Yamagata–Matsumiya source materials.

In sum, then, each of the published editions I consulted was inadequate by itself. Only Iizuka provides a detailed biographical study of Daini plus primary sources related to his monument inscriptions. Only Kawaura, Iizuka, and, to a lesser extent, Nishida include annotation to the text. Only Takimoto presents all the crucial Yamagata–Matsumiya source materials. And only

Kawaura and Iizuka contain detailed introductions or commentaries, though these are seriously flawed by nationalistic bias. Of the two postwar editions published, Naramoto's gives nothing beyond the literary Japanese text. Nishida's limited annotation is useful for correcting a number of ideologically inspired prewar errors. But even Nishida fails to free himself entirely from the heavy hand of the past, and his single-page commentary to the text contains misleading statements. As a result, I was forced to combine the particular strengths of each published edition in preparing this translation.

In trying to render Master Ryū's tract into contemporary English, I have followed Daini's classical Chinese text closely, but not at the cost of readability. Thus I sought to preserve the terseness of Daini's original language, yet strove to be more direct, precise, and forceful. I hope that my efforts will allow students and general readers in the West to engage Master Ryū and his polemics with unflagging interest throughout. Specialists in the field of Japanese political thought are urged to consult the primary texts listed above in order to check the fidelity of my English translation against the letter and spirit of Daini's original treatise.

PART TWO

Master Ryū's New Thesis

I. Making Name and Actuality Conform

Master Ryū said:

Something may have a name yet not be actual.[1] But nothing actual ever lacked a name. We cannot do without names; that is why the sages couched their teachings in these. In antiquity, the Duke of Chou made officials perform as their office titles dictated, and all states submitted to benevolent rule. Confucius made the conduct of state ritual and music accord with their ceremonial names, and all under heaven praised the efficacy. The *Tao te ching* says, "The myriad things were begotten by the named."[2] The *Chuang tzu* says, "Reality accompanies name as guest does host."[3] Confucians and Legalists have mastered many teachings revealed in names.

The divine emperor Jimmu founded our eastern land [in 660 B.C.] and ruled by the dictum, "Nourish the peoples' livelihood and eliminate hardship from their lives."[4] His radiant virtue extended throughout the four quarters for over a thousand years. [Shōtoku Taishi] set up a system of graded court caps and robes [in 603] to discriminate ranks and so enacted ritual and music to teach proper government.[5] We had counterparts to the Dukes of Chou and Shao, and to the Regents Yi Yin and Fu Yueh; so our civilizing dynastic powers of moral suasion left no commoner untouched.[6] Later, nobles such as Fujiwara no Mototsune [836–891] and Yoshifusa [804–872] made state affairs conform to the Taihō Code and thereby carried on the glorious institutions first established by Shōtoku, the Sharp-Eared Prince.[7] Our long-lived dynasty attained such great heights that its flowering civilization rivaled the Three Dynasties of high antiquity.[8]

Imperial rule deteriorated by Hōgen-Heiji times [1156–1159], and government fell to the hands of [Minamoto] eastern barbarians owing to civil strife in the Juei-Bunji eras [1182–1189].[9] After that, the military dictated state affairs. Underlings seized power and installed or deposed sovereigns at will, so the former sages' ritual and music were lost.[10] Later still, when the Ashikaga arose, warrior power increased further; and they waxed impudent toward the throne despite their lowly title of "general-in-chief."[11] But the illustrious virtue of former sage-emperors had so permeated the peoples' hearts that even these brutal subjects dared not give their presumption free rein. The imperial regalia remained with His Majesty, and the dynastic line survived "like a thread."[12]

> Matsumiya Kanzan: Japan's customs dictate that the imperial regalia remain with His Majesty. You Confucian scholars cannot understand that. The status of sovereign and of subject are immutable—like heaven and earth. All within the realm recognize the titles, ranks, and calendar prescribed by our imperial court. How can you say that it survived "like a thread"?[13]

Local warlords arose with the passing of generations. They ran amok like tigers and dragons, stealing and killing to no end. Villainous rebels hatched every sort of conspiracy while warrior-barbarians plundered at will. They donned neither cap nor headcloth; their garments lacked collar and sleeves. The arrogant touted their virtue; the violent took pride in their deeds. A few of them truly pitied the masses, but they carried on the evils of a Warring States era.[14] How could they know the sages' teachings? And how could lowly commoners remain in their native abodes to enjoy a stable livelihood?

What are the greatest of those evils? First is the grand disarray of state offices. The Way is valid in all times and places: Civil rule maintains order under normal conditions; martial rule deals with emergencies. People do not distinguish civil from martial rule. Those who are supposed to deal with emergencies maintain order in normal times. That should not be.

> Matsumiya Kanzan: Government in ancient times was not divided into civil and military functions. The same man served as minister in court and general on campaigns. How can a rustic like you presume to "deal with emergencies" or "maintain order in normal times"? Misguided superficial remarks violate the dictum that "the superior man is discreet in speech."[15]

The daimyo are provincial rulers who inherit lands, pass on hereditary titles, and administer states and peoples.[16] They assume the airs of military commanders and issue arbitrary decrees unauthorized by recorded precedent. Even cooks and clerks, who never wield arms, presume to be warriors and oppress the people. That is the first evil inimical to the Way of government. All daimyo, great officials, and others who hold the fifth court rank or above receive the post of provincial governor and are appointed to one of the eight imperial government ministries.[17] But these are in name only; reality differs.

> Matsumiya Kanzan: True, "provincial governor" is just a formal title devoid of reality.[18] So it may seem wrong in principle. But this is an expedient way for a small state to enhance its imperial majesty and awe barbarians into submission. One should not always cling rigidly to fixed principles. Here is a wonderful kingly policy.[19]

And the discrepancy is even worse below the fifth rank. Why? I do not know. But we cannot avoid duplicity when using one form of government [military] to perform the functions of another [civil]. Here is a second evil: Government offices lack meaning and order. Generals are masters; court counselors, their servants.[20] Princes of the fifth rank hold posts tied to the fourth. The tail wags the dog; we wear shoes on our heads and hats on our feet. So power justifies pretension. Here is a third evil: Hierarchy is subverted and the base become exalted.

People in antiquity always went by surname or coming-of-age name, and they addressed each other with the decorum proper to senior and junior. Today, high nobles call each other by office title, not properly by name.[21] Warriors, commoners, and vagabonds incorporate central or provincial-government titles in their names. Peasants, artisans, merchants, menials, indentured servants, even the meanest and most despised classes—actors, outcastes, beggars, and untouchables—suffix their names with "bei" (middle palace guard), "emon" (outer palace guard), "suke" (assistant), or "jō" (ministerial secretary).[22] Imperial law codes stipulate that false or unauthorized use of government titles warrants the harshest punishment. But if we enforced them strictly, who in the realm today would *not* be guilty?[23] Here is a fourth evil: Titles and names are hopelessly confounded.

Of course such customs did not arise overnight. Chinese characters for "palace," "shape," "chariot driving," "inquiring," "serving in office," or "extending or arriving at" have acquired peculiar new meanings; so nobles today have no idea what these connote in proper usage.[24] This holds true in all spheres of life, and it might be amusing if it were not so pathetic.

Matsumiya Kanzan: Every people in the world considers its own language to be right and proper. You Confucian scholars alone insist that Chinese standards be rigidly adhered to. You turn things topsy-turvy by condemning your native tongue and calling us all "eastern barbarians" instead of Japanese. Did the sages intend to standardize languages when they insisted that "name and actuality conform"? Even by purely Confucian standards, the Way is more or less being practiced here without our having altered traditional customs.[25]

But people are used to this situation and think it normal, so they just follow along. They could not communicate if they used language correctly; so they confuse coarseness for refinement and ugliness for beauty. Trying to fix usage now would be like sorting hairs to comb or counting rice grains to boil. Stupid, unlettered commoners just ape their betters in speech and action. They have no capacity for reason. The trees and grasses have names based on what they are; that accords with reason. Are men inferior to trees and grasses? Confucius deplored conditions in Wei, saying: "Name and actuality must conform. If not, officials will speak inaccurately, their work will go undone, state ritual and music will not flourish, punishments will not fit crimes, and commoners will be unsure of what they may and may not do."[26] What would he say about us?

Imperial rule lasted over two thousand years.[27] Its moral suasion pervaded the realm, and its virtue permeated the peoples' hearts. How long-lived, extensive, and fathomless it was! But it atrophied: "Deprived of water, the white dragon fell prey to a fisherman"; and [Emperor Godaigo] traversed a thousand miles drenched in dew and rain.[28] How trying indeed! Restored to power by one or two loyal subjects, he ruled only a small provincial state,[29] but still he maintained his ancestral tombs. The imperial line remains eternal; it has survived over four hundred years to the present.[30] Though power has fallen to underlings, the Way remains intact above and the canons of former sage-emperors are in the imperial law codes for all to see. If someone but fostered love for the people, he could make name and actuality conform, make ritual and music flourish, and end the need for punishments. How sad that no such man exists in the realm. We cannot fully restore things to what they were in antiquity, but neither can we fully reform things as they have come down to us. Why this inability to act except by halves? Perhaps we value things too much as they are, and not as they ought to be. Perhaps we are too self-serving, and do not serve the whole realm. Or perhaps we fail at learning and administration, so that our "skill and cleverness" fall short of the task.

> Matsumiya Kanzan: "Self-serving" men pursue personal gain. Those who "serve the whole realm" embody benevolence and righteousness. Our hegemon [in Edo] practices this tenet; our king [in Kyoto] symbolizes it. That is the ultimate in political virtue and beauty. He who occupies the throne should *not* possess "skill and cleverness." But he would have to if we took your thesis to its logical conclusion. Yours is a contemptible argument.[31]

II. Attaining Oneness

Master Ryū said:

"Heaven is clear, earth is stable, kings and lords exemplify fidelity to the realm—all for having attained oneness."[32] Can this pertain only to them? Great officials cannot regulate their clans, officials cannot support wives and children, commoners cannot enjoy secure livelihoods, fathers cannot edify sons, and sons cannot serve fathers—unless they attain oneness. "Heaven does not have two suns, a people does not have two kings."[33] "A loyal subject does not serve two masters, a chaste wife does not marry twice."[34]

One disciple said:

Please explain in detail.

Master Ryū went on:

In states suffering decay and disorder, rulers and subjects lack unity because rank and stipend come from different sources. Those who seek prestige go to one; those who seek personal gain go to the other. Since honors and wealth come separately, people's desires are divided. Which side should we follow? [Kyoto] bestows honors but is poor, [Edo] dispenses wealth but enjoys no prestige. Authority is divided because people cannot gain both. Which side should we follow? One must be sovereign; the other, subject.

> Matsumiya Kanzan: The superior man favors state ritual. The contemptible man covets personal gain. Our imperial court now administers office and rank only, not finances. It deals with ritual, which superior men favor, not personal gain, which contemptible men covet. This Way has allowed sage-emperors to employ wise ministers throughout the ages. For if ministers sought ritual *and* wealth, they might not act properly.[35]

Those charged with policymaking equivocate, unable to sort out the merits of each side; those charged with problem solving waver, as if stuck in the middle of a vast plain or broad stream. One should act with benevolence and loyalty—but based on what, and directed to whom? Lords, officials, and commoners all ask: "Which side should we follow?" Men debate makeshift policies and adopt stopgap measures; some approve and some censure. But commoners mutter, "Decrees and bans change daily. Orders issued at dawn are rescinded by dusk. Laws contradict each other as day does night. Which side should we follow?"

There is a beast called "Half-Flanks." To run, each of the pair must align with a mate of the opposite flank. There is a bird called "Single-Wings." To fly, each of the pair must align with a mate of the opposite wing.[36] In each case, the halves must form a whole in order to function; if either half went its own way, running or flying could not occur. That is the nature of these creatures; and they are not inferior to other animals, though humans might think them deformed, for we could not exist that way. Both halves cooperate to form a whole, and that allows them to run or fly and to sustain themselves. But they serve no master above and exact labor from no subjects below; they need only live out their own lives. The Way forbids that to men. Duplicity in serving a ruler is unconscionable and violates the former sages' immutable moral tenets; duality in exacting labor from subjects shows a lack of benevolence, and the masses would not accept that. Today we revile as "lewd" any woman who gives herself over to two men, but we think nothing of a subject who serves two masters. So there must be many chaste wives and no faithful officials.

> Matsumiya Kanzan: It is fine to talk about heaven attaining oneness, but I have never heard of our eastern and western capitals [Edo and Kyoto] forming one entity; so this thesis is flawed from the start. Obedience or disobedience was an issue in ancient times,

when there were two kings and two imperial courts in the land: the Northern and Southern. But now one is sovereign and the other is subject. So what is the problem? Wen's goodness lay in serving the Shang dynasty even though he held sway over two-thirds of the realm. The shogun adheres to subject status even though he holds sway over all the realm. This beautiful Japanese custom, without parallel anywhere, is something you Confucian scholars cannot appreciate. Hold your tongue, follower of alien doctrines! The superior man is always on guard against insolent pride.[37]

All men feel pangs of conscience and tugs of desire; but superior men obey conscience, while contemptible men succumb to desire. So, in times of decay and disorder, a superior man maintains his lofty disdain, renounces the world from a cave in the hills, or follows his noble impulses in the woods; but the contemptible man is smug in his sinecure and neglects administrative duties while filling out his tenure.

Long ago, Huang Hsien went to Ch'i. Spotting a group of fishermen there, he noticed one of them clasping the hands of another, ardently expounding on affairs of the day. Huang then noted, "Superior men do not serve in office here; the days of Ch'i are numbered." Seeing that one superior man had failed to attain his aspiration, Huang knew that Ch'i was in decay.[38] If given a glimpse of our land, he would dash away with trailing sleeves. Why would he stay to serve? Given our present situation, the sages themselves would be at a loss. Those now in charge of states must restore government so that officials do what office titles dictate, and they must make state ritual and music flourish so that these function effectively. Eliminate duplicity and duality between ruler and subjects—that is, revive a unified power—and decrees will be obeyed. Then the need for laws will end. With the sovereign on his throne, even contemptible men will know whom to follow. This is the Way to attain oneness.

III. Man and Adornment

Master Ryū said:

Men are born naked and without distinctions of nobility and baseness. That is their heaven-endowed nature. Grubbing for food and giving free rein to desires, they resemble birds and beasts. But each bird or beast has its own talent, such as flying or running; its own mark of adornment, such as feathers or fur; and its own size category, such as big or small. Even scaled and shelled insects form distinct groups comparable to the classes of trees and grass. But men differ. None has a peculiar talent, such as flying or running; and none has feathers or fur. Each has a nose, mouth, and limbs of identical shape. All of their languages employ the same patterned marks. A beautiful sound or face arouses the same desires in all. This shows that men were originally equal, without distinctions of noble and base. "The strong overpowered the weak, the haughty despised the infirm."[39] Men would harm, wound, oppress, kill, rob, and pillage; and did so to kinsman or stranger, elderly or young alike.[40] "They dwelt in caves and slept on grass."[41] They died among the birds and beasts, rotted amid the trees and grass. Such was life in primeval times. "Yet of the myriad creatures, man is most possessed of divine spirit."[42] So superior beings arose from the masses. Not only could they survive and nurture themselves, they enabled all others to do so too. They grew food and sewed garments for the realm's peoples and taught the arts of farming and spinning. They "nourished the peoples and eliminated hardship from their lives" so that nothing was wanting.[43] Then the peoples submitted to those sages "as little stars defer to the North Star."[44]

When men grub for food and give free rein to desire, they cannot tell noble from base or kinsman from stranger. That is why the sages ranked people by status name—sovereign or subject, parent or child, husband or wife, senior or junior; by talent—wise or foolish, worthy or unworthy; and by occupation—peasant, artisan, or merchant. Only that kept the strong from overpowering the weak and the haughty from despising the infirm; only that stopped the harming, wounding, oppressing, killing, robbing, and pillaging. The sages codified ritual and music, decreed specific duties, and created dress codes; that is how status ranks, state offices, and graded court caps and garments came to be. "Sages" created these, "worthies" conveyed these, and "the sovereign" administers these. "Great officials" submit to him, "officials" work under them, and "the peoples" come under the moral suasion of all. No one, from the Son of Heaven above to the commoner masses below, lacks cap or garment; that is why men do not herd with the birds and beasts. None of this derived from nature; all was established by sages.

Caps adorn the head, garments embellish the body. To lack these is to follow barbarian ways and sets one apart from "peoples of the sages." Men exist wherever sun and moon shine, wherever boats and carts travel. But they partake of civilization and adornments only where this moral transformation of customs occurs. Only there can they adopt sagely institutions and acquire sagely virtue. Cap and garment do not just fend off the cold. They derive from a sense of shame: that naked, barefoot men are no different from the birds or beasts. So the sages created and enforced cap, garment, and skirt regulations. The *Book of Rites* enjoins: "Do not tuck up one's skirt unless fording a stream"; "Do not bare one's chest unless laboring at a parent's command";[45] and "Do not remove one's cap even on the emperor's death."[46]

These rules derive partly from a sense of shame about unseemliness and partly from a need to adorn the head and body. But dress codes discriminate ranks, offices, and administrative functions; they also help to conduct ritual, music, and punishments. As well, they help to elevate folkways and customs, promulgate decrees, maintain state order, and induce barbarians to submit. Only when dress codes exist may we speak of benevolence and the Way. Only thus did the ancient sage-kings bring the realm under their moral suasion. "Yao and Shun dangled their garments and skirts, and all under heaven was well ordered."[47] Could it have been otherwise?

A ruler who ignores the Way acts differently. To him, cap and garment are shackles, ritual and music are empty adornments. He relies on laws and punishments to rule, and that produces upheaval and revolt. How unlike the sage-kings! After an era of decay and disorder, rulers must thoroughly examine ancient practices to make sure that existing dress codes distinguish civilization from barbarism as true adornments should. Because discrimination now is based solely on what a person owns, there is no way to tell the noble from the base or the esteemed from the lowly. If someone travels at the head of a grand procession comprising many carts and followers, people think him rich and noble. No one can tell a duke or marquis from a count, or a lord from a great official. This is because palace robes all follow the same style and courtiers choose any patterned colors they like for their garments. Among lesser officials and commoners, too, discrimination depends solely on what a person has. The rich wear beautiful silks and the poor, coarse hemp.[48]

So distinctions of noble and base are confounded. We find no one [like Tzu-lu]: "In tattered cotton-padded garments, he felt no embarrassment next to men wearing fox-fur or badger-skin coats."[49] When a man is acutely embarrassed about something he lacks, he longs for it; and if this desire goes uncurbed, no income will suffice. Then officials and people become insolvent. Being noble or base has nothing to do with furs or skins. But people look only at clothes in differentiating men. They esteem those in fine apparel and despise those in shabby rags. To avoid being despised, all men vie to obtain beautiful wardrobes; and so, extravagant ways become ever more firmly rooted.[50] Worse still, true discrimination of high from low is lost. So the canons of behavior integral to civilized life break down. Despairing of their poverty, officials and people forget righteousness; giving full rein to their desire, they trigger disastrous upheavals. Countless such evils flourish owing to disorder in cap and garment and to the dearth of adornments marking civilized life.

High officials today may wear proper caps and garments during religious rituals or observances. But way-clearers in front of official processions tuck up skirts, bare buttocks, swing arms, kick feet, and scream crassly. Everyone thinks this a display of grandeur, and such antics are established folkways. But I find them more repulsive than the sight of a peasant clod sweating in the summer sun.[51] Cropped hair was common in the realm by Ashikaga times, but only among base fighting men whose calling required short hair. After the great upheaval [the Ōnin War], however, even state officials such as court nobles and generals-in-chief cropped their hair and shaved their foreheads, thereby baring their scalps.[52] And they lacked dress codes for good measure! The civilized custom of cap and garment was thus transformed to barbaric folkways—with all the ugliness that these entail. When [Liu Pang] pacified the realm in days of yore, he appointed wise ministers to establish court rituals [in 201 B.C.]. Only after implementing these in his regime did he "come to know imperial majesty" as Kao-tsu, the first Han-dynasty emperor.[53] Men covet wealth because it buys goods, and they covet noble status because it brings prestige; otherwise they would covet neither. But no prestige accrues to one who dons cap and garment, enters court service, and conducts government. So how can anyone learn about the Way to bring the realm under moral suasion? Do we have methods to create order and peace, or practices suited to an age of decay and upheaval? Do we have here the moral tenets of Middle Kingdom civilization, or barbaric folkways? How should we cope with this situation?

After the Chin and Yuan invaded the Sung, Mongols won control of the realm [in 1264]. But they still could not transform civilized customs; regulations for court cap and garments and for state offices remained in effect. So the Way of the ancient sage-kings did not lapse. When Ming [T'ai-tsu] rose to power [in 1368], all violent outlaws submitted to chastisement and all things reverted to olden forms. And to this very day [not just officials but] even commoners escape the barbaric customs of "wearing hair down and folding robes to the left."[54] Our land presents a contrast. Even if sages should appear to conduct the ritual and music of antiquity, make state offices conform to ancient practices, and revive a system of court cap and garments, even then the barbaric folkways of cropped hair, bared buttocks, and exposed feet would remain. Without long-term inducements to purge these, how could we emulate the people of Middle Kingdom civilization [China]? Officials and people cannot endure their shackles, but they receive no relief. Indeed, the evils of this degenerate age are so rife that, try as I may, I cannot stifle deep sighs of despair.

IV. Main Guidelines

Master Ryū said:

He who would rule all states under heaven must first establish main guidelines; details will work themselves out later. He must promote great benefits and eliminate great evils in the realm. A benevolent ruler, wise ministers, and good men in office make for "great benefits." A violent ruler, foolish ministers, and petty men in office make for "great evils." When great benefits are promoted, great evils disappear; when good men are elevated to office, contemptible men defer to them. The ancients said: "One cannot cheat in weighing things when scales are hung right, in marking lines when ink strings are stretched right, or in drawing figures when compass and slide are crafted right."[55] The sages' Way is like those instruments. It ensures that things are weighed, lines are marked, and figures are drawn without cheating. Then benefits are promoted and evils are eliminated. "Evil-hearted men withdrew when Shun promoted Kao Yao, and when T'ang promoted Yi Yin, from a field of many contenders for office."[56] Such is the Way to govern states by promoting benefits and eliminating evils.

That does not occur in eras of upheaval and decay. No one with virtue has high rank. No one with talent holds office. Some mishandle affairs through excessive attention to details. Some ruin matters through disorderly haste. But no one follows the Way or relies on proper methods, so states escape ruin only by a fluke. Men in office today cannot devise policies or create ideas on their own. They adhere to the customs of bygone eras without a thought to validity, saying, "That's how it's always been." But if this is so, one cannot question a thing's proper nature or function. Of course there are good customs we should follow—those set down by sages, conveyed by worthies, and proved over time to be harmless in government and helpful in conducting affairs. When a custom does not work, we must examine the original intent behind it and the current circumstances surrounding it. We must amend it so as not to contravene antiquity or contradict the present, and only then implement it. Why should we stick blindly to a custom just because it exists?[57]

Wicked sovereigns like Chieh of Hsia and Chou of Shang lived in bygone eras. If those ruling houses had stayed intact and their descendants had remained kings during later generations, should they have clung to the customs set down by Chieh and Chou? If so, that means good government requires lewd music in state ceremonies, nightlong naked orgies amid pools of wine and forests of meat, and law codes calling for fire-pit executions by amused rulers.[58] No ruler, not even a boy, who grieves over his people's welfare would ever approve of such customs; their evil is too great and obvious. But clinging to customs is also absurd when their evil is slight and inconspicuous. Some customs worked before, but not now; some will work now, but not later on. That is why Confucius said: "The Shang built on Hsia rituals, and the Chou built on Shang rituals; but we know what each augmented and deleted."[59]

Yu and T'ang were sages, and the Hsia and Shang were sagely eras in antiquity. But if they had followed the past uncritically, affairs would have gone poorly. So they devised dynastic ritual and music only after augmenting and deleting what was suitable. This point is most pertinent for us, carrying on as we do, the evils of a Warring States era. Our ritual and music were devised over a thousand years ago [in 603]. Today we live in a different world, under a different state; so we have no dynastic rituals to build on or proper methods to follow.[60] Customs today are really leftover folkways from an age of disunity and civil war, the residue of barbarism. Few of these would be harmless in guiding the realm's peoples. Some leaders do see that our customs are unsuitable and must be changed.[61] But they pursue hit-or-miss policies based on short-term gain that work fine at dawn and go awry at dusk, or cure today's ills but not tomorrow's. Policies come and go like waves on a beach, plans change like the weather; but nothing gets resolved when men debate in droves without rhyme or reason. The common rabble upbraids them for prevaricating and procrastinating—fashionable activities in the realm today.

That leads each official to pursue what will help—and to shun what will harm—himself alone. Each seeks only to avoid wrongdoing for which he could be reprimanded. Why should he take risks in devoted state service? Toadies prey on him, eager to ingratiate themselves with money and gifts. Bribery is rife both inside and outside government. A poor man's good works, legion though these be, count for less than a rich man's single bribe. An official seeking promotion does not think about talent: if adept at greasing palms, he succeeds; if inept, he fails. Men feel elated at success and dejected by failure; so they beat frequent paths to the door of some powerful magnate, hoping that these courtesy calls will somehow pay off.[62] An aspirant may exhaust his fortune, lose his salary, and sell off his wife and children. Coming to ruin through such greed is the height of folly. Such fools know nothing of classical learning or accomplishments. How can they devise measures for bringing peace and order to the realm? If placed in office, their sole aim would be self-enrichment. When men of such aims get the power to fulfill these, vile practices will never end. Here is a great and obvious evil if there ever was one, but no one seems to notice it. How stupid can we be?

Tung Chung-shu [179–104 B.C.] wrote: "The key to ruling is like tuning a harp. When it is badly off-pitch, undo the strings and stretch them taut again. Only then can one play."[63] Today the realm's harp is badly off-pitch. So it is time to undo the strings and stretch them taut again. We must not lose this chance! There is nothing wrong as such with elevating lesser officials to ministerial posts, or with making foot soldiers into generals. And there is no better method for achieving that than to foster ritual through justice, control men through ritual, recruit wise and virtuous men to office, punish self-serving sycophants, eliminate graft, and instill a sense of shame in officials. Only then may we speak of peace and order and the Way. Only that would be government befitting the entire realm.

V. The Civil and the Martial

Master Ryū said:

Five hundred years have passed since government moved to the Eastern Plain.[64] The ill-bred assume sway over all, subvassals monopolize power, and everyone esteems the martial *(bu)* while disdaining the civil *(bun)*. To disdain the civil harms government because ritual and music break down, and people cannot endure the ensuing crudities. To esteem the martial harms government because laws and punishments take force, and people cannot endure the ensuing cruelties. Run-of-the-mill officials say, "Civil refinement is too roundabout; rely on martial prowess, which is direct. Ritual is too complex; rely on law, which is simple. Why examine antiquity or study the Way?" Only barbarians would say this—those who cannot see that "the culturally refined are steeped in martial prowess,"[65] and that no one, however strong, can overcome ritual and music because these follow antiquity in their simplicity and the Way in its easy execution. Civil and martial are like the ends of a scale. Rising and falling, they reveal order and chaos; heavy or light, they reveal prosperity and decline. How could either be eliminated? One loosens, the other tightens; one softens, the other hardens. Stillness follows movement; weakness follows strength. Rulers pacify the realm, and its peoples enjoy their pleasures and make the most of their gains. To this day, no one fails to praise the virtues of civil and martial. The *Book of Odes* says: "With many solemn officials, King Wen was secure." This shows why Wen was named "the Cultured." And that classic also reads: "surrounded by many warriors who defend the lords." This shows why King Wu was named "the Martial."[66] The Chou dynasty would not have enjoyed so flowery a civilization given Wu's martial prowess alone, without Wen's cultural refinement. Nor would it have enjoyed such glorious exploits given Wen's cultural refinement alone, without Wu's martial prowess. Clearly, then, neither the civil nor the martial can be done away with.

People today fail to grasp this truth. How could they? They have never seen a sacred text. Only the absurd or the mad would speak without knowing; and we may ignore them. But the realm's peoples grieve over the crudities, and fear the cruelties, inflicted by rulership that they cannot endure. How can I bear to look on and do nothing? The superior man "offers up his life to perfect his virtue."[67] There is no brighter cultural refinement than ritual and music. But owing to the crude and vulgar folkways prevailing in recent eras, people say that ritual and music diverge from human sentiment. They are ignorant of the intricate ceremonies for coming of age, marriage, funerals, and ancestor worship. Some have never seen, much less mastered, the long- and short-stringed harps, or the nineteen- and thirteen-piped flutes. States have no rituals for nourishing the elderly; counties have no laws for regulating feasts to honor the worthy.[68] People do not know the correct number or position of performers in works of court music and dance.[69] How could they know about court caps and garments or about the other adornments of civilized life? When ignorance grows this great, we revert to primeval times.

People cannot do without institutions and rituals. So they replace the sagely-created ones with those arbitrarily devised; and that is how barbarian ritual came to be. Barbarians swagger, strut, and toss elbows at court. Decadent tunes, fierce customs, and fleshly dexterity grace their actions in ancestral ritual halls. Defiled rites and lewd music should have no place before the former sage-kings' ancestral tombs. But such rites and music are now established throughout the realm. One can only expect unlettered commoners to think these beautiful; that is what they have grown up with. But there is no greater shame than for supposedly discriminating state officials to view this depravation with indifference. Such are the great evils caused by disdaining the civil.

I also look askance at men who "esteem the martial."[70] A state has both civil and military officials because neither can perform both functions; in this they are comparable to horses and oxen. By nature, horses can run far and oxen can pull heavy loads. But if we made either do the opposite, neither could bear the task. Men entrusted with civil affairs study classical texts—the *Odes, Documents, Rites,* and *Music.* So they develop warm dispositions that become character traits. The highest are ministers; the lowest, local clerks. But that is the work they can do. If we put them in the ranks and gave them armor and weapons, we could never hope for the exploits of a Meng Pin or Hsia Yu.[71] By contrast, men entrusted with military affairs wield arms—the halberd, shield, hatchet, and battle-ax. So they develop fierce dispositions that become second nature. The highest are generals; the lowest, horsemen or footmen. But that is the work they can do. If we gave them sacrificial implements and dressed them in court garments, we could never expect the capacity for ceremonial of a Tzu-yu or Tzu-hsia.[72] Clearly, then, neither civil nor military officials can perform both tasks.

Today there are too many government posts; idle officials grow in number; and worse, they hold neither civil nor military office in a true sense. They just handle affairs as convenience dictates. What are they to take charge of? They know nothing of ceremonial implements. Yet few know enough of military affairs to devise stratagems, and some never touch weapons. Their hands are silky-smooth, their faces, petal-soft. They cannot travel without palanquins or sit without cushions. If we gave them swift horses and stout bows and sent them to face a foe, their buttocks could not endure the saddle, and their fingers could not draw a bowstring. Some footmen may fight well with long- or short-shafted weapons, but commanders are not trained in the *Liu T'ao* or the *Yu ch'ien p'ien*.[73] So they could not direct troops with regular methods. Men do not advance to the drum or retreat to the gong, and cannot tell the various command flags apart. So defeat would be certain. How can we expect leadership in the ranks? Only a few generals after the imperial dynasty's fall *(shōkoku)*[74] have not been like this.

In antiquity, the Kantō barbarian chief Taira no Masakado [d. 940] and the south-sea pirate-chieftain Fujiwara no Sumitomo [d. 941] insolently claimed the title "emperor" and ran amok through several provinces. But when Fujiwara no Hidesato roused himself to lead armies against them, these evil rebels were vanquished, their forces were put to flight, and their heads were severed.[75] Akuro no Takamaru too proclaimed himself "king" [in 802].[76] He plundered the eastern barbarians and schemed to seize the imperial throne. But when Sakanoue no Tamuramaro [758–811] led forces through the Eastern Sea Circuit, bandit gangs went into hiding and stalwart foes were gripped with fear. Tamuramaro and Hidesato lived in the wilds—on mountain plains and remote isles—where they honed their courage and cunning. They learned to secure fortifications and to enlist and lead troops; so they easily crushed great enemies. Their exploits were matchless throughout the realm. Their fierce valor was, and always will be, legendary. They exemplified military prowess in antiquity—long before the slogan "esteem the martial" came into being. Field commanders in our far-flung militia reported to the War Ministry in the capital and took orders from local civil officials.[77] Their garrisons were crack units—disciplined, brave, and well led. They scored swift victories whenever dispatched to conquer foes.

Thus "the culturally refined are steeped in martial prowess," and no one, however strong, can overcome what ritual and music teach. Those claiming to "esteem the martial" delude themselves; for neither the civil nor the martial may be done away with. Confucius said: "When guided by edicts and regulated by punishments, commoners feel no shame about wrongdoing; they just keep from being caught."[78] That holds not only for commoners. Lords and high and lesser officials too just try to keep from being caught; thus servile fawning is now a national pastime. When people lack all sense of shame, how can they call themselves "superior men" fit to govern? Have today's evils come to this? It all results from esteeming the martial and disdaining the civil.

VI. Heaven-Mandated Peoples

Master Ryū said:

Antiquity had four heaven-mandated peoples: officials, farmers, artisans, and merchants.[79] Officials served states, exhorting the realm to virtue. Farmers planted and harvested, ensuring the realm's food supply. Artisans crafted utensils, supplying the realm's needs. Merchants exchanged goods, dispersing wealth throughout the realm. All four received heaven's mandate from above and exerted themselves for peoples below in a spirit of mutual love, help, sustenance, and respect for achievement. Each was essential; none could be eliminated. The former sage-kings viewed their peoples as parents do their children, and those peoples viewed the sages as children do their parents. Parent teaches child, child sustains parent; and therein lies the Way. High and low were amicable, without the slightest enmity. States were well ordered, and peoples were content. But the sages worried nonetheless. So they set up state offices, decreed the functions of these offices, led peoples with ritual and music, and edified them through edicts. The sages enriched peoples with state grants, honored them with court ranks and titles, adorned them with court cap and garment, and kept them in fearful awe with the weapons of war. The sages judged men's talents and decreed fitting types of work, led men by righteous example, and employed them in the proper seasons.[80] They rewarded or punished in good faith, they promoted or demoted as canons dictated. Only then did the masses respond with affection and the four quarters submit to moral suasion.

State officials head the four peoples. They discharge their heaven-ordained duties by honoring the ruler's decrees to issue edicts for commoners. They help him rule the masses by practicing benevolence and righteousness, personifying loyalty and good faith, and dispensing virtuous teachings. But officials now are dissolute and lack a sense of shame. They are derelict in obeying heaven's mandate above and inept at promoting the common good below—as their dismal reform efforts show. They grub after profit like merchants, obstruct farming, damage industry, and wax pompous in their plush lifestyles—oblivious to the injuries they cause. Day in and day out, they consume food grown by farmers and goods crafted by artisans—with no thought of gratitude. Easy living makes them poor. They spend beyond their means, pile up debts, and bicker over unmet payments. It is only natural that merchants are crafty about profit; they have been so since childhood. Aiming to snare their victim, they first portray themselves as helpless. Then comes a sales pitch to blunt a "Mu-yeh blade" or make the stout Wu Huo waver.[81] And merchants grow even bolder when they are in the right and officials are in the wrong. How can we outwit them? The greatest own myriad treasure-filled storehouses and employ thousands of outcaste menials.[82] Debtor-officials have nothing, merchant-princes have everything: houses, furnishings, fine clothes, and jewels. So feudal lords cringe before them in submissive awe. The court ranks and titles decreed by former sages, and the teachings of righteousness and virtue, are at an end—all because government lacks proper policies.

Farmers plant in the spring and harvest in the fall. They live amid the grasses and sleep drenched in dew. The flesh on their limbs grows cracked and sore as they labor to pay taxes and raise families with what remains. Their lives consist of steady, constant toil. A man may be of the highest nobility or own all the world's wealth, but he cannot live without food. So, in a sense, farmers hold the power of life and death over him. That is why the sage-kings took charge of agriculture in antiquity. They urged men to plow, taught women to weave, enriched farmers by keeping taxes low, and stabilized farm livelihoods by reducing corvée demands. They lovingly cared for farmers so that even solitary souls without kin received blessings.

Such is not true in later ages. Farmers work infertile fields for months on end. After wrenching a crop from the thin soil, they must battle tax officers who demand sixty to seventy percent of the harvest plus corvée and taxes in kind.[83] Some farmers work rich lands that leave a surplus for personal use—until officials demand further exactions. Those surcharges, plus corvée duty, lead farmers to destitution and death. But what do officials care?

Whether soils are rich or poor, whether harvests are good or bad, farmers shiver and starve; and, ultimately, they give up farming. At the end of their rope, some seek ill-gotten gain in superfluous mercantile activities.[84] Others beg for food, die in ditches, or turn to felony. Tillers become scarce and fields turn to wasteland. So even good-grade, five-acre plots outside major towns yield but a twenty-bushel harvest. When droughts or floods come, people just sit by and wait to die. Those good at selling grow rich; those good at farming go hungry. How different from the canons of the former sages! Yet ignorant officials value money and goods alone, forsaking virtue for gain. Above, merchants hold kings and nobles in contempt. Below, they ride roughshod over state officials, treat artisans as outcaste menials, and view farmers as lackeys. So the sagely Way for "nourishing the peoples" is at an end—all because government lacks proper policies.

Artisans fashion utensils to eliminate hardship for the realm's peoples, but they also vie for petty profit with merchants. They use shoddy materials to craft inferior goods—quick to make and quick to break—because they want products to sell briskly, not be durable. They could produce high-quality goods if they wished, but that would make them poor. So they turn out cheap goods and get rich. Worse still are state-run workshops that employ "apprentices" who are really outcaste menials. Unable to use compass and slide themselves, they have others do the actual crafting and finishing. They don beautiful robes, relish fine foods, and strut about like master craftsmen. But in fact, they are just merchants who purvey goods. Here again, name and actuality do not conform. Men are not what they purport to be; and those who really are, gain no reward. Profits go to those who claim to do what they cannot. So the truly capable do not survive. Artisans today are just merchant underlings. Why quibble over degrees of skill? The sages' Way to "eliminate hardship from the peoples' lives" is at an end—all because government lacks proper policies.

The more people toil, the poorer they get. Commoners say: "Tilling a field puts no food on my table, spinning at a loom puts no clothes on my back." Officials too say: "Studying does not get me ahead, working does not help my family." Both ignore their heaven-mandated tasks and eagerly adopt evil ways. Why do so many seek ill-gotten gain in superfluous mercantile activities, while so few work hard at their proper callings? The ancients said, "Whatever the ruler likes, his people are disposed to even more."[85] The former sage-kings knew this. So they esteemed virtue and scorned riches in order to keep the masses from doing evil. Their moral tenets were manifest above. So folkways were purified below. Today we must set up state offices, determine their proper functions, suppress what is superfluous, revive what is primary, eliminate mercantile power, and foster agriculture. Only then will officialdom reform. If everyone is content in his livelihood, each of the four peoples will find its proper place in society, and all under heaven will be at peace.

VII. Mutual Surveillance Groups

Master Ryū said:

Techniques for governing in antiquity always included mutual surveillance groups. But if these are set up improperly, people will not enjoy a stable livelihood in their native abodes and will abscond in great numbers; then states will be beset by outlaws. There can be no greater affliction for government than that.[86] In our own day, following an age of decay and disorder, mutual surveillance techniques are lost and domicile registers are in disarray. People are strangers even in hamlets of ten or so households. Cities teem with vagrants, and each year thousands more flee from the countryside, leaving broken homes behind. Once a man has begun life anew elsewhere, his past will never catch up with him. Many live out their lives in secure anonymity, escaping arrest forever in the city. More than a few are lucky enough to start prosperous enterprises. And once their names go into the new domicile registry, they are indistinguishable from prominent families native to that area.

Many of these migrants fall into poverty. They beg on back roads or die in ditches—while people watch unperturbed. Some shave their heads to become itinerant priests—all for a meal. Petty thieves wound people in robbery attempts and suffer punishment far from home. They find no help in trouble, no sympathy in distress. People do not care if someone is noble or base, kinsman or stranger; they judge by appearances.[87] People ought to be neighbors; but in fact they are worse than enemies. They clamor like swine and bicker like dogs. How lamentable indeed! Even so, out-of-the-way rural communities preserve old, simple ways. People there still view officials and the law with fearful awe, so conditions remain within bounds. Urban masses are different. They hold kings and princes in contempt, and despise state officials as being so many helpless babes waiting to have belongings pilfered or families abducted. Treachery signifies cleverness and armed robbery proves courage to these masses. They form illicit bands, assume high-sounding names, and enjoy immunity from state control or legal punishment. Indeed, governments need them to apprehend other outlaws, "using a thief to catch a thief,"[88] so to speak. Made bolder by such official backing, they oppress the realm's peoples even more. Truly, this is "providing arms for the brigand and provisions for the bandit."[89] What could be more lamentable?

Some men turn into "samurai at large," who change masters often, peddling their martial arts for a living. Many gain fame and do quite well by such earnings. Others become "clerics," who earn their livelihood by setting up pulpits and preaching to lonely, helpless souls. Still others turn into "shamans," who build shrines and altars from which to cast spells or tell fortunes for a hefty fee. Their ilk always exist in times of peace and order. Revered by villagers and other petty men, they do perform useful services of a sort. But no matter what they call themselves—samurai at large, clerics, or shamans—they lie beyond the reach of local officials and their names go unrecorded in domicile registers. So outlaws or vagabonds easily mix in and outnumber them. These elements swagger and boast, indulge in debauchery, harbor renegades, run gambling dens, lead youths astray, work their wiles on naive folk, and so lure law-abiding subjects into evil—all with stark impunity.

Punishments for noncapital offenses under current law may be meted out by tattooing, shaving the head, or lashing with the bamboo, plus banishment and confiscation of property. This has scattered throughout the realm vast numbers of violent criminals who are undeterred by minor punishments and have nowhere to turn. Unable to return to proper callings, they seek help from family and friends. But because they are spurned and ostracized, they cannot keep body and soul together. "[Unlike superior men,] petty men with their backs to the wall lose control,"[90] especially given their violent natures. How can smoldering embers not burst into flame? Such men flock to villages by the legion. Looting and plundering, they obstruct the people's work; cheating and defrauding, they harm the people's livelihood. They eat away at commoners like weevils in grain, and so bring states to ruin.[91] Conditions, then, are *not* normal.[92] We must revive mutual surveillance groups and ascertain proper methods of domicile registration. Superiors must direct inferiors and inferiors must follow superiors without exception. All must be made to obey. Only then will people again enjoy settled livelihoods in their native abodes. Only then will punishments revert to being purely symbolic in nature. These changes, I pray, can be implemented under the Way of government.

VIII. Exhorting Officials

Master Ryū said:

Farmers, artisans, and merchants are the good peoples—"good" in that they "nourish others and eliminate hardship." They assist and foster each other and thus benefit their states. The former sage-kings loved these peoples as parents do children. They set up teachers to edify them and officials to rule over them. Mutual surveillance groups were instituted, and corvées regulated, properly. The sages elevated and grouped these good peoples with state officials. Hence the name "the four peoples" *(shimin)* and its rationale. Performers, entertainers, and their ilk pursue riches and money by dealing in sensual pleasure. They feed only themselves and produce nothing to feed or clothe the realm's peoples. States gain nothing by their presence and would lose nothing in their absence. That is why the former sage-kings excluded them from the four peoples, recorded their names in separate domicile registries, and banned their intermarriage with the good classes. The sages viewed peoples with gradations in love, [not equally]. They segregated the four peoples by occupation and allowed each to make a living through devotion to that calling. Therein lies the Way of benevolence.

Such was not true in later ages. Pure and foul waters mingled in the same stream; sweet and putrid incense shared the same urn. Good and base peoples lived together. High and low status lost meaning. Household registries fell into disarray. Thus sagely government died out. Worst of all, performers and entertainers came to receive official stipends, thereby gaining wealth without achievement and honor without virtue. These toadies would change occupations outright—to become state officials—because they came to win the ruler's favor.[93] Once they got their way, they worked their wiles on him and waxed fat at the expense of commoners. They slandered, truckled, raged, lied, and victimized the good classes. How grievous indeed.

Petty officials consort with entertainers, frequenting playhouses daily. They see alluring sights and hear charming words. They envy these entertainers and come to believe that such talents are unrivaled in the realm. They lose all sense of shame and emulate the ways of actors. They soon become glib and slick and are fully transformed to base ways. Discipline breaks down, and officials popularize vile, lewd customs. The music of entertainers is indecent, if not wild. It stirs up passions deep in the listener's breast. It is more lethal to "the virtues of equilibrium and harmony"[94] than any venom or sharp weapon. Great and lesser officials not only watch these performers and listen to such music, they take lessons in emulation. Worse still, they play this music—not the odes prescribed by Shun and King Wu—in ancestral ritual halls or at court. Nobles dance to that music as performed by state ministers. And everyone thinks this the ultimate in beauty.[95] Their singing has no patterned measure; its rhythm is repulsive and grossly off-pitch. Their hoots and howls make the cawing of crows and grunting of apes seem elegant. Their dances lack regular movements and belong to neither the civil nor the martial genre. Their odes are senseless shriekings devoid of taste—the weird products of a bad dream. What can these possibly signify? Their strings and pipes are supposed to create harmony, but instead produce a dizzying lewdness. Their lyrics cannot be endured. In fact, the grunts of man and woman in bed are less grating to the ear.[96]

But "whatever the ruler likes, his people are disposed to even more."[97] So he debases folkways "faster than by decrees sped through post stations."[98] He feels no shame at what is disgraceful, no contempt for what is detestable. As a result, officialdom degenerates to a nadir. No official can manage his affairs without loyalty, faithfulness, and a sense of shame. One cultivates these virtues through acts of will, and practices them through force of character. When the scalp wastes away, hair cannot grow. When will and character waste away, an official—though skilled, talented, and adorned in court cap and garment—is as bogus as Meng the actor.[99] How can we deem him a superior man or a high-ranking minister? These evils stem from the lack of mutual surveillance groups and from the mingling of good and base peoples. Still, diviners, physicians, craftsmen, and artisans differ from pseudo-officials; at least they benefit their states. People may like or dislike, be good or poor at, certain kinds of work. If one likes something and is good at it, he is called a prodigy. If one likes but is poor at something, he may practice and pretend, but will fool no one. When the former sage-kings prescribed their tenets, they established state posts for teachers and officials. They sought out, employed, and promoted talented men to those posts; and they overlooked no one in the realm.

Such is not true in later ages. Once a man renowned for some skill is lucky enough to gain a post, it is passed on as a hereditary calling even when the house's head is unqualified.[100] Though wishing to quit, he cannot; forced to carry on the calling, he feels shackled by it. Indeed, exceptions to this rule prove it. How can anyone master craft secrets and win a name for himself? That is why governments in later eras have enjoyed the services of few truly able men, and why most artisan-servants of the state are just content to collect their pay. Then, too, men addicted to an art may be worse than those given over to wine and women. They "grow destitute learning how to butcher dragons."[101] Or they undertake other noble quests to master some exquisite yet useless technique—only to hustle and jostle each other in the world. Are there really no men of talent in poor households today? Or do they chafe in silence "like the horses of northern Chi waiting in vain for Po Lo's coming?"[102] Who knows how many live out their days in resentful obscurity?

In antiquity, the King [Chao] of Yen heeded Kuo Wei's counsel that the bones of a swift horse are worth a thousand gold pieces; and, as a result, no worthy man in the realm declined his summons to serve.[103] What efficacy! When the ruler shows such a desire to obtain talented officials, they appear as a shadow follows form, or an echo follows sound. If a ruler today showed the same desire as the King [Chao] of Yen, how could worthy men not rush to serve him eagerly? With no system of civil service examinations,[104] we thwart able men who seek to get ahead and make unqualified men do work they dislike. Yet we complain that there are no good men in government. How foolish! We suppress men who would benefit their states and impede those who would serve the realm. Can this be the Way to exhort officials or give repose to the peoples?"[105]

IX. Giving Repose to the Peoples

Master Ryū said:

Fish in garden ponds yearn for rivers and seas; birds in bamboo cages long for hills and woods. Why? Because that is where they find repose. The same holds for peoples in the realm. The former sage-kings knew this. So they viewed the realm's peoples as parents do their children, and cared for them as they would their own bodies—by ensuring the attainment of repose and enjoyment in life. These peoples in turn viewed the sages as children do their parents. Would any of them not submit to such benevolence? As the *Book of Odes* says: "Beaming with his smile, the ruler is a father and mother to the realm's peoples."[106]

Clerics preach that those who do good in life go to heaven after death and find all sorts of happiness, but those who do evil go to hell and find no end to suffering. All who hear this eagerly pursue good and fearfully shun evil. Why? Because they seek repose. No one has ever seen heaven or hell, and we are not sure of going to either. Yet men are joyful when they hear about heaven, and fearful when they hear about hell. Nor is that all. In extreme cases, they will abandon family and fortune, accept hunger and cold, disdain the torturer's blade, and scorn death itself—or even hope for its quick arrival.[107] Why? Because they despair of finding repose after death unless they act this way while alive. They give up real, compelling needs for an uncertain repose; and their craving is far more intense than a fish yearning for rivers and seas or a bird longing for hills and woods. One who faces certain woe or insufferable shame will say, "It is better to die." Thus the man who jumps off a cliff in a famine seeks to escape certain woe, or the general who kills himself after a defeat seeks to avoid insufferable shame. This surely proves that men yearn for repose and pleasure more than for life itself, and shun danger and pain more than death itself.

The realm's lords rule their states in their own way, and their peoples possess different customs. Ignorant, inept officials pursue short-term gain over long-range planning. They lower no taxes, repeal no laws, and end no punishments. They issue decrees and commands inconsistently, and mete out rewards and punishments unfairly. People cannot enjoy a stable living, but flee hither and yon to avert ruin. Fugitives swarm at large in states all over the realm. Men do not long for a secure livelihood in their native abodes. Instead, they flock about like renegades. Confucius said: "When guided by virtue and regulated by ritual, commoners will have a sense of shame and act properly. When guided by edicts and regulated by punishments, they feel no shame about wrongdoing; they just avoid getting caught."[108] Or: "When the ruler concentrates on virtue, petty men think of their native abodes; when he concentrates on the law, they think of chance fortune."[109] If we truly grieved over the peoples' welfare, how could we not practice these tenets?

The execution of laws and punishments today may diverge from the former sage-kings, but that is not wholly out of line with realities at present. Nonetheless, burning at the stake, crucifixion, and executing a guilty man's kin are barbaric acts—the ultimate in cruelty.[110] One man burns at the stake for arson; another and his kin meet death for killing an animal.[111] What sentence do we reserve for "ransacking imperial tombs"?[112] But either way, they die; and populations fall by the day and month. That might be tolerable if all harm were limited to the state in question. Some states reduce the death sentence to banishment and confiscation of property. That may seem merciful, but it is really a cruel stopgap measure carried over from an era of disunity and civil war, not an institution that befits unified rule.[113] So felons flee from state A to state B; or, expelled from state C, they end up in state D. That does punish them in a way. But without work or money, they must turn to theft or plunder. How can such measures eliminate these evils? Summary execution by strangling or beheading is better than robbing a man of his livelihood by denying him work.

The destitute increase daily, and our benevolence avails them nothing. Bandits, too, increase daily, and our laws avail us nothing. Subversives are sure to surface because men do not seek repose where they ought to or fear what they ought to. Of course, this does not mean that officials and peoples show no love at all for rulers. But unless men find repose in their callings and enjoy security of livelihood, they will harbor evil schemes to garner ill-gotten riches through commerce. Why? Because they hate the lack of security in one calling and move to wherever it can be had— "like fire toward dryness or liquid toward dampness."[114] No one would give up a calling that ensured repose and security for one that did not.

Someone asked:

Then, how can we ensure the peoples' repose and security?

Master Ryū answered:

Rulers today generally squeeze taxes to benefit themselves, and farmers are their worst victims by far. Employ conscientious tax officers who do not plunder the surplus from field and loom. Then the realm will not lack supplies of food; for the peoples would find repose in their proper livelihoods. Employ conscientious tax officers who stop merchants from garnering ill-gotten gains. Then the realm will not lack supplies of goods; for state officials would find repose in their heaven-mandated calling. When officials and peoples find repose, states are strong and rich. Strong, rich states are a blessing to the realm; for only then can ritual and music be promoted, and rewards and punishments be clarified. This is truly the Way to give repose to the peoples. It is for all eternity.

X. Adhering to One's Calling

Master Ryū said:

Under the former sage-kings, peoples remained in their callings, fathers passed these occupations on to sons, and each family enjoyed a stable livelihood devoted to work in its native abode. In high antiquity, all accepted this as the Way and pursued their callings diligently. Food was plentiful, implements were sturdy, and goods circulated freely, so that users incurred no loss and producers suffered no want.

Later ages are not like that. Official stipends amount to less than a farmer's surplus. Farmers fall behind artisans and merchants, who in turn fall behind diviners and physicians, who in turn fall behind clerics. Meanwhile, actors and courtesans form a class of their own; and the adherents of alien cults and barbarian learning create a separate realm for themselves.[115] Do slaving commoners remain true to their calling and diligent in their work? No, they seek personal gain by changing occupations at will. Yesterday they plowed fields, today they peddle goods; at dawn they brewed spirits, by dusk they cast spells or tell fortunes. Warrior-officials in imposing attire envy the garb of actors; monks in the bliss of nirvana convert to the doctrines of Jesus.[116] Commoners are wholly undiscriminating. How can they tell right from wrong? They know only that they are at risk in one calling and secure in another, that they have nothing to lose and everything to gain by changing occupations; for by nature, they yearn for profit and shrink from loss. How can today's run-of-the-mill officials hope to end all of this?

In the capital and other cities, palaces and mansions line each street in splendor. Surrounded by high walls, their towers aspire to touch the sky. State ministers live here, and court nobles serve here. With robes that blur like curtains flowing in the wind, endless processions of mounted retainers and four-horse chariots traverse the avenues. Entertainers line up row on row: actors, buffoons, dancing girls, lads and lasses, trained bears and monkeys, dwarfs and deformities, the blind and deaf.[117] Shamans peddle charms. Clerics chant sutras. Crowds push and shove to get a better look, showering treats and coins at their feet. Here residents offer no tribute and hawkers pay no duties. Marketplaces are bedecked to look like Persia.[118] No one minds the strange robes and alien tongues. Storerooms house lovely treasures of gold and brocade. Stalls that serve tea and intoxicants extend for miles on end—with no green grass or brown earth in sight. "Like ants racing to putrid meat,"[119] the realm's peoples all flee their states and native abodes for the capital. Who can begin to guess their numbers? As more persons crowd into less space, the area outside palace walls barely supports one man per two square yards. All crave personal profit and strive to garner ill-gotten gain in superfluous mercantile activities. Those who toil diligently in primary occupations at the plow or loom are nowhere to be found. Fed and clothed in the capital, the city masses spend lavishly day by day. They eat gold for food and burn money for fuel, yet they still feel deprived.

By contrast, farmers in the countryside exhaust themselves and their resources by shipping tax grains over long distances. They perform corvée duty for years. So their fields turn to wasteland through neglect. Men discard the plow and women abandon the loom—all seeking ill-gotten personal gain in superfluous commercial activities. How can they show concern for their families? The ancients said: "When a farmer quits his field, someone in the realm feels pangs of hunger; when a woman quits her loom, someone in the realm shivers from the cold."[120] Desperadoes now employ the occult to lead stupid commoners down evil paths; and those commoners plunder the homes of local leaders or appeal directly to provincial lords—all because these men have nothing to lose and everything to gain. Run-of-the-mill officials live in the capital from birth. They see its riches firsthand, but know nothing of rural poverty. Of course they will claim: "Times have never been better" or "Our land is supreme in the realm." Little do they fathom the immutable laws that govern heaven and earth: Neither yin nor yang, "security nor stagnation," remains constant; there can be no "increase and benefit" in one place without "decrease and loss" elsewhere.[121]

Should some crisis arise, war flags will flutter before our eyes, battle drums and gongs will boom in our ears, spears will advance from the front, and missiles will fly from the rear. The foe will attack on horseback and foot, unleashing fire and flood. How will we respond? Officials and troops are responsible for repulsing any attack. But our mishmash units fight at their own behest. They will lash their horses to gallop away, or flee on foot with banners in hand. Menials and camp followers are really fugitives and renegades with no sense of honor or obligation. They are hooligans who enlist only to stave off hunger. How can such units be true regiments? Only a fool would rely on them in wartime. We pursue trivial short-term gains, yet ignore grave future problems. We watch destitute commoners suffer, yet directly cause their woe. In antiquity, those who ruled the four quarters dispensed benefits impartially to help afflicted persons in states all over the realm. Only then did commoners enjoy a secure livelihood and devote themselves to their callings in their native abodes. That is why regimes of old were long-lived in upholding peace and order, and why their states grew ever more wealthy and populous. The *Book of Documents* says: "Nonpartisan and impartial, the Kingly Way is broad; fair and impartial, the Kingly Way is level."[122] Thus ruling the people means to be "broad," and ruling a state means to be "level." "Leveling," then, must be the aim of those in government today.[123]

XI. The Need to Circulate Goods and Currency

Master Ryū said:

The Way for ensuring enough food is to promote farming; the policy for distributing wealth is to "level" prices. Assess no high taxes, and farming will advance. End merchant profiteering, and prices will level off. The sage-kings promoted farming in antiquity: "The Hsia had the *kung* tax per fifty *mou*, the Shang had the *chu* per seventy *mou*, and the Chou had the *ch'e* per one hundred *mou*. These systems differed, but none levied more than ten percent of the crop."[124] In later eras [the Wei and Chin], taxes assessed on grain and goods totaled ten or twenty percent. But as wise and noble men then argued, even that rate violated the Way of antiquity. Chou-era officials charged with leveling prices were: the Director of Markets, Mercantile Controller, Market-Shop Supervisor, Overseer of Merchants, and Treasurer for Market-Taxes.[125] Sales taxes on salt, iron, tea, and horses always provoked fierce debate in later dynasties. [In Japan] of late, taxes run from fifty to sixty percent of the crop, plus levies on goods and demands for corvée.[126] Whatever stays with the farmer does not meet his expenses. So he neglects farming and his fields turn to wasteland. Neglect leads to want, want to desperation, and desperation to flight. For a lack of tillers, fields produce no crops and food supplies decrease.

Merchants are different. They hoard when prices are low, sell when these are high, and so make easy money. Merchant princes support thousands: outcaste menials[127] and underlings who wear brocade, eat fine meats, and enjoy time on their hands. What merchants do cannot be called work. Their stockrooms brim with luxury playthings—items of gold and sculptures of jade unrivaled in the realm. Their tables are served by scores of lovely women— with alluring smiles and enticing brows. Their storehouses conceal countless valuables—tons of gold and mountains of brocade. They buy up homes and lots, and some come to own a thousand houses. They rent out shops and dwellings, and some become millionaires. They enjoy life to the hilt. At home, they hoard goods without loss. In society, they throw state revenues into chaos by their timely hoarding and selling. No present measures can combat their wily machinations, so they wax impudent as their wealth rivals that of feudal lords. Rare plants, exotic creatures, and marvelous objects; brocades, tapestries, fabrics, silks, and delicate knits; objects of pearl, jade, gold, and iron; choice grains, fine meats, luscious fruits, and sweet wines; shamans, artisans, physicians, tradesmen, entertainers, buffoons, and courtesans of every rank—all fall into merchant clutches.

Thus goods and currency grow scarce and fail to circulate in the realm. A lovely old brocade may cost one thousand gold pieces per square inch; a fine sword guard may come to ten thousand *koku* of rice. The salary of an official will never permit him to wear such brocade or his descendants to mount such a sword guard. And this holds for more than clothes and luxury items. Firewood and grass, fish and salt, products of the earth, goods forged at the hearth and kiln, the various trades and crafts—all come under merchant control. So prices rise steeply and the realm's money lands in merchant coffers. Dukedoms and marquisates of a hundred *li*, ministries in large, populous states—all lack resources to save the helpless and abandoned in their charge. High officials cannot maintain their clans, lesser officials cannot support their families, and farmers and artisans cannot pay their debts. So they all borrow from merchants. One year's interest may run from two hundred to five hundred percent. So borrowers must pawn their clothes and possessions, or force their wives and children into indentured servitude. What evil to the realm could be greater than this? Run-of-the-mill officials spend days on end debating these problems, but arrive at no solutions. They just squeeze taxes from commoners to line their rulers' pockets, exacting from the good peoples while exempting the base. They take no merchants to task, just engage in busywork not worth the price of a meal ticket.

Well, what should we do? Merchants are base but wealthy in the realm. They relish fine foods and don exquisite clothes prohibited to their status. They hoard or sell at will, thus expanding or constricting the realm's supply of goods and money. Their crimes are great indeed. What should we do? Create agencies and issue edicts to make them eat the same food as farmers and live on a par with artisans. Confiscate their luxury playthings and stately mansions. Punish anyone who refuses to mend his ways and obey. If sellers are many and buyers few, the goods now hoarded in storerooms will go up for sale everywhere. When many goods go up for sale, they sell poorly and prices fall. Then we could tell the genuine from the fake and the good from the shoddy. We could fine profiteers and confiscate from hoarders. Prices could not but level off; goods and money could not but circulate.

What about farmers? Taxes do not have to be ten percent on one hundred *mou* as in Hsia times in order to be deemed light. In later ages, they were forty percent on good, thirty-five percent on fair, and thirty percent on poor fields. With allowance made for good and bad harvests, that was not heavy compared with rates today. In recent decades, poor farmers obtain no fertilizers and their fields have turned to wasteland. Harvests are down twenty or thirty percent; and coupled with stiffer assessments by tax officials, this leaves farmers with little. So they keep under half of what they did under the fallen dynasty *(shōkoku)*.[128] Field fertility is one of nature's givens. Although human effort may enhance it, neglect also detracts from it. And when floods or droughts take their toll as well, it is as the ancients said: "Rich fields are worth less than poor." How much more so if human effort is concentrated on barren fields and taxes rise on fertile fields. Today, good fields have less value than poor; for buyers prefer the poor to the good. Whether a field is good or poor ought to depend on its harvests. But here we have the opposite, though I cannot see why.[129] We must redraw field boundaries and revise classifications as to "good" and "poor." Then we could calculate annual yields over the years and set up a new tax system. If we kept officials from abusing it, farmers would enjoy stable livelihoods in their proper calling and agriculture would advance. That would ensure enough food and boost the circulation of wealth throughout the realm.

But there is much more to promoting great benefits in the realm. Great and lesser officials now gain office and status by politicking and gift-giving. So men of tainted aspiration seize court posts, and greed reigns supreme near the throne.[130] Owing to such gift giving, lesser officials and commoners bankrupt their families, and ministers and great officials exhaust a full year's salary. Money piles up in the homes of powerful officials because many men come calling with gifts, yet few take any away. How can one hope to rise in the world and still support a family on a small fief or salary? Those seeking promotion lose all sense of shame and succumb to greed and envy. This is one evil in the realm; it impairs the state's powers of moral suasion. The high-ranking and powerful are not free from desire, and those who bring them gifts do so for a reason; so accepting these is to be expected.[131] But fine lines blur if the practice becomes frequent. When posts open up, receivers recommend givers without regard to qualifications. Supposedly, this is "screening candidates." Actually, it is the selling of office. This is a second evil in the realm; it impairs administration.

Those who are now in office got there by gift giving. So they will expect no less from others. They favor men who bring much and spurn those who bring little. Palace eunuchs and women exploit such greed to satisfy their ambitions. Loyal officials of good faith withdraw, leaving dissolution behind.[132] This is a third evil in the realm; it impairs folkways and customs. When a man needs something done, he plays on the wants of others and suborns them to do his bidding. So visitors will flock to the gate of a powerful incumbent, but "only sparrows break his solitude" after he leaves office[133]. This is a fourth evil in the realm; it impairs men's sensibilities. Naturally, followers and consorts of a powerful minister will enjoy his favor. But lowly menials and their ilk gain his ear too. They acquire riches, eat fine meats, sport fancy brocades, idle their time away, and indulge in luxuries not allowed to their status. This is a fifth evil in the realm; it impairs state policies and decrees. Goods and currency are scarce and fail to circulate in the realm because of these evils. Why do we not end them?

I earnestly hope the realm's lords will use the rules of propriety to limit and regulate gift giving, remove schemers of tainted ambition, rectify covetous ways, and punish offenders so that the high-ranking will be men of integrity and the lowly will be men of honesty. Only then will lords uphold their states, ministers and high officials retain their offices and salaries, and lesser officials and commoners enjoy security of livelihood in support of their families. These are truly great benefits for the realm, but officials reject them. They disgrace the court and officialdom by grubbing for profit with commoners. They toady to powerful ministers above and heel to merchant control below. They ensure that food grows scarce and that goods and money fail to circulate in the realm. Thus they create the source of their own destitution. Can there be greater fools?

Among those present was one fond of debating politics who said:

I take no issue with your views on the Way to ensure food supplies and distribute wealth. But it seems to me that the price of a thing does not depend solely on its abundance or scarcity. One *koku* of rice sold for two *ryō* in antiquity, yet no one deemed it expensive. Its price is less than half that now, yet twice as many people go hungry. They look malnourished and some starve in their fields. With all due respect, I ask why.

Master Ryū answered:

That is easy. It is like food or currency tipping a scale. When either is abundant, its value falls; when scarce, its value rises. This stands to reason. Yet why does the opposite seem true? Harvests today are less than half of what they were in antiquity, and the starving lie about like disheveled hemp. But currency is less than one-third of what circulated in antiquity. So food is certainly scarce, but it still prevails over money. The scale, then, does operate. Rapacious tax collectors make this situation worse by stripping the fat off farmers in the name of state needs. People esteem currency, despise grains, and amass riches and treasure. Merchant princes hoard rice, the source of their wealth, and watch it rot in storage rather than dispense it to the hungry poor. Ideal measures like the ever-normal granary system might as well not exist because we could never implement them now. So people can only sit back and wait for death to claim them. Can anything be more lamentable? That holds not only for commoners. Officials on state salaries must sell rice cheaply and buy goods dearly. So their daily expenses turn into merchant profits, and their yearly incomes end up in merchant clutches. How can it be the natural order of heaven and earth for the flow of goods and currency to stagnate? That is the fault of men! And unless we do something to change it soon, one *koku* will not fetch a single copper even in famine years. This has nothing to do with high or low prices, or with good or lean harvests; it stems from our lack of policies to ensure that food and currency circulate in the realm.

XII. Benefits and Evils

Master Ryū said:

The key to government is: Strive to promote benefits and eliminate evils in the realm. Benefits are not for oneself alone. All peoples must partake of the ruler's virtue; all must have enough food, gain wealth, and be relieved of anxiety and suffering. By teaching "equilibrium and harmony" we bring repose to the common masses. Then they can cultivate benevolence and filial submission so that "all are morally uplifted to the level of overlords."[134] These indeed are the great benefits I speak of. Whatever precludes them are evils to be eliminated. Rulers who governed states well in antiquity strove to promote benefits and eliminate evils. Only then did their peoples follow them. One promotes benefits through ritual, music, and the cultured adornments of civil rule *(bun)*. One eliminates evils through administrative regulations and the statutory punishments of martial rule *(bu)*. The ruler himself leads by exemplifying *bun;* he admonishes by employing *bu*. Only then will the realm's peoples obey him. He does not lead and admonish for his own sake; his is a heaven-mandated duty.

In antiquity, Yu led forces to conquer the Miao.[135] He proclaimed: "Foolish people of Miao, led by one so stupid and impudent, so haughtily sure of his own sagacity. He violates the Way and impairs virtue, grants official posts to despicable men, and ignores superior men. Abandoned by his people, he will suffer heavenly chastisement. I now accept heaven's decree and assault this evildoer." Or when T'ang struck down Chieh, he avowed: "I lead no revolt. Hsia-dynasty crimes are many, and heaven bids me to terminate it." T'ang assumed the throne after his victory, and when heaven sent a prolonged drought, he showed a desire to sacrifice himself by praying: "If others in the realm have done evil, I alone should be punished; but if I have done evil, let no one else suffer."[136] Neither Yu nor T'ang sought wealth, honor, fortune, or joy for himself. Neither sought personal repose or happiness; both promoted benefits and eliminated evils for the realm.

Sagely and wise sovereigns were like that in antiquity. One may try to emulate them; but if one strays from the Way, benefits will not derive and evils will not end: The Way *must* be followed. Teach equilibrium through ritual, teach harmony through music: "When equilibrium and harmony reach their apogee, heaven is high, earth is low, and the myriad things are nurtured."[137] There is no other Way to promote benefits. But commoners are stupid. If they stray from the Way that must be followed—and so create harmful disorder—they must be punished to eliminate evils. Only thus can one chastise them for vice and encourage them to goodness. When many persons do good and few do evil, benefits derive to the realm. Ritual and music are instruments of cultured adornment in civil rule; laws and punishments are matters of martial rule. Civil rule maintains order under normal circumstances; martial rule brings emergencies under control. Civil rule creates good administration; martial rule suppresses the chaos of war. Civil rule is the norm; martial rule is a last resort.[138] When this norm and last resort are applied, each as required, the realm is led to goodness. A ruler's virtue is judged by how he performs duties in the Way; his worthiness, by whether he knows the Way; his benevolence, by how far he manifests the Way. The Man of Benevolence promotes benefits and eliminates evils in the realm.

As generations passed and states declined, no sagely and wise sovereigns appeared above and no loyal and upright ministers served below. Ritual became defiled, music became lewd, and laws and punishments were meted out far too often. How can a ruler be virtuous, worthy, or benevolent if he strives only to eliminate evils and not promote benefits, only to control emergencies and not dispense good government? Laws and punishments exist to stop people from doing evil. Anyone who harms the realm will be punished—even the ruler of a state. Troops should be raised to chastise him if he does not mend his ways. Manifest cases in point are T'ang's destruction of the Hsia, and Wu's of the Shang. If a deposer ends up as emperor, he is deemed to possess the Way; if he ends up at the level of a state head—or, indeed, anything lower—he is deemed to lack it. If he deposes for a good cause, he becomes a sovereign; if not, he becomes a bandit. If T'ang and Wu had sought only to eliminate evils and not promote benefits, they would have been usurpers out for personal gain. How could they be deemed benevolent? Their deposing of rulers *(hōbatsu)* accorded with the Way in eras when others repudiated it. That is why deposers may be deemed sovereigns, and the deposed, bandits. If performed for the good cause of eliminating evils and promoting benefits, even a minister's deposing of his ruler *(hōbatsu)* qualifies as benevolence because it coincides with popular will. So, for heads of states in the realm, martial prowess is contingent on cultural refinement, and laws and punishments should only supplement ritual and music. To ignore this and employ corporal or capital punishments alone is to legalize disfigurement and murder.

It is sad that those charged with governing in ages of decay and decline employ *neither* the civil nor the martial; so *both* ritual and law die out. They do not strive to promote benefits; worse still, they do not even wish to eliminate evils. They benefit themselves and harm others. Can any tyranny be greater? When states suffer disorder, rulers benefit their own lands and harm other lands, great officials benefit their own clans and harm other clans, lesser officials benefit themselves and harm their colleagues. At their worst, rulers benefit themselves and harm their peoples, and great officials benefit themselves and harm their clans. Such recklessness can only lead to extinction. I see nothing of value in our nation's rule since Juei and Bunji times [1182–1189].[139] The sages created ritual and music to establish the virtues of equilibrium and harmony precisely because they grieved over conditions like this. They wanted to promote benefits and eliminate evils, protect the masses, and "morally elevate commoners to the level of overlords"—so as to bring happiness to all peoples under heaven.

Thus the *Book of Odes* says: "Ah, the former sage-kings will never be forgotten."[140] But alas, today we carry on institutions from an era of warring states; so we cannot return to what was before.

What must be done? A ruler needs but find worthy men for office. That is very easy. What is very hard is for those men to make themselves known to him. In antiquity, King Ling of Ch'u liked slim-hipped consorts, so women starved to death trying to become slender; and the King of Yueh liked brave troops, so men did not flinch from leaping aboard burning ships at the beat of a battle drum.[141] Nothing is more painful than starving to death by trying to become slender, or leaping aboard a burning ship. But if that is what the ruler likes, people will do it without being ordered. The reason is simple: it is very hard for men to make themselves known to a ruler, so they eagerly perform the most painful acts to catch his notice. How much more eager they would be if what he likes is not painful at all. If he but wants something done, endless streams of men will come forth to do it. But if a ruler rejects this dictum and keeps things as they are, it shows he does not want to promote benefits in the realm.

XIII. Wealth and Strength

Master Ryū said:

"Wealth" means to have enough food; "strength" means to have enough troops. To have both greatly benefits the realm, for then the ruler has no worries. The former sage-kings valued rice and millet, not pearls and jade; they loved their peoples, not their queens and consorts. They kept what is worthless from harming what is beneficial. There is no wealth in a thousand acres of stone, no strength in a million scarecrows; for acres of stone yield no grain and scarecrows repulse no foes. An extensive state poor in grain, a huge yet useless population—these are the same as a thousand acres of stone or a million scarecrows.

This holds true for the realm as a whole, for lords in their states, for great officials in their clans, and for lesser officials in their families. The sage-kings did not fret over being cold; they kept their peoples warm. They did not mind going hungry; they kept their peoples fed. That is why "no one faulted their coarse diet and shabby dress."[142] The *Book of Changes* says: "Take away from the ruler above and add to the people below," to gloss its image for "increase and benefit." It says: "Add to the ruler above and take away from the people below," to gloss its image for "decrease and loss."[143] These ultimate principles of heaven and earth find canonical sanction as a matter of course. But a foolish ruler or fourth-rate sovereign tries to weaken his state and impoverish his people. If he has charge of the whole realm, all peoples hate him; if he has charge of one state, its people hate him.[144] With hatred comes revolt, and with revolt comes chaos. Then disaster is bound to occur.

The ancients said: "Without a nine-year stock of food, a state is poor; without a six-year stock, it is destitute; without a three-year stock, it should not call itself a state."[145] That stock of food is not to sustain the ruler alone. It is to succor his people and provide for emergencies. State rulers in later ages lack even one year's food supply, and in extreme cases they tax their peoples years in advance. That not yielding enough, they make up the deficit by taking away from high officials, who in turn make up theirs by taking away from lesser officials, who in turn make up theirs by taking away from family members. To say that such a regime "should not call itself a state" is to labor the obvious. If the ruler stripped state officials of rank and made them pay their debts, they would have to pawn their children for food and burn corpses for fuel. Yet even that would provide but a meal or two. How, then, could they defend their monarch or consolidate their territories? Day by day, the state's officials grow more destitute and its people, more rebellious. Resentment and anger explode. The people cannot help conspiring against the ruler. His state is poor and its army is weak to start with; for men of firm resolve are kept from rousing themselves to action and remain out of sight. That precludes true planning on the realm's behalf.

Yet the stupid ruler views others as poor and himself as rich; others as lowly and himself as exalted. He thinks that his foundations are rock-solid, that his position is as secure as Mount T'ai. He fancies that his methods to maintain peace and order leave nothing to be desired. Nefarious ministers and villainous officials charm him by lining his pockets with revenue squeezed from the people. Toadies ingratiate themselves and make him their stooge. The cleverest liken his government to that of Yao, Shun, and the Three Dynasties; or they compose court music and odes to praise him. But never do they caution him about evil ways. They make him gloat over his wisdom and virtue, while keeping him ignorant of conditions in the realm as well as the changing times. A benighted fool by nature, he becomes even more so—until he fails to see the demise lying just ahead.

When a tall tree falls over, it is because termites have eaten through the trunk; when a huge dike collapses, it is because cracks have penetrated the wall. Although the tree will not fall and the dike will not collapse unless struck by fierce rains or strong winds, only a fool ignores termites in the trunk or cracks in the wall because the weather is fair and the winds are gentle.[146] No one can drive a horse past the point of thirst and hunger; if it sees water or grass, it bolts. No one can tame a tiger to the neglect of feedings; if it sees meat, it rages. This holds true not only for horses and tigers. "Birds peck and beasts claw when cornered"; and "caterpillars constrict in order to lunge forward."[147] Dragons and serpents lie low in order to preserve themselves.

If great heroes should "offer up their lives to perfect virtue"[148] and lead men to righteousness, then loyal, wise, and brave patriots would exhort and direct the realm's peoples. In turn, those peoples would exert themselves, yet follow commands compliantly. The resulting fury would be as irresistible as a starving tiger pouncing on meat or a thirst-crazed horse bolting toward water. The righteous and brave would rouse themselves to action— inspired to avenge the wronged, vindicate the disgraced, and recompense blessings received from above. Deposing a tyrant (hōbatsu) would be as easy as a strong wind toppling a termite-infested tree or a fierce rain dissolving a cracked dike. Only then would the ruler see that his state, presumed to be as "secure as Mount T'ai," is really "a nest built on a tent."[149] Only then would the principles of "increase and decrease, benefit and loss" to the realm become clear; survival or demise depends on them. If the man in charge of a state does not harm the beneficial by pursuing the worthless, his heaven-bestowed duties as a ruler of men will be discharged.

In antiquity, the Duke [I] of Wei liked cranes; so his ministers perched them on their carriages. But when faced with an invasion [in 660 B.C.], his people abandoned him, saying: "Make use of your cranes."[150] Today's ruler may not know it, but he shows fondness and favor in the same way. How? His ministers squeeze taxes from the people and encourage his greed, while selfish officials gloss over his wrongdoing and divert sagely advice from his ears. That enhances neither his wisdom nor his virtue. The ancients knew how hard it was to see themselves, so they used mirrors to view their faces; they knew how hard it was to know the limits of wisdom, so they used the Way to rectify their conduct. A ruler's best course of study is not to master the refinements of the Six Arts, not to recite the doctrines of the Hundred Schools.[151] He should just accept the need to believe in the Way. Then those who have mastered it will come forth to serve him. If he but places his trust in them, how could villainous rebels ever arise in his state? All troubles in the realm would then cease.

Afterword

My family lived for six generations near a bend in the Kamanashi River south of Komagatake.[152] But early in the Kyōhō era [1716–1735], our home suffered so much flooding that rebuilding it became pointless. So we moved and converted our house site into farmland on which to grow beans and wheat. There my father unearthed a stone box containing coins minted in pre-Yuan and pre-Ming times. Underneath these there was an old manuscript entitled *Master Ryū's New Thesis*. It crumbled at the touch and was very hard to read. So father copied the text of its thirteen chapters, which, he said, someone had already punctuated.

Father died more than twenty years later, and the tract was passed on to me. Reading it, I saw much merit in the author's provocative contentions about good and bad political systems. His work seems to date from medieval times; from his attacks on "barbarian learning" and "the doctrines of Jesus," I would guess him to be a contemporary of Oda Nobunaga [1534–1582]. The annals and biographies in our national histories narrating eras before the imperial dynasty's fall *(shōkoku)* list many clans whose surname contains the ideograph "Ryū."[153] Therefore, it is not possible to identify the author for certain. But whoever he was,

I feel sorry for him; for his tract, composed in an age of decay and upheaval, has been lost to the world until now. Nevertheless, this volume, smudged as it is from my father's frequent handling, is a treasured keepsake; and so I dare not show it to strangers. Instead, I have made another copy and placed the two in a small box, hoping that some good friend will assess the treatise's worth one day, and that it will remain a family heirloom forever.

Yamagata Masasada of Kai province
Second lunar month of 1759

Abbreviations

BG	*Bungaku* 文学
DKJ	*Daikanwa jiten* 大漢和辭典
HJAS	*Harvard Journal of Asiatic Studies*
IKNR	*Iwanami kōza Nihon rekishi* 岩波講座日本歴史
KNKS	*Kōza Nihon kinseishi* 講座日本近世史
KNR	*Kōza Nihon rekishi* 講座日本歴史
NKBT	*Nihon koten bungaku taikei* 日本古典文学大系
NKS	*Nihon keizai sōsho* 日本経済叢書
NR	*Nihon rekishi* 日本歴史
NS	*Nihon no shisō* 日本の思想
NSK	*Nihonshi kenkyū* 日本史研究
NSSK	*Nihon shisōshi kenkyū* 日本思想史研究
NST	*Nihon shisō taikei* 日本思想大系
RGK	*Rekishigaku kenkyū* 歴史学研究
RH	*Rekishi hyōron* 歴史評論
RK	*Rekishi kōron* 歴史公論
TNKS	*Taikei Nihonkokka shi* 大系日本国家史
YDSJ	*Yamagata Daini sensei jiseki kō* 山県大弐先生事蹟考
YDSJS	*Yamagata Daini sensei jiseki kō shiryō* 山県大弐先生事蹟考 資料

Notes

Part One
Chapter 1: Yamagata Daini

1. Matsumoto Sannosuke, *Kokugaku seiji shisō no kenkyū*, p. 14.
2. See Matsumoto and early postwar works representative of Marxist historians such as Tōyama Shigeki, *Meiji ishin;* and Inoue Kiyoshi, *Nihon gendaishi I: Meiji ishin.*
3. Nezu Masashi, *Tennō to Shōwa shi (jō)*, pp. 89–90; Ōuchi Tsutomu, *Fuashizumu e no michi*, pp. 369–370.
4. Murao Jirō and Tanaka Takashi are the Hiraizumi protégés specifically mentioned in Irokawa Daikichi, *Meiji no seishin*, pp. 239–240; Murao is mentioned in Nagahara Keiji, *Kōkoku shikan*, p. 15.
5. Tōyama, "Watashi no rekishi kenkyū to tennōsei," p. 118; Nagahara, *Kōkoku shikan*, pp. 16–17.
6. I have used two popular annotated editions: Miura Tōsaku, ed., *Kokutai no hongi: Seikai*, and Kamata Shigeo, *Dare nimo wakaru Kokutai no hongi*, a modern Japanese translation with annotation and commentary. There is a not-so-reliable English translation by John Gauntlett, *Kokutai no Hongi.*
7. Nagahara, *Kōkoku shikan*, pp. 15–20.
8. See Miura, *Kokutai no hongi*, passim.
9. Sakamoto Tarō et al., eds., *Nihon shoki jō*, pp. 146–147; see also the supplementary note on pp. 571–572.
10. Hayashi Fusao and Kobayashi Hideo, "Rekishi ni tsuite," *Bungakkai* (December 1940), reprinted in Koyama Atsuhiko, ed., *Fukuroku ban: Shōwa daizasshi, senchū hen*, p. 114.
11. Kiryū Yūyū, *Chikushōdō no chikyū*, p. 42.
12. Mikami Sanji, *Sonnōron hattatsu shi*, pp. 1–21, 49–54, and 455–464.
13. George Sansom, *A History of Japan: 1615–1867*, p. 178.
14. Delmer Brown, *Nationalism in Japan*, p. 59.
15. Edwin O. Reischauer and John K. Fairbank, *East Asia: The Great Tradition*, p. 664.

16. Peter Nosco, *Remembering Paradise,* pp. 125–126.

17. W. G. Beasley, *The Meiji Restoration,* p. 144.

18. H. D. Harootunian, *Toward Restoration,* pp. 122 and 254.

19. Herschel Webb, *The Japanese Imperial Institution in the Tokugawa Period,* p. 251.

20. Ibid.

21. David Magarey Earl, *Emperor and Nation in Japan,* pp. 64–65.

22. Ibid., p. 65.

23. Ibid., p. 245 (bibliographic entry).

24. Ibid., p. 217.

25. Tetsuo Najita, "Restorationism in the Political Thought of Yamagata Daini," pp. 17–30.

26. Ibid., pp. 17–18.

27. Ibid., pp. 25–26 and 28.

28. Ibid., pp. 21–22.

29. Ibid., p. 23.

30. Ibid., p. 19.

31. Najita, *Japan,* pp. 54–55, 59–68, 127–137; see also Najita, "Ōshio Heihachirō (1793–1837)," pp. 155–179; and Najita, "Nakano Seigō and the Spirit of the Meiji Restoration in Twentieth-Century Japan," pp. 375–421.

32. Kate Wildman Nakai, *Shogunal Politics,* pp. 172–212 and 227–242; Nakai, "Tokugawa Confucian Historiography," pp. 62–91.

33. Joyce Ackroyd, trans., *Lessons from History,* pp. xlvii and xlvi.

34. This work was composed in essay form in the early 1940s but published in book form in 1952 as *Nihon seiji shisōshi kenkyū;* it has been ably translated by Mikiso Hane as *Studies in the Intellectual History of Tokugawa Japan.*

35. Maruyama, *Studies,* pp. 276–280; *Nihon seiji shisōshi kenkyū,* pp. 278–282.

36. Hayashi Motoi, "Hōreki-Tenmei ki no shakai jōsei," pp. 105–154.

37. Ibid., pp. 124–131, 142–144.

38. Thus Hayashi Motoi criticized John W. Hall by name for depicting Tanuma Okitsugu as a "forerunner of modern Japan" when that role had really been played by "the people" who were ancestors of "our country's proletariat." See Hayashi, "Hōreki-Tenmei," pp. 123–124.

39. My synopsis below derives from Ichii Saburō, *Meiji ishin no tetsugaku,* pp. 3–144 and 226–231; "Yamagata Daini no shisō," pp. 1–12; and "Ishin henkaku no shisō," pp. 97–150.

40. Ichii, *Meiji ishin no tetsugaku,* pp. 3–15.

41. Ibid., pp. 12–24; see also Ichii, "Yamagata Daini no shisō," pp. 1–2.

42. Ichii, *Meiji ishin no tetsugaku,* pp. 25–26; and *Rekishi no shinpo towa nanika,* pp. 138–148.

43. Ichii, *Meiji ishin no tetsugaku*, pp. 34–53; Ichii, "Ishin henkaku no shisō," pp. 100–107.

44. Ichii, *Meiji ishin no tetsugaku*, pp. 34–53; and Ichii, "Ishin henkaku no shisō," pp. 107–116.

45. Ichii, *Meiji ishin no tetsugaku*, pp. 45–53 and 120–144; Ichii, "Ishin henkaku no shisō," pp. 108–112.

46. Oda Makoto, *Yonaoshi no rinri to ronri: ge*, pp. 148–149.

47. Kōno Yukitaka, ed., *Yamagata jinja shi*, p. 74.

48. The average daily wage for a manufacturing laborer was 1.76 yen; see Nakamura Takafusa, *Economic Growth in Prewar Japan*, p. 220.

Chapter 2: Life, Letters, and Illusion

1. Hirose Kōichi, ed., *YDSJS*, p. 31.

2. The following biographical sketch derives from Hirose Waiku and Hirose Kōichi, *YDSJ*, pp. 1–58; Iizuka Shigetake, *Yamagata Daini seiden*, pp. 3–286; Tokutomi Iichirō (Sohō), *Kinsei Nihon kokuminshi 22: Hōreki-Meiwa hen*, pp. 423–523.

3. Gamō Kumpei, *Kaien yawa*, in Hirose, *YDSJS*, p. 24.

4. Hirose and Hirose, *YDSJ*, p. 14.

5. Kitajima Masamoto, ed., *Taikei Nihonshi sōsho: Seijishi II*, pp. 242–243.

6. Iizuka, *Yamagata Daini seiden*, pp. 57–58.

7. Hirose and Hirose, *YDSJ*, p. 15.

8. Tokutomi, *Hōreki-Meiwa hen*, pp. 446 and 460.

9. Hirose, *YDSJS*, p. 29.

10. The following account of the incident relies on Hirose, *YDSJS*, Hirose and Hirose, *YDSJ*, and Fukuchi, *Yamagata Daini*, as critically examined with reference to the historical detective work by Yokoyama, "Meiwa jiken kō," pp. 200–241. Fukuchi's *Yamagata Daini* is often called a "novel," but it would come to about a hundred pages in a modern *bunko* edition—more like a short story. Fukuchi is a useful source when used with caution, and the transcript of a lecture on Yamagata appended to the work is particularly interesting. I owe this source to Professor Watanabe Hiroshi of Tokyo University.

11. Gamō Kumpei quoted in Hirose, *YDSJS*, p. 25.

12. Ichii, "Ishin henkaku no shisō," pp. 102–104.

13. Ōishi Shinzaburō, "Nōmin tōsō yori mita Genroku-Kyōhō-Meiwa ki ni tsuite," p. 21.

14. Aoki Kōji, *Hyakushō ikki no sōgō nenpyō*, pp. 128–129. Ichii, however, links Daini with them; see *Meiji ishin no tetsugaku*, pp. 34–36.

15. Hirose, *YDSJS*, pp. 24 and 26.

16. Hoshino Mamoru, *Takenouchi Shikibu gimi jiseki kō*, p. 114.

17. This last point is based on Fukuchi, *Yamagata Daini*, pp. 64–68, and so may be questionable.

18. Miyagi Kimiko, *Ōshio Heihachirō*, p. 258.

19. Yokoyama, "Meiwa jiken kō," pp. 228–230.

20. Kondō Keizō, ed., "Yamagata Daini oshioki ikken," p. 401.

21. Hirose, *YDSJS*, p. 46.

22. Kondō, "Yamagata Daini oshioki ikken," p. 400.

23. Ibid.

24. Ibid., p. 401.

25. Hirose, *YDSJS*, pp. 30–32.

26. Ibid., p. 29.

27. Quoted in Hirose and Hirose, *YDSJ*, p. 35.

28. Hirose, *YDSJS*, p. 29.

29. *Kumoru tomo, nanika uramin, tsuki koyoi, hare o matsu beki, mi ni shiaraneba.* See Hirose, *YDSJS*, p. 27. See also Najita, "Restorationism," p. 27.

30. Quoted in Naramoto Tatsuya, *Nihon no rekishi 17: Chōnin no jitsuryoku*, p. 336.

31. Sugita Gempaku, *Nochimigusa*, pp. 109–110.

32. Letter to Hagiwara Motoe in Ōkubo Tadashi, ed., *Motoori Norinaga zenshū*, vol. 17, pp. 125–126.

33. One manuscript is found in the Tokyo University Library; Professor Watanabe Hiroshi kindly supplied me with a photocopy.

34. This expression follows Tokutomi, *Hōreki-Meiwa hen*, pp. 7 and 517.

35. Kawakami Kizō, ed., *Utsunomiya Mokurin, Yoshida Shōin ōfuku shokan*, p. 179.

36. Ibid., p. 238.

37. Kusaka, "Shisai takuroku," p. 401.

38. Ibid.

39. Ibid., p. 31.

40. Hirose, *YDSJS*, p. 33.

41. This view is shared by Iwahashi Junsei, *Sorai kenkyū*, pp. 498–504, and by Imanaka Kanji, "*Ryūshi shinron* to sono shisōshiteki keiretsu ni tsuite," pp. 50–63.

42. Takano Toshihiko, "Bakuhan taisei ni okeru kashoku to ken'i," pp. 259–260.

43. The following paragraphs, on works by Daini other than *Ryūshi shinron*, follow Iizuka, *Yamagata Daini seiden*, pp. 210–268.

44. For a brief introduction to this theory see Shigeru Nakayama, *A History of Japanese Astronomy*, pp. 100–105.

45. Iizuka, *Yamagata Daini seiden,* p. 250.

46. See Numata Jirō et al., eds., *Yōgaku jō,* p. 144.

47. Tokutomi, *Hōreki-Meiwa hen,* p. 430. For the date of this work's composition, see Kanaya Osamu, ed., *Sonshi,* p. 9.

48. Kawaura Genchi, ed., *Ryūshi shinron,* pp. 116–119 (original *kambun*); Takimoto Seiichi, ed., *Sango,* pp. 350–355.

49. Kawaura, *Ryūshi shinron,* pp. 50–53; Takimoto, *Keizai roku,* pp. 52 and 178–181.

50. See Kawaura, *Ryūshi shinron,* pp. 27–28; Takimoto, *Keizai roku,* pp. 185 and 193.

51. Dazai Shundai, *Sango,* p. 396.

52. Kawaura, *Ryūshi shinron,* p. 81.

53. Hirose, *YDSJS,* p. 27.

54. Tokutomi, *Hōreki-Meiwa hen,* p. 446.

55. Ichii, "Ishin henkaku no shisō," pp. 97–116; Najita, "Restorationism," pp. 17–30; Noguchi Takehiko, "Tō-bu hōbatsu no aporia," pp. 43–62; Yamada Tadao, "Kinsei ni okeru 'hōbatsu' shisō no oboegaki," pp. 36–41; and Kawaura, *Ryūshi shinron,* pp. 74 and 79.

Chapter 3: Textual and Contextual Analysis

1. See Uete Michiari, *Nihon kindai shisō no keisei,* pp. 197–231; Ozawa Eiichi, *Kinsei shigaku shisōshi kenkyū,* pp. 370–400; Matsumoto Sannosuke, *Kinsei Nihon no shisōzō,* pp. 3–48; and Tahara Tsuguo, "Kinsei chūki no seiji shisō to kokka ishiki," pp. 297–329.

2. Kawaura, *Ryūshi shinron,* pp. 73–74. Here I follow Nishida's modern Japanese translation; see Nishida Ta'ichirō, ed., *Ryūshi shinron,* p. 418.

3. Bitō Masahide, "Sonnō jōi shisō," pp. 46–48; Kate Wildman Nakai, "Tokugawa Confucian Historiography," pp. 67–69.

4. As opposed to this "domestic" aspect of sovereignty, the "external" aspect consists of power to defend national territory against alien incursion plus recognition by foreign governments.

5. In deference to the court, however, Japanese in the Tokugawa period continued to speak in terms of traveling "up to" *(nobori)* Kyoto and "down to" *(kudari)* other areas including Edo. Only after the imperial court was transferred to Tokyo in Meiji times could one speak of traveling "down to" Kyoto.

6. Yamaga Sokō, *Takkyo dōmon,* p. 320.

7. Ibid., pp. 320 and 507.

8. Ibid., p. 320.

9. Yamaga Sokō, *Takkyo zuihitsu,* p. 508.

10. Yamaga Sokō, *Takkyo dōmon,* p. 320.

11. Yamaga Sokō, *Takkyo zuihitsu*, p. 508.

12. Ibid., p. 320.

13. "*Jindai, ōdai,* and *buke no yo.*" See Gotō Yōichi et al., eds., *Shūgi washo*, p. 99. In this particular passage, however, Banzan describes the three stages in relation to the development of "civilization" in Japan, signified by the introduction of Chinese-style bans against marriage between first and second cousins or people of the same surname.

14. Banzan apparently is referring to ex-Emperor Goshirakawa's decree of x/1183, which sanctioned Yoritomo's claim to *shōen* proprietorships in central Japan and police powers in the east. See Ishii Susumu, *Nihon no rekishi 7: Kamakura bakufu*, pp. 96–102; Jeffrey Mass, *Warrior Government in Early Medieval Japan*, pp. 74–77.

15. Gotō et al., *Shūgi washo*, pp. 10–11.

16. Ibid., pp. 150–151.

17. Ibid.

18. Ibid., pp. 151–152.

19. On the Ansai school and its place in early Tokugawa thought, see Herman Ooms, *Tokugawa Ideology*, pp. 194–286.

20. Muro Kyūsō, "Yusa Jirōzaemon ni kotauru no sho," pp. 250–251.

21. Muro Kyūsō, *Akō gijin roku*, p. 271.

22. Yusa Bokusai, *Yusa Bokusai shokan*, pp. 378–379.

23. Ibid., p. 380.

24. Muro Kyūsō, "Yusa Jirōzaemon ni kotauru no sho," p. 250.

25. Ibid., p. 145.

26. Ogyū Sorai, *Seidan*, p. 305.

27. Ogyū Sorai, *Sorai shū*, p. 491. See also Yoshikawa Kojirō, *Jinsai, Sorai, Norinaga*, pp. 219–221.

28. Ogyū Sorai, *Seidan*, pp. 349–350.

29. Ogyū Sorai, *Sorai shū*, p. 491; Arai Hakuseki, *Dokushi yoron*, p. 369. Joyce Ackroyd interprets "*kyōshu*" as the emperor "being on a level with" the Ashikaga shogun. For another discussion, see Kate Wildman Nakai, *Shogunal Politics*, pp. 208–211.

30. For Shundai's use of the term, see Dazai Shundai, *Bunkai zakki*, pp. 609 and 655; for Daini's, see Kawaura, *Ryūshi shinron*, pp. 39, 66, and 81.

31. Kawaura, *Ryūshi shinron*, p. 35.

32. Ibid., p. 20.

33. Ibid., p. 19.

34. Ibid., pp. 15–17.

35. Ibid., pp. 15–16 and 39.

36. Ibid., p. 19.

37. Dazai Shundai, *Keizai roku*, p. 4.

38. Kawaura, *Ryūshi shinron*, p. 16.

39. Ibid., pp. 31–32.

40. Ibid., p. 32; emphasis added.

41. Takimoto, *Ryūshi shinron*, p. 64.

42. Ibid., pp. 64–65.

43. See Matsumoto Sannosuke, *Kinsei Nihon no shisōzō*, pp. 35–36.

44. Dazai Shundai, *Bendōsho*, pp. 275–277.

45. Kawaura, *Ryūshi shinron*, p. 24.

46. See Wakabayashi, "Katō Hiroyuki and Confucian Natural Rights," pp. 469–492.

47. Kawaura, *Ryūshi shinron*, p. 24.

48. Ogyū Sorai, "Utsunomiya Sankin ni atauru sho," p. 284.

49. Dazai Shundai, *Bendōsho*, pp. 275–276.

50. Ibid., p. 276. This culmination would be either Kōbun (r. 671–672) or Temmu (r. 673–686), depending on whether Shundai included Jingu in the list.

51. Kawaura, *Ryūshi shinron*, p. 15.

52. I do not use the English term "empress" here in order to avoid confusion with *kōgō*, the wife of a reigning emperor.

53. Kawaura, *Ryūshi shinron*, p. 29.

54. Later, in the nineteenth century, the term "long-locks" was applied to the Taiping rebels, who let their forelocks grow in defiance of Manchu law.

55. Mitamura Taisuke, "Manshū kara kita ōchō," pp. 205–206.

56. Ibid.

57. Kawaura, *Ryūshi shinron*, p. 28.

58. Ibid., p. 29.

59. East Asians, as opposed to the Western historians who study them, emphasized the forehead shaving, not the pigtail, as signifying Chinese subservience to the Ch'ing.

60. Kawaura, *Ryūshi shinron*, p. 18.

61. Ogyū Sorai, "Yakusha kiyaku," p. 240.

62. Dazai Shundai, *Keizai roku*, pp. 4–5.

63. Iwahashi Junsei and Yoshikawa Kōjirō argue that such criticism of Sorai as a "China-worshiper" was inaccurate and unfair. Nevertheless, that is how contemporaries perceived him. See Iwahashi, *Sorai kenkyū*, pp. 242–249; and Yoshikawa, *Jinsai, Sorai, Norinaga*, pp. 201–242.

64. Takimoto, *Ryūshi shinron*, p. 68.

65. Ibid., p. 66.

66. Kawaura, *Ryūshi shinron*, p. 27.

67. Ibid.

68. Ibid., p. 16.

69. Ibid., pp. 36 and 79.

70. Ibid., pp. 17 and 72–73.

71. Ogyū Sorai, *Sorai sensei tōmonsho*, p. 200.
72. Kawaura, *Ryūshi shinron*, p. 48.
73. Ibid., pp. 45–46.
74. See Hirose and Hirose, *YDSJ*, p. 24.
75. Iizuka, *Yamagata Daini seiden*, p. 188.
76. Nishikawa, *Chōnin bukuro*, pp. 132–133.
77. Kinugasa Yasuki, *Kinsei jugaku shisōshi no kenkyū*, pp. 111–131.
78. The term "naturalize," though used in a different context, is taken from Kate Wildman Nakai, "The Naturalization of Confucianism in Tokugawa Japan," pp. 157–199.
79. Ogyū Sorai, *Seidan*, pp. 283–284.
80. Kawaura, *Ryūshi shinron*, p. 50.
81. This is the position taken by Iizuka, *Yamagata Daini seiden*, pp. 350–351.
82. Kawaura, *Ryūshi shinron*, p. 18.
83. See Mase Kumiko, "Kinsei no minshū to tennō," pp. 229–266; Takano Toshihiko, "Bakuhan taisei ni okeru kashoku to ken'i," pp. 234–276; and Miyaji Masato, *Tennōsei no seijishiteki kenkyū*, pp. 17–66. For a critique of these studies, see Yamaguchi Kazuo, "Shokunin zuryō no kinsei-teki tenkai," pp. 57–74.
84. These paragraphs are based on Wakabayashi, "In Name Only," pp. 38–45.
85. For a detailed explanation of how *jōruri* players obtained imperial court ranks and office titles, see Yasuda Tokiko, "Kinsei zuryō kō," pp. 561–650.
86. Mase, "Kinsei no minshū to tennō," pp. 245–248.
87. One is translated into English; see Susan Matisoff, trans., *The Legend of Semimaru*. For studies of the genre, see Moriyama Shigeo, *Chikamatsu no tennō geki*, and Kidani Hōgin, *Chikamatsu no tennō geki*.
88. Chikamatsu Monzaemon, *Yōmei tennō shokunin kagami*, pp. 58–120.
89. Quoted in Mase, "Kinsei no minshū to tennō," p. 230.
90. In this passage, the Nishida text includes "stupid" *(tsuiro)*; Nishida, *Ryūshi shinron*, p. 348. In Kawaura's text, the commoners are just "unlettered"; Kawaura, *Ryūshi shinron*, pp. 19 and 101. Kawaura renders *tsui* "by extension" *(sui)*; but this does not fit the context and probably stems from a corrupted text because the ideographs *tsui* and *sui* are almost identical and the *ro* was dropped.
91. Kawaura, *Ryūshi shinron*, p. 46.
92. Ibid., p. 28.
93. Ibid., p. 72.
94. Ibid., p. 60.

95. Kinugasa, *Kinsei jugaku shisōshi no kenkyū,* pp. 119–131; Buyō Inshi, *Seji kembun roku,* p. 745.

96. Kawaura, *Ryūshi shinron,* p. 30.

97. Ibid., p. 72.

98. Ibid., p. 61.

99. Ibid., pp. 61 and 77.

100. Ibid., p. 77.

101. Dazai Shundai, *Keizai roku,* pp. 52–53.

102. Kawaura, *Ryūshi shinron,* p. 62.

103. Ibid., p. 45.

104. Ibid., p. 60.

105. Ibid., pp. 62–70.

106. Ibid., pp. 77–78.

107. Ibid., p. 78.

108. Ibid., p. 80.

109. Ibid., p. 53.

110. Ibid., p. 28.

111. Ibid., pp. 75–76.

112. Kondō Mitsuo, ed., *Sengokusaku ge,* pp. 304–317. For a contemporary Japanese reference (1763) to the "thousand-mile steed," see Hiraga Gennai, *Fūryū shidōken den,* p. 214.

113. Kawaura, *Ryūshi shinron,* p. 53.

114. See Ichii, "Yamagata Daini no shisō," pp. 7–8.

115. Kawaura, *Ryūshi shinron,* p. 34.

116. Ibid., pp. 71 and 75. Daini's phrase is *"hioku hōzubeshi."*

117. Honda Wataru, ed., *Chūgoku koten bungaku taikei 13: Kanjo, Gokanjo, Sangokushi retsuden sen,* pp. 101–115, especially p. 105. For the original see Nagasawa Kikuya, ed., *Wakokubon seishi Kanjo,* vol. 2, pp. 719–729, especially p. 721.

118. See Robert Borgen, *Sugawara no Michizane and the Early Heian Court,* pp. 173–178, and Kitayama Shigeo, *Nihon no rekishi 4: Heian-kyō,* pp. 272–276.

119. Rai Sanyō, *Nihon seiki,* pp. 100 and 155–157; Date Chihiro, *Taisei santenkō,* pp. 428–432.

120. Kawaura, *Ryūshi shinron,* p. 36.

121. Ibid., p. 37.

122. Ibid., p. 21.

123. Ibid., p. 22.

124. See Nagasawa Kikuya, ed., *Nan pei ch'ao k'an pen Erh ya,* pp. 87–88; also *DKJ,* vol. 6, pp. 805 and 802. *"Chu"* in the compound *"chu-hsu"* on p. 802 of vol. 6 is a homonym for character number 37481 in vol. 10, p. 910, and is also found under character number 39288 in vol. 11, p. 214.

125. Ogyū Sorai, *Seidan*, p. 348.
126. Arai Hakuseki, *Dokushi yoron*, p. 369.
127. Ogyū Sorai, *Seidan*, p. 348.
128. Takimoto, *Ryūshi shinron*, p. 68.
129. Ibid.
130. Kawaura, *Ryūshi shinron*, pp. 21–22.
131. Ibid., p. 22.
132. This problem remains unsolved today, when the emperor is not a "monarch," "sovereign," or "head of state" in name but increasingly assumes these functions in fact. See, for example, Yokota Kōichi, *Kempō to tennōsei*, pp. 1–33 and 77–107.
133. Kawaura, *Ryūshi shinron*, pp. 37–38.
134. Ibid., pp. 35–36.
135. Ibid., p. 73.
136. "*Gunkoku no sei*" is used in Kawaura, *Ryūshi shinron*, p. 75; "*sengoku no sei*" is used passim.
137. Yokoyama, "Meiwa jiken kō," pp. 226–227.
138. Quoted in Iizuka, *Yamagata Daini seiden*, pp. 88–89.
139. Ibid., pp. 119–120.
140. Ueda Masaaki, *Jimbutsu sōsho 49: Yamatotakeru no mikoto*, pp. 72–87 and 120–173. See also Sakamoto Tarō et al., eds., *Nihon shoki jō*, pp. 600–601, supplementary note.
141. Sakamoto, et al., *Nihon shoki jō*, pp. 302–303.
142. Kawaura, *Ryūshi shinron*, p. 39.
143. Hirose, *YDSJS*, p. 34.
144. Kawaura, *Ryūshi shinron*, p. 75.
145. Ibid., pp. 78–79.
146. In Han Fei-tzu's day, a *chang* was 2.25 meters and a *ch'ih* was 22.5 centimeters. For this passage see Takeuchi Teruo, ed., *Shinshaku Kambun taikei 11: Kampishi jō*, pp. 277–278.
147. Kawaura, *Ryūshi shinron*, p. 80.
148. See Kamata Tadashi et al., eds., *Shunjū sashiden*, vol. 1, pp. 246–247.

Chapter 4: A New Appraisal

1. Uete, *Nihon kindai shisō no keisei*, pp. 197–231.
2. Bito Masahide, "Sonnō jōi shisō," p. 62.
3. Two studies of this "*tennō* drama" genre, by Kidani Hōgin and Moriyama Shigeo, exist for Chikamatsu Monzaemon; both are titled *Chikamatsu no tennō geki*. For Chikamatsu Hanji, see Uchiyama Mikiko, "Meiwa hachi-nen no Chikamatsu Hanji," pp. 67–81.

4. Many modern historians have uncritically relied on such sources. See Yokoyama, "Meiwa jiken kō," pp. 200–212.

5. For a different interpretation of "restoration" in the late Tokugawa period, see Harry Harootunian, *Toward Restoration,* passim.

6. On the idea of nostalgic nativism see Nosco, *Remembering Paradise,* passim.

7. *Futen sotsudo ōmin ōdo ni arazaru nashi* and *ikkun banmin.* See his debate with Yamagata Taika in 1856–1857; Yamaguchi-ken kyōikukai, ed., *Yoshida Shōin zenshū,* vol. 3, pp. 547–552.

8. See Wakabayashi, *Anti-Foreignism and Western Learning in Early-Modern Japan,* passim.

9. Ōshio Heihachirō, *Gekibun,* p. 101.

10. The following paragraphs on early Tokugawa Confucianism and Sorai closely follow Watanabe Hiroshi, *Kinsei Nihon shakai to Sōgaku,* pp. 161–164 and 179–213; see also Wakabayashi, "Tokugawa Sociopolitical Thought," pp. 169–170. But Watanabe's understanding of Daini's thought differs from mine. He sees Daini as carrying on Sorai's emphasis on creating rites and music, but by the imperial court rather than the bakufu, and as advocating "the logic of rebellion" along with Ōshio Heihachirō. See Watanabe, *Kinsei Nihon shakai to Sōgaku,* p. 185, and Watanabe, *Seiji shisō II: Kinsei Nihon seiji shisō,* pp. 72–76.

11. Matsudaira Nobutsuna and Ikeda Mitsumasa are so quoted in Watanabe, *Kinsei Nihon shakai to Sōgaku,* pp. 15 and 197.

12. Ibid., pp. 102 and 207.

13. Ibid., p. 186.

14. Sakamoto Tarō et al., eds., *Nihon shoki jō,* pp. 146–147; see also the supplementary note on pp. 571–572.

15. Ibid., p. 146.

16. Ibid., pp. 117–118 and 152.

17. The following paragraphs are based on Ueyama Shumpei, *Kamigami no taikei,* pp. 72–107 and 148–194.

18. I use "principal wife," rather than "empress" to translate *"kogo"* in order to avoid confusion with *"jotei,"* rendered "female sovereign."

19. A *sesshō* served a child emperor; a *kampaku* served an adult emperor. But I do not distinguish the two in my discussion because the distinction was immaterial from the Fujiwara standpoint.

20. Under the influence of Mitogaku, the fifteenth *tennō*—the female sovereign Jingū—was dropped from the official list in the Edo period. This was not because she was mythical, but because she had never undergone proper accession ceremonies.

21. Saigyō (1118–1190) had ninety-four verses in the *Shinkokinshū,* but these were selected posthumously.

22. Perhaps the most lucid analysis is by Nagahara Keiji and Ōsumi Kazuo, "Chūsei no rekishi kankaku to seiji shisō," pp. 18–34, and I follow it closely here. Also consulted were Delmer Brown and Ishida Ichirō, *The Future and the Past*, pp. 1–14 and 403–450; Taga Munehaya, *Jien*, pp. 135–176; and Akamatsu Toshihide, "Kaisetsu," pp. 3–31.

23. Okami Masao and Akamatsu Toshihide, eds., *Gukanshō*, p. 165; Brown and Ishida, *Future and the Past*, p. 51.

24. *Gyosui gattei* or *kunshin gattei gyosui no gi*. See Okami and Akamatsu, *Gukanshō*, pp. 33, 147, and 329; Brown and Ishida, *Future and the Past*, pp. 35, 210–211, and 215.

25. Jien's terms were *bumbu kenkō no shissei* and *bumbu kenkō no setsuroku*. See Okami and Akamatsu, *Gukanshō*, pp. 336–337, 344, and 346–349; Brown and Ishida, *Future and the Past*, pp. 218, 225, and 228–230.

26. See Akamatsu, "Kaisetsu," p. 3.

27. Okami and Akamatsu, *Gukanshō*, pp. 245, 347, and headnote 59 on p. 347; Brown and Ishida, *Future and the Past*, pp. 226 and 228.

28. Okami and Akamatsu, *Gukanshō*, p. 349; Brown and Ishida, *Future and the Past*, p. 230.

29. Okami and Akamatsu, *Gukanshō*, pp. 344–345; Brown and Ishida, *Future and the Past*, pp. 225–226.

30. I rely here on analyses by Nagahara and Ōsumi, "Chūsei no rekishi kankaku to seiji shisō," pp. 37–63; Varley, *Chronicle of Gods and Sovereigns*, pp. 1–45; and Satō, *Nambokuchō no dōran*, pp. 10–17, 70–88, 226–234, and 290–294.

31. Iwasa Tadashi et al., eds., *Jinnō shōtōki, Masukagami*, pp. 88–89; Varley, *Chronicle of Gods and Sovereigns*, pp. 117–118.

32. Satō, *Nambokuchō no dōran*, pp. 70–82.

33. Iwasa et al., *Jinnō shōtōki, Masukagami*, p. 116 and headnote 13; Varley, *Chronicle of Gods and Sovereigns*, p. 160.

34. Iwasa et al., *Jinnō shōtōki, Masukagami*, p. 255; Varley, *Chronicle of Gods and Sovereigns*, p. 180.

35. Iwasa et al., *Jinnō shōtōki, Masukagami*, p. 134; Varley, *Chronicle of Gods and Sovereigns*, p. 188.

36. Jien has already been cited in these contexts. For Chikafusa see Iwasa et al., *Jinnō shōtōki, Masukagami*, pp. 119–123; Varley, *Chronicle of Gods and Sovereigns*, pp. 166–172.

37. Okami and Akamatsu, *Gukanshō*, pp. 159 and 329; Brown and Ishida, *Future and the Past*, pp. 47 and 211.

38. Okami and Akamatsu, *Gukanshō*, pp. 347–348; Brown and Ishida, *Future and the Past*, p. 229.

39. Gomizuno-o, "Shinkan gokyōkun sho," pp. 198–199.

40. See Wakabayashi, "In Name Only," pp. 28–29.

41. Fujita Yūkoku, "Seimeiron," in Kikuchi Kenjirō, ed., *Yūkoku zenshū,* p. 229.

42. But in actuality this article was abused along with state Shinto and peace preservation laws to make the emperor a manifest deity beyond criticism.

43. Historians with political views as radically different as Ienaga Saburō and Itō Takashi agree that Article 3 made it impossible to charge Emperor Shōwa with war crimes under Japanese law. International law, however, would be a different matter. See Ienaga, *Sensō sekinin,* pp. 257–258; Itō and Ōe, in "Rekishiteki 'sekinin' no shozai," pp. 44–45.

44. *"Hohitsu"* is usually mistranslated "giving advice." See, for example, George M. Beckmann, *The Making of the Meiji Constitution,* p. 154. Contrast *"hohitsu"* with Article 6 of the present constitution: "The emperor, with the advice *(jogen)* and approval of the cabinet. . . ."

45. See, for example, Konoe, *Ushinawareshi seiji,* pp. 131–132. He arrived at the figure twenty-six hundred by going back to Jimmu's accession in 660 B.C.

46. Hosokawa Morisada, *Hosokawa nikki ge,* p. 61.

47. Takahashi Hiroshi and Suzuki Kunihiko, *Tennōke no mitsushi tachi,* pp. 11–14; emphasis added.

Chapter 5: About the Original Texts

1. See Hirose, *YDSJS,* pp. 58–59.
2. Iizuka, *Yamagata Daini seiden,* p. 296.
3. In Tsuda Hideo, ed., *Kinsei kokka no tenkai,* pp. 200–241.
4. Nishida, *Ryūshi shinron,* p. 342.

Part Two
Master Ryū's New Thesis

1. This set of paired opposites, "name and actuality" (mei/kei), is crucial to Daini's thesis. Here kei (Ch. hsing) does not mean "form." In classical usage, as in the Chuang Tzu and Han Fei Tzu, the homophones kei, "form" and "punishment," both mean "the true situation" or "reality." See Fukunaga Mitsuji, ed., *Sōshi gaihen chū,* pp. 24 and 31–32; Takeuchi, ed., *Kampishi,* pp. 49, 52, 71, 78, 80, 83, and 656. Creel holds that kei means the function or performance of an office or official, H. G. Creel, *What Is Taoism?,* pp. 79–91 and 104–109. Fukunaga and Watson concur; Fukunaga, *Sōshi gaihen chū,* pp. 13, 27, and 33; Burton Watson, trans., *The Complete Works of Chuang Tzu,* p. 145n. In some cases, as in the ensuing passage, Daini seems to follow this meaning.

2. Fukunaga Mitsuji, ed., *Rōshi jō*, p. 31; D. C. Lau, trans., *Tao Te Ching*, p. 57.

3. Fukunaga, ed., *Sōshi naihen*, pp. 44–46.

4. Jimmu, mythical founder of Japan's imperial dynasty, supposedly ruled from 660 to 585 B.C.; and the ideal of virtuous government, *"Riyō kōsei,"* was expounded by the sage-king Yu, founder of the Hsia dynasty, as described in the (spurious) "Counsels of Great Yu" chapter of the *Book of Documents*. See Ikeda Suetoshi, ed., *Shōsho*, pp. 545–546.

5. Shōtoku Taishi (574–662) established this twelve-rank system of court caps and garments patterned after Chinese models.

6. The Dukes of Chou and Shao were ministers under Chou-dynasty King Ch'eng (r. 1115–1079 B.C.), who was a grandson of King Wen. Shao administered the western part of the empire, and Chou, the eastern. Yi Yin and Fu Yueh were regents during the Shang dynasty. Yi Yin served under Kings T'ang (r. 1766–1753 B.C.) and T'ai Chia (r. 1753–1720 B.C.). Fu Yueh served under King Wu Ting, or Kao Tsung (r. 1720–1691 B.C.). The *Book of Documents* stresses that meritorious service by these four ministerial exemplars accounted for the ideal government of those times.

7. Shōtoku Taishi earned the name "Toyo*satomimi* no mikoto" because, according to legend, he could understand ten people speaking to him at the same time.

8. The Hsia, Shang (or Yin), and Chou dynasties of ancient China are traditionally dated 2205 to 771 B.C. For Confucians, this represented a golden age.

9. Daini sees the Juei-Bunji eras (1182–1189) as beginning the decline and fall of imperial rule. Thus he ignores Yoritomo's receipt of the title "Barbarian-Quelling Great General" *(seii taishōgun)* in 1192, the Kenkyū era.

10. After the 1221 Jōkyū War, Hōjō Yoshitoki forced Emperors Juntoku and Chūkyō to abdicate; later he banished the ex-Emperors Tsuchimikado, Gotoba, and Juntoku.

11. Ashikaga Yoshimitsu (1358–1408) became shogun in 1368 at the age of eleven. In 1381 he became Minister of Central Affairs and Minister of the Left; his "Palace of Flowers" was about twice the size of the imperial palace. In 1394 he became Grand State Minister *(dajōdaijin)*, then unprecedented for a warrior, when he bequeathed the shogunal post to his son. In 1401 he proclaimed himself "King of Japan" and "vassal" to the Ming emperor to obtain lucrative trading rights with China.

12. *"Ito no gotoku,"* a phrase taken from the *Sorai shū*, p. 491.

13. See Takimoto, *Ryūshi shinron*, p. 64. All notes by Matsumiya Kanzan are taken from this Takimoto edition.

14. Daini wants us to believe that his tract dates from the age of Oda Nobunaga, when Japan was emerging from the Warring States period

toward unification; see his afterword. Modern historians date that period as being from 1467 to 1568, but evidence in his text shows that Daini interpreted it to have begun either in 1185, when Minamoto hegemony was established, or in the 1330s. "Imperial rule lasted over two thousand years," he says later, after which the imperial house split into Northern and Southern branches when Ashikaga rule began.

15. Takimoto, *Ryūshi shinron*, p. 65.

16. Throughout his tract Daini depicts the *bakuhan* system as roughly analogous to the Chou-era *feng-chien* system. Thus his "realm," or "all under heaven" *(tenka)*, comprises numerous *kokka*, "states" or daimyo domains. Hence I render "rulers" and "states" in the plural except where Daini writes of rulership in the abstract or clearly refers to the shogun or emperor.

17. All daimyo and high-ranking bakufu bannermen who held the fifth court rank, over three hundred in number, theoretically qualified for the post of provincial governor. See Kodama Kōta, *Nihon no rekishi 18: Daimyō*, p. 197. The eight central-government ministries set up by the ancient imperial law codes were Central Affairs, State Ceremonial, Popular Affairs, Civil Administration, War, Justice, Treasury, and Imperial Household.

18. The bakufu petitioned the imperial court to issue the title "Provincial Governor of XX." One example was Daini's famous contemporary, the bakufu bannerman Ōoka Tadasuke (1677–1751). In 1712 he received junior fourth rank, lower grade, plus the title "Provincial Governor of Notō"— though he never set foot there. In 1717 he received the more prestigious title "Provincial Governor of Echizen" and is best known by that name, Echizen no kami. See Tsuji Tatsuya, *Ōoka Echizen no kami*, pp. 93–95.

19. Takimoto, *Ryūshi shinron*, p. 65.

20. Strict adherence to the rank-office concordances stipulated by the old imperial law codes would mean that the Tokugawa shogun as a "general" could hold junior third rank at most. That would place him below a grand counselor *(dainagon)*, who held senior third rank. But the Tokugawa branch houses of Kii and Owari held the grand counselor title; so they ought to have outranked the shogun, their patriarch and overlord. Moreover, Tokugawa Ieyasu received junior first rank in 1602, even before being granted the shogunal title.

21. A rough analogy might be English surnames derived from office titles such as "chamberlain" or "chancellor." An example of a Japanese office title adopted as a personal name would be Takenouchi *Shikibu*, who used the title "Ministry of Ceremonials." Another would be Asano *Takumi no kami* Naganori of *Chūshingura* fame, who adopted the title "Chief of the Bureau of Artisans." Informally they were called "Shikibu-dono" and "Takumi-

dono." As we shall see, Daini also objected to this use of *"dono"* because this Chinese character ought to mean "palace" or "hall."

22. Examples would be "Toku*bei*," "Ichiza*emon*," "Sanno*suke*," "Kiku-no*jō*," and so forth. "Bei" represents a euphonic change from "Hyōe."

23. The Ritsu imperial penal codes were first compiled under Temmu (r. 673–686) and, later, in 701 and 718. For the specific articles Daini wants enforced, see Inoue Mitsusada et al., eds., *Ritsu-Ryō*, pp. 20–23.

24. The sinophile and linguistic purist Daini here criticizes his country-men for deviating from the original meanings of Chinese ideographs. For example, "palace" or "hall" *(tono, dono)* came to mean "my lord" or "Lord X," and the other ideographs mentioned here were used as honorifics or humble forms in everyday Japanese speech. Nishida's modern Japanese translation should not be followed here.

25. Takimoto, *Ryūshi shinron*, p. 66.

26. Yoshikawa, *Rongo ge*, pp. 107–110.

27. The failure of Godaigo's imperial restoration led to warrior Ashikaga rule in the late 1330s. Since imperial rule began in 660 B.C. for Daini, another "two thousand years" would have ended in 1340.

28. According to a parable in a Han-dynasty work, the *Shuo yuan*, a white dragon possessed of spirit once turned itself into a fish, entered a clear cold pond, and was speared by a fisherman unaware of its true iden-tity. Wu Tzu-hsu, advisor to the King of Wu, used this fable to dissuade him from traveling about disguised as a commoner. For the original phrase see Morohashi, *DKJ*, vol. 8, p. 38. The white dragon became a stock meta-phor for a king or nobleman who should stay in his palace rather than invite harm by roaming about incognito. Takizawa Bakin employed the metaphor in this fashion; see Koike Tōgoro, ed., *Nansō Satomi hakken den*, vol. 5, p. 27. Both Nishida and Kawaura interpolate Godaigo as the "white dragon" without explanation. I agree, based on the context (see note 29 below), but this is problematic on strictly textual grounds. One could also argue that Gomurakami, not Godaigo, is the white dragon. The *Taiheiki* passage alluded to by Daini deals with Gomurakami's flight in 1352 from Otokoyama-Yawata to Yoshino-Anō: "The emperor is surrounded by large enemy [bakufu] forces, and reinforcements are exhausted. If the divine dragon should disguise himself [among commoners] and be snared, we would have no one under heaven to serve in battle." See Gotō, Okami, and Kamata, eds., *NKBT 36: Taiheiki 3*, p. 200, and also their supplementary note on p. 499, where they cite the same *Shuo yuan* parable of the white dragon.

29. Daini wrote to Matsumiya: "In that era, only Lord Kusunoki will-ingly 'sacrificed himself to perfect benevolence' (like a *shishi*)"; Kawaura, *Ryūshi shinron*, pp. 88–89. Hence the "white dragon" is probably Godaigo.

However, "he only ruled a small provincial state" implies that the realm as a whole no longer submitted to Godaigo's imperial dynasty; thus by Confucian standards it was defunct and could not claim legitimacy.

30. An instructive slipup. Godaigo died in 1339. Adding "over four hundred years" would place the author in the mid-eighteenth century; so he could not have been "a contemporary of Oda Nobunaga" (1534–1582) as Daini claims in his afterword. Kawaura takes "over four hundred years" to mean "from the founding of Kamakura rule [1185] to the time of Nobunaga"; see Kawaura, *Ryūshi shinron*, p. 156. But that interpretation does violence to the context.

31. Takimoto, *Ryūshi shinron*, p. 66. Kanzan sardonically alludes to the passage in *Mencius* where Daini's term "skill and cleverness" *(jutsu-chi)* appears: "It is often through adversity that men acquire virtue, wisdom, skill, and cleverness [*jutsu, chi*]. The estranged subject or son of a concubine . . . succeeds where others fail." See Kanaya Osamu, ed., *Mōshi*, p. 446; Lau, *Mencius*, p. 185. Daini's thesis is "contemptible" because "skill and cleverness" are suitable for such Chinese rulers of base origin—but not for Japan's divine emperor, who embodies political ideals that the shogun-hegemon actually implements.

32. Quoted from the *Tao te ching*; see Fukunaga, *Rōshi ge*, pp. 19–28.

33. Mencius so cites Confucius quoting from the *Book of Rites*. See Kanaya, *Mōshi*, pp. 299–300; Lau, *Mencius*, p. 140; Ichihara et al., *Raiki jō*, pp. 492–493; Ichihara et al., *Raiki ge*, pp. 204–205 and 513.

34. Ssu-ma Ch'ien so quotes a certain Wang Chu, whose city of Hua in Ch'i came under attack by Yen armies in the Chou period. Wang killed himself rather than accept a command in the Yen army. See Watson, *Records of the Historian*, p. 34. This sentence and the one before it were later incorporated in the *Lesser Learning*, attributed to Chu Hsi's editorship in the twelfth century. They were moral maxims in Japan until 1945.

35. Takimoto, *Ryūshi shinron*, p. 68. I insert this note at an appropriate place in Daini's text rather than attach it to the end of this section as Takimoto does.

36. Imaginary animals found in the *Erh ya*, an ancient Chinese primer that lists glosses for obscure terms. It dates from the third century B.C. and was supposedly compiled by the Duke of Chou. For the original source see Nagasawa Kikuya, ed., *Nan pei ch'ao k'an pen Erh ya*, pp. 87–88. See also *DKJ*, vol. 6, pp. 805 and 802. "*Chu*" in the compound "*chu-hsu*" on p. 802 of vol. 6 is a homonym for character number 37481 in vol. 10, p. 910; it is also found under character number 39288 in vol. 11, p. 214.

37. Takimoto, *Ryūshi shinron*, p. 68. Again I insert the note at an appropriate place in the body of Daini's text.

38. According to Nishida, Huang's biography is in the *Hou Han shu*, but

this episode is not; so it is unknown where Daini got this information. See Nishida, *Ryūshi shinron*, p. 355.

39. This is a variation on passages, often quoted by Tokugawa writers, from the *Hsun tzu* and *Book of Rites* that describe the presocial state of nature as envisioned by Confucians. For the loci classici, see Kanaya et al., *Junshi ge*, pp. 239–240; Ichihara et al., *Raiki chū*, pp. 413–414.

40. This behavior violated the Confucian ideal of graded distinctions in love and respect.

41. Adapted from the "H'si Tz'u Commentary" to the *Book of Changes*. See Honda, *Eki*, p. 533; Wilhelm and Baynes, *The I Ching*, p. 334.

42. Quoted from the (spurious) "Great Declaration" chapter of the *Book of Documents*. See Ikeda, *Shōsho*, p. 607.

43. See note 4 to the translation (above).

44. Quoted from the *Analects*. See Yoshikawa, *Rongo jō*, pp. 27–30; Lau, *The Analects*, p. 63.

45. See Ichihara Kyōkichi et al., eds., *Raiki chū*, pp. 156–157.

46. According to the *Tso chuan*, Tzu-lu, Confucius' disciple, served the King of Yen and died in a civil war. True to the rites, he retied the strings of his court cap before expiring. See Nishida, *Ryūshi shinron*, p. 358; Kawaura, *Ryūshi shinron*, p. 157.

47. Quoted from the "H'si Tz'u Commentary" of the *Book of Changes*. See Honda, *Eki*, pp. 529–530; Wilhelm and Baynes, *The I Ching*, p. 332.

48. This paragraph is from Dazai Shundai, *Keizai roku*, p. 185.

49. Quoted from the *Analects*. See Yoshikawa, *Rongo jō*, pp. 296–297.

50. This paragraph is from Dazai Shundai, *Keizai roku*, p. 185.

51. This paragraph is from Dazai Shundai, *Keizai roku*, p. 193.

52. Takenouchi Shikibu reportedly ridiculed the Tokugawa shogun as "Grand Minister of the Center with a Half-Shaved Head" *(sakayaki no naidaijin)*; Tokutomi, *Hōreki-Meiwa hen*, p. 154.

53. Based on the "Biography of Shu-sun T'ung" in Ssu-ma Ch'ien's *Shih chi*; see Watson, *Records of the Historian*, pp. 222–226.

54. As described by Confucius; see Yoshikawa, *Rongo ge*, pp. 161–162; Lau, *The Analects*, pp. 126–127.

55. Adapted from the *Book of Rites*; see Ichihara et al., *Raiki ge*, pp. 156–157.

56. See Yoshikawa, *Rongo ge*, pp. 100–102; Lau, *The Analects*, p. 117. Confucius based these observations on the *Book of Documents*; see Ikeda, *Shōsho*, pp. 77–78, 91–118, and 543–555 for Kao Yao; pp. 176–177 for Yi Yin. But Yi Yin is best known for serving as regent under T'ang's grandson, T'ai Chia.

57. Contrast Daini with Motoori Norinaga's rigid adherence to established methods: "In general, affairs in society are beyond human wisdom

and manipulation no matter how wise you may be. So do not implement new methods readily. If you rule by following the times and holding to established ways in all things, you will make no serious errors, even though some flaws remain." See *Hihon tamakushige*, p. 331.

58. According to Ssu-ma Ch'ien, the wicked last Shang king, Chieh, and his court cronies debauched amid "pools of wine and forests of meat" and enjoyed viewing "fire-pit executions." See Noguchi et al., *Shiki jō*, pp. 32–33. Interestingly, the bakufu's 1613 prohibition of Christianity stipulates "fire-pit executions" *(hōraku)* for violators; see Hayashiya Tatsusaburō et al., eds., *Shiryō taikei Nihon rekishi 4: Kinsei I*, pp. 234–235.

59. Yoshikawa, *Rongo jō*, pp. 52–53; Lau, *The Analects*, p. 66.

60. This implies that a true central government for the realm should set up new dynastic rituals.

61. Hakuseki and Sorai argued that the bakufu should establish its own state rituals and merit ranks apart from the imperial court; see "Buke kan'i shōzoku kō," in Ichijima Kenkichi, ed., *Arai Hakuseki zenshū*, vol. 6, pp. 472–473; and *Seidan*, in Yoshikawa Kōjirō et al., eds., *NST 36: Ogyū Sorai*, pp. 347–350. See also Nakai, *Shogunal Politics*, pp. 173–190 and 202–212, and Ooms, *Tokugawa Ideology*, p. 169. But, as Daini notes further on, nothing got resolved. Hakuseki's proposals were overturned by Shogun Yoshimune, and Sorai's were never taken up.

62. Iizuka argues that such passages on bribery and official corruption accurately reflect shogunal politics under Ieshige and, moreover, that Daini learned of such practices firsthand under Ōoka Tadamitsu from 1745 to 1760—the same years that Ieshige was shogun. See Iizuka, *Yamagata Daini seiden*, p. 319. Tadamitsu wielded near-dictatorial power as grand chamberlain and sole confidant of Ieshige, who was physically and mentally infirm.

63. Quoted from *History of the Former Han*. See Nagasawa, *Kanjo*, vol. 2, pp. 617–618.

64. In 1185, Minamoto no Yoritomo (1147–1199) founded a military regime at Kamakura on the Kantō plain. Noguchi Takehiko holds that Daini took the five-hundred-year figure from a passage in *Mencius*: "Without fail, a true king will arise each five hundred years. . . . But now over seven hundred years have elapsed since the Chou; so the time is more than ripe." According to Noguchi: Daini, like Mencius, saw himself as a harbinger of revolution, and this particular sentence caused the bakufu to execute him. See Noguchi, "Tō-Bu hōbatsu no aporia," pp. 45–47. But as Noguchi himself half-admits, such a reading is "far-fetched" (p. 47). The five-hundred-year figure was a conventional unit of time used by Confucians and Buddhists to measure warrior rule. For examples of its use by Kumazawa Banzan and Fujiwara Seika, see Ishida Ichirō and Kanaya Osamu, eds., *NST 28:*

Fujiwara Seika, Hayashi Razan, p. 245 and the note on p. 389. Moreover, Daini dated the start of bakufu rule from 1185, not 1192; and 1185 is also significant because most Tokugawa historians mistakenly believed that is when Yoritomo received imperial sanction to appoint provincial protectors *(shugo)* and land stewards *(jitō)* throughout Japan. See Ishii, *Kamakura bakufu,* pp. 181–184 and 199–211.

65. Confucius as quoted in Ssu-ma Ch'ien's *Shih chi;* see Noguchi et al., *Shiki chu,* p. 62.

66. Tsukamoto Tetsuzō, ed., *Shikyō,* pp. 316 and 8–9.

67. Confucius so defined a *shishi;* see Yoshikawa, *Rongo ge,* p. 199.

68. Described in the *Book of Rites;* see Ichihara et al., *Raiki ge,* pp. 456–478.

69. Confucius condemned the Chi family thus: "They use eight rows of eight dancers each to perform in their courtyard." See Yoshikawa, *Rongo jō,* pp. 55–56; Lau, *The Analects,* p. 67. The position and number of dancers per row was set by rank: 64 (8 × 8) for the emperor, 36 (6 × 6) for feudal lords, 16 (4 × 4) for great officials, and 4 (2 × 2) for officials. The Chi were of the great official class, so they should have limited themselves to sixteen dancers. This violation had grave political implications for Confucius. The Chi were subverting the social order or even harboring designs on the throne.

70. The spirit behind the Kyōhō Reforms under Shogun Yoshimune (r. 1716–1745).

71. Ssu-ma Ch'ien quotes: "As they say, 'Even though things be of the same class, abilities differ.' Thus we praise Wu Huo for his power, cite Ch'ing Chi for his swiftness, and emulate Meng Pin and Hsia Yu for their valor"; Noguchi et al., *Shiki ge,* p. 226. Meng Pin also appears in *Mencius.* See Kanaya, *Mōshi,* pp. 78–79; Lau, *Mencius,* p. 76.

72. Singled out by Confucius for "culture and learning." See Yoshikawa, *Rongo ge,* pp. 5–7; Lau, *The Analects,* p. 106.

73. Ancient Chinese military classics. The *Liu T'ao* is usually ascribed to Lu Shang of the Chou. He helped King Wu overthrow Chieh, evil last king of the Shang, and was rewarded with enfeoffment in Ch'i. See *DKJ,* vol. 2, pp. 69 and 914. The *Yu ch'ien p'ien* is conventionally cited with the *Liu T'ao,* but its date and authorship are unknown.

74. Nishida's interpretation based on a passage from the *Offices of Chou.* "*Shōkoku*" denotes "the fallen dynasty" because the present regime "achieved victory over" and displaced the previous ruling house; Nishida, *Ryūshi shinron,* p. 374. Reflecting the nationalistic bias of his time, Kawaura simply glosses the term as "the previous age" with no hint of a dynastic overthrow in Japan; Kawaura, *Ryūshi shinron,* p. 160. The *DKJ* supports Nishida; see *DKJ,* vol. 2, p. 400.

75. In fact, Fujiwara no Hidesato, whose dates are unknown, quashed Masakado's revolt but not Sumitomo's.

76. Akuro (or Akuji) no Takamaru was a legendary figure often identified as an eighth-century aboriginal leader who revolted against the central government at Takkoku no Iwa, near Hiraizumi in present-day Iwate prefecture. The first reference to him, an *Azumakagami* entry for IX/28 1189, says he was defeated by Sakanoue no Tamuramaro and Fujiwara no Toshihito; see Kishi Shōzō, ed., *Zen'yaku Azuma kagami*, vol. 2, p. 123. The real rebel, named Aterui, put up a stiff fight before succumbing to Sakanoue in 802. See *KDJ*, vol. 1, p. 105; see also Takahashi Takashi, *Sakanoue no Tamuramaro*, pp. 101–106. After this mistaken identity became established, Akuro appeared in many war tales, ballads, plays, and chapbooks. See the early Muromachi *Tale of Yoshitsune*; Kajiwara Masaaki, ed., *Gikeiki*, pp. 110 and 534. Daini probably learned of Akuro from these fictional sources. Like most prewar scholars, Kawaura accepts Akuro as historical; Kawaura, *Ryūshi shinron*, p. 160. For a detailed discussion of the Akuro legend see Hori Ichirō, *Wagakuni minkan shinkōshi no kenkyū*, vol. 1, pp. 664–686.

77. The form of military service under the eighth-century Ritsu-Ryō state. On how these units were formed, especially in light of international strategic considerations, see Sasayama Haruo, *Kodai kokka to guntai*, pp. 48–72.

78. See Yoshikawa, *Rongo jō*, pp. 30–31; Lau, *The Analects*, p. 63.

79. This and other sections on political economy derive from Dazai Shundai's *Sango;* see Takimoto, *Sango*, pp. 350–355.

80. That is, they did not hinder farmwork by demanding corvée service during the planting and harvesting seasons. Besides being benevolent, this was wise fiscal policy because less agricultural output meant less tax revenue.

81. Wu Huo was a strongman of the Ch'in era (221–207 B.C.) able to lift one thousand pounds; see Kanaya et al., *Junshi jō*, pp. 294–297; and Kanaya, *Mōshi*, p. 400; Lau, *Mencius*, p. 172. Mu-yeh was a swordsmith in Wu during the Spring and Autumn period (722–481 B.C.). After sacrificing his wife to the hearth god, he made a famous pair of strong, sharp swords, one of which came to be known as "Mu-yeh." See *DKJ*, vol. 9, p. 687. For an early Chinese reference, see Kanaya et al., *Junshi jō*, pp. 424–430; see also Watson, *Hsun Tzu: Basic Writings*, p. 58. Mu-yeh and his sword were often cited in Japanese literary works. See Yamada Yoshio et al., eds., *NKBT 23: Konjaku monogatari 2*, pp. 260–262; and Ichiko Teiji and Ōshima Tatehiko, eds., *NKBT 88: Soga Monogatari*, pp. 170 and 305. Mu-yeh also appeared on the Edo-era theatrical stage. See *Kanjinchō*, in Gunji Masakatsu, ed., *NKBT 98: Kabuki jūhachiban shū*, p. 185; see also Chikamatsu, *Kokusenya kassen*, in Shuzui Kenji and Ōkubo Tadakuni, eds., *NKBT 50: Chikamatsu jōruri shū ge*, p. 271. This last play has been translated into

English; Donald Keene, trans., *The Battles of Coxinga,* p. 140, where Mu-yeh is romanized "Mo Yeh."

82. Daini's term is *nuhi.* They were not slaves but a base class of people stipulated by the Ritsu-Ryō law codes. Both the Kawaura and Nishida editions read "tens of. . . ." But Nishida notes this as a textual error; Nishida, *Ryūshi shinron,* p. 378. The Naramoto edition reads "thousands of . . ."; Naramoto, *Ryūshi shinron,* p. 403. In "The Need to Circulate Goods and Currency," Daini writes: "Merchant princes support thousands." So I emend "tens" to read "thousands."

83. In "The Need to Circulate Goods and Currency," Daini claims the current tax rate was fifty to sixty percent.

84. Here and in "Adhering to One's Calling" Daini draws the Confucian physiocratic distinction between farming as the people's proper calling ("the root") and nonessential, ethically tainted, mercantile activities ("the branches").

85. Kanaya, *Mōshi,* p. 147; Lau, *Mencius,* p. 96.

86. Daini took many of his ideas on mutual surveillance groups, domicile registries, and deurbanization from Ogyū Sorai; see *Seidan,* pp. 263–302.

87. Nishida interprets the passage as "they only keep in mind whether a person is rich or poor"; *Ryūshi shinron,* p. 383.

88. These were *okappiki* or *meakashi*—local roughnecks employed by constables *(yoriki)* such as Daini under the jurisdiction of bakufu city magistrates. As the *okappiki* were more or less criminals themselves and received scant pay for their services, relying on them to uphold order and apprehend criminals obviously had serious drawbacks. See Ishii Ryōsuke, *Shimpen Edo jidai mampitsu jō,* pp. 23–37.

89. Quoted from the *Hsun Tzu;* see Kanaya et al., *Junshi ge,* pp. 347–348.

90. Uttered by Confucius in Ch'en, a small state suffering famine and facing attack by Wu; see Yoshikawa, *Rongo ge,* pp. 192–194; Lau, *The Analects,* p. 132.

91. The passage beginning "Punishments for . . ." is adapted from Dazai Shundai, *Keizai roku,* pp. 230–231 and 237–238. Here and in "Giving Repose to the People," Shundai and Daini carry on Sorai's arguments against banishment as a remnant from the Warring States period; see Ogyū Sorai, *Seidan,* p. 429.

92. Compare with Daini's definition of the Way of government: "Civil rule maintains order under normal conditions." See Kawaura, *Ryūshi shinron,* pp. 17 and 72.

93. Eminent *kabuki* actors, *jōruri* chanters, and gay-quarter "courtesans" received imperial court rank and office titles such as *Harima no jō,* or they affixed the suffix *-dayū* to their names. See Iizuka, *Yamagata Daini seiden,*

pp. 350-351. Goyōzei (r. 1586-1611) apparently was the first emperor to grant such titles officially to actors and chanters.

94. A key concept taken from the *Doctrine of the Mean.* See Shimada Kenji, ed., *Daigaku, Chūyō,* pp. 178-180; and Wing-tsit Chan, ed., *A Sourcebook of Chinese Philosophy,* p. 99. See Daini's "Benefits and Evils," Section XII, where he discusses the political implications of these "virtues."

95. Singing and dancing to the samisen, a practice that bakufu and domain governments prohibited during periods of reform.

96. This paragraph is from Dazai Shundai, *Keizai roku,* p. 152.

97. Kanaya, *Mōshi,* p. 147; Lau, *Mencius,* p. 96.

98. Mencius quotes Confucius: "The influence of his virtue disseminates faster than decrees sped through post stations." See Kanaya, *Mōshi,* p. 75; Lau, *Mencius,* p. 75.

99. Yu Meng from Chu donned the court garments of a deceased minister in order to gain the ear of, and remonstrate with, his sovereign. See Noguchi et al., *Shiki ge,* pp. 298-301.

100. Here Daini seems to criticize social stratification based on hereditary occupations. This contradicts the main thrust of his treatise, which is to uphold that principle.

101. A Taoist metaphor for an exceedingly difficult, expensively acquired skill that ends up being useless: there are no dragons to butcher. See Fukunaga, *Sōshi zappen ge,* pp. 156-158; and Watson, *Complete Works of Chuang Tzu,* pp. 355-356.

102. Northern Chi was famous for horses, and Po Lo of the Spring and Autumn era was legendary for his ability to judge them. See *DKJ,* vol. 1, p. 677. In the *Chuang Tzu,* however, Po Lo is treated satirically—as killing the horses he picked to train. So the ones he missed were actually better off. See Fukunaga, *Soshi gaihen jō,* pp. 58-59; see also Watson, *Complete Works of Chuang Tzu,* p. 104.

103. A famous episode from *Intrigues of the Warring States;* see Kondō Mitsuo, ed., *Sengokusaku ge,* pp. 312-317.

104. "*Kakyo no hō*": civil service examinations used in imperial China from Sung times on to recruit talented men for office. For a concise survey see Miyazaki Ichisada, *China's Examination Hell.*

105. The passage beginning from "When the former sage-kings prescribed their tenets..." is adapted from Dazai Shundai, *Keizai roku,* pp. 178-181.

106. Tsukamoto, *Shikyō,* p. 354.

107. Daini alludes to Pure Land doctrines and rebellions by the Ikkō sect in order to add a sixteenth-century flavor to his text and make it appear to date from Oda Nobunaga's time.

108. See note 78 to the translation.

109. Daini construes this passage following Ogyū Sorai. The "gentlemen" and "small men" here should be taken to mean "the ruler and ruled"—not a moral distinction between men "within the class of the ruled," as Lau holds in *The Analects*, p. 73. For the Sorai interpretation, see Sorai, *Rongochō*, pp. 88–89, and Yoshikawa, *Rongo jō*, pp. 96–97.

110. Many cruel and punitive laws, and even much punishment as part of collective responsibility, had been ameliorated by the Kyōhō era (1716–1735). See Ishii Ryōsuke, *Shimpen Edo jidai mampitsu jō*, pp. 311–313; see also Tsuji, *Ōoka Echizen no kami*, p. 138.

111. Iizuka claims this is a criticism of Tsunayoshi's "Laws of Compassion for Living Things," which, in extreme cases, carried the death sentence for people who killed or mistreated animals. See Iizuka, *Yamagata Daini seiden*, p. 358. On Tsunayoshi's laws see Donald Shively, "Tokugawa Tsunayoshi, the Genroku Shōgun," pp. 95–97. For a revisionist view with emphasis on how people perceived the relationship of animals to humans in Tokugawa times, see Tsukamoto Manabu, *Shōrui o meguru seiji*.

112. The punishment should fit the crime; see the *Shih chi*; Noguchi et. al., *Shiki ge*, p. 97.

113. See Ogyū Sorai, *Seidan*, p. 429. He too inveighs against banishment as a leftover medieval practice.

114. Quoted from the "Wen-yen Commentary" of the *Book of Changes*; see Honda, *Eki*, pp. 17–18, and Wilhelm and Baynes, *The I Ching*, p. 9.

115. "Alien cults" *(gedō)* refers to the Catholicism spread by Iberian missionaries in the fifteenth and sixteenth centuries. Daini uses the Chinese-translated Jesuit term for "geometry," *"chi-ho,"* to render "barbarian learning." By using these terms, he tries to show that his text was written "by a contemporary of Oda Nobunaga."

116. Daini's term is *"Yaso no oshie."*

117. For a socioanthropological analysis of such "special status people," and especially monkey trainers, see Emiko Ohnuki-Tierney, *The Monkey as Mirror*, pp. 95–127.

118. Again Daini is trying to make his text appear to date from the era of Oda Nobunaga. He describes medieval free markets *(za)* and portrays foreign nationals preaching and trading in Kyoto. He also uses the Chinese term, *"Po-ssu,"* for Persia. The Chinese and Persians traded as early as the sixth century; contact was especially frequent in T'ang times, when Zoroastrianism was known as "the Doctrine of Persia" *(Po-ssu chiao)*. See DKJ, vol. 6, p. 1061, and vol. 8, p. 423.

119. Quoted from the *Chuang Tzu*; see Fukunaga, *Sōshi zappen jo*, pp. 149–150; Watson, *Complete Works of Chuang Tzu*, p. 276. Ants attracted to stinking mutton are sardonically likened to the masses who seek out the sage-king Shun.

120. Quoted from the *History of the Former Han;* see Nagasawa, *Kanjo,* vol. 1, p. 278.

121. These concepts from the *Book of Changes* figure prominently in Daini's thought, especially in "Wealth and Strength," Section XIII.

122. Ikeda, *Shōsho,* pp. 252–253.

123. Ibid. Daini deemed "leveling prices," as revealed in this *Book of Documents* passage, to be a key objective of every government. See the next section, "The Need to Circulate Goods and Currency."

124. Quoted from the *Mencius;* see Kanaya, *Mōshi,* pp. 150–151; Lau, *Mencius,* pp. 97–98.

125. The *Ssu-shih, Chih-jen, Ch'an-jen, Ku-shih,* and *Ch'uan-fu.* All are listed in the *Rites of Chou.* See Nishida, *Ryūshi shinron,* p. 405. My English translations follow Charles Hucker, *A Dictionary of Official Titles in Imperial China,* pp. 455, 150, 107, 282, and 198.

126. In "Heaven-Mandated Peoples," Section VI, Daini writes that the current tax rate was sixty to seventy percent of the crop.

127. *"Dorei."* See also "Heaven-Mandated Peoples," where Daini uses the term *"nuhi"* to describe this class of menial tradesmen working for rich merchants.

128. Contrast this with Motoori Norinaga's views on the poverty suffered by present-day peasants compared with those in antiquity under the imperial dynasty: "[Today] they are just resigned to paying taxes at present [high] rates. . . . It hasn't yet dawned on them that taxes are too high. I sympathize with them, but they have to go on paying." In sum, Norinaga held that peasants had been downtrodden since the inception of warrior rule and maintained that taxes should not be raised further; but these should not be lowered, either. See *Hihon tamakushige,* pp. 338–340.

129. Iizuka argues that Daini here criticizes "the *kemi* system of tax assessment set up by the preceding shogun, Yoshimune," which created this paradoxical situation; Iizuka, *Yamagata Daini seiden,* p. 381. But in fact Yoshimune implemented the *jōmen* system to replace the *kemi.* So instead this passage probably criticizes the bakufu's policy of offering capital outlays or tax reductions to encourage either the development of new fields in hitherto nonarable areas, such as mountainous or swampy regions, or the cultivation of infertile marginal fields that normally would lie fallow.

130. The "court" *(byōdō)* and "throne" *(renkoku no moto)* here signify the bakufu, not the imperial court.

131. Ogyū Sorai explained the origin of this practice thus: "In the Keichō through Kan'ei eras [1596–1643], the shogun was wary of daimyo revolts. So the *rōju* made it a policy to get daimyo to spend lots of money. That is why they did not hesitate to accept money and gifts from the daimyo. Quite to the contrary, they thought it was part of their job." See *Seidan,* pp. 321–

322. Of course, many *rōju* in Daini's time continued accepting bribes for that ostensible reason: it impoverished the daimyo and so constituted loyal service to the bakufu.

132. Daini again describes the bribery and corruption that supposedly characterized Ōoka Tadamitsu and Tanuma Okitsugu. This image has been popularized by Tokutomi Iichirō in *Kinsei Nihon kokuminshi 22: Tanuma jidai*, by Tsuji Zennosuke in *Tanuma jidai*, and, to a lesser extent, by John Hall in *Tanuma Okitsugu*. Tsuji's 1915 work, reissued in 1936 and 1980, has been crucial in this regard. But Ōishi Shinzaburō has long argued that the image of corruption is not substantiated by reliable sources; Ōishi, "Tanuma Okitsugu ni kansuru jūrai no shiryō no shimpyōsei ni tsuite," pp. 24–33; *Nihon no rekishi 20: Bakuhansei no tenkan*, pp. 369–381; and *Edo jidai*, pp. 190–215.

133. Literally: "he could set up a net to catch sparrows outside his gate." See the locus classicus in Ssu-ma Ch'ien's *Shih chi*; Noguchi et al., *Shiki ge*, p. 256.

134. "*Hioku hōzubeshi,*" taken from the "Biography of Wang Mang" in the *Han shu*; see Nagasawa, *Kanjo*, vol. 2, p. 1019. This conveys Daini's Confucian idea of elevating the masses and shows the limits of his egalitarianism. Such betterment is to take place primarily in the cultural and moral spheres.

135. A barbarian tribe on ancient China's southern frontier.

136. These three quotations are from the "Speech by T'ang" and the (spurious) "Counsels of Great Yu" and "Announcement by T'ang" in the *Book of Documents*; Ikeda, *Shōsho*, pp. 177, 552, and 573.

137. Quoted from the *Doctrine of the Mean*. See Shimada, *Daigaku, Chūyō*, pp. 178–180; Chan, *Sourcebook of Chinese Philosophy*, p. 99.

138. This set of paired opposites means to "accord with" *(jun)* or "run counter to" *(gyaku)* reason or the Way. But here Daini argues that martial rule is in fact needed for government; so I translate the terms as "norm" and "last resort."

139. In what surely must be a misprint, Nishida renders this as "Juei [1182–1185] and Heiji [1159–1160] times." See Nishida, *Ryūshi shinron*, p. 419. Note also that the imperial court did not appoint Minamoto no Yoritomo "Barbarian-Quelling Great General" *(seii taishōgun)* until 1192—in the Kenkyū era.

140. Quoted from the *Book of Odes*; Tsukamoto, *Shikyō*, p. 406.

141. Famous examples of subjects who give a ruler what he wants, taken from the *Han Fei Tzu*. See Takeuchi, *Kampishi jō*, p. 73; Watson, *Han Fei Tzu: Basic Writings*, p. 33.

142. Adapted from the *Analects*; see Yoshikawa, *Rongo jō*, pp. 262–264; Lau, *The Analects*, p. 95.

143. These quotations underscore Daini's emphasis on "increasing benefits" expressed in "Adhering to One's Calling" and "Benefits and Evils." The same *Book of Changes* ideograph *(i)* denotes both "increase" and "benefit." See Honda, *Eki,* pp. 313–322 and 305–313; my translation differs from Wilhelm and Baynes, *The I Ching,* pp. 162–165 and 158–161.

144. This implies "the shogun ruling all of Japan or a daimyo ruling a single domain." Again Daini depicts the current *bakuhan* system as roughly analogous to the *feng-chien* system of Chou times. Hence "the realm" or "all under heaven" *(tenka)* comprised a plurality of states *(kokka).*

145. Quoted from the *Book of Rites;* see Ichihara et al., *Raiki jō,* pp. 336–337. Daini emphasizes the need to rectify names: unless a regime properly performs the ruling functions inherent in its name of "state," it cannot claim that title and, by extension, is not a legitimate government.

146. Daini took this "large dike" metaphor and the need to solve problems while they are still small from the *Han Fei Tzu;* see Takeuchi, *Kampishi jō,* pp. 277–278.

147. Quoted from the *Hsun Tzu* (Kanaya et al., *Junshi ge,* pp. 408–409) and *Book of Changes* (Honda, *Eki,* pp. 537–538).

148. Confucius' definition of a *shishi;* Yoshikawa, *Rongo ge,* p. 199.

149. Quoted from the *Tso chuan;* see Kamata et al., *Shunjū sashiden,* vol. 4, pp. 1148–1149.

150. See Kamata et al., *Shunjū sashiden,* vol. 1, pp. 246–247.

151. The Six Arts—the rites, music, archery, chariot riding, calligraphy, and ciphering—formed the core of education for the Chou aristocracy. The Hundred Schools flourished in China during the fifth through third centuries B.C., the high point of classical Chinese thought.

152. In present-day Kōfu city, Yamanashi prefecture. See Iizuka, *Yamagata Daini seiden,* pp. 3–4.

153. Families with the character "Ryū," or "Yanagi," in their surnames, such as Yanagimoto, Yanagawa, Yanagihara, Yanagisawa, and Yanagida.

Glossary

This list of major Japanese and Chinese terms does not include postwar Japanese scholars or titles found in the bibliography.

Aizawa Seishisai　会沢正志斎
Akao　赤尾
Akihito　明仁
A-heng/Akō　阿衡
Akō (incident)　赤穂
Akuro (Akuji) no Takamaru　悪路
　　(事)高丸
Amaterasu　天照
Amenofutotama no mikoto
　　天太玉命
Amenokoyane no mikoto
　　天児屋根命
Andō Shōeki　安藤昌益
Ansei　安政
Arai Hakuseki　新井白石
Asano Naganori　浅野長矩
Ashikaga bakufu　足利幕府
Ashikaga Yoshimitsu　足利義満
　　　　　　Takauji　尊(高)氏
Aterui　阿弓流為
Azuma　吾嬬

bakuhan　幕藩
Bakumatsu　幕末
bansei ikkei　万世一系
bei (hyōe)　兵衛
Bendō sho　弁道書
Bengi roku　弁疑録
Bidatsu (emperor)　敏達
bu/wu　文

buke no yo　武家の世
bun/wen　武
Bungo no kami　豊後守
bunko　文庫
bunsai　文采
Buretsu (emperor)　武烈
Buyō Inshi　武陽隠士
byōdō　廟堂

Chao (king)　昭
Chan kuo ts'e　戦国策
Ch'an-jen　廛人
chang　丈
Ch'ang Chung-ching　張仲景
ch'e (tax)　徹
Chi　冀
Ch'i　斉
ch'ih　尺
Chih-jen　質人
chi-ho　幾何
Chieh-Chou　桀紂
Chigusa Tadaaki　千種忠顕
Chikamatsu Hanji　近松半二
　　　　　　Monzaemon　門左衛門
Chikugo no kami　筑後守
Chin　金
Chin　晋
Ch'in　秦
Ch'ing　清
chōtei　朝廷

Chou 周
chu (tax) 助
Ch'u 楚
Chu Hsi 朱熹
chu-hsu 岠虛
Chūkyō (emperor) 仲恭
Chūai (emperor) 仲哀
Ch'uan-fu 泉府
Chuang Tzu 莊子
chūkō 中興
Chung-hua/Chūka 中華
Chung-kuo/Chūgoku 中国
Chūshingura 忠臣蔵
chūwa 中和

dainagon 大納言
dajōdaijin 太政大臣
Danzaemon 弾左衛門
Date 伊達
　　　Chihiro 千広
Dazai Shundai 太宰春台
Dewa 出羽
dochaku 土着
dorei 奴隷
dōri 道理

Echizen no kami 越前守
Edo 江戸
Emishi 蝦夷
emon 衛門
Erh-ya 爾雅

feng-hsien 封建
Fu Yueh 傅説
fudai 譜代
Fujii Umon 藤井右門
Fujita Tōko 藤田東湖
　　　Yūkoku 幽谷
Fujiwara no Fuhito 藤原不比等
　　　Hidesato 秀郷
　　　Kamatari 鎌足
　　　Kōmyō 光明
　　　Miyako 宮子

Morosuke 師輔
Mototsune 基経
Sumitomo 純友
Yoshifusa 良房
fukei no itari 不敬の至
fukeizai 不敬罪
Fukuchi Gen'ichirō 福地源一郎
fukusho 副署
futen sotsudo ōdo ōmin 普天卒土
　　王土王民
futodoki shigoku 不届至極

Gachū-fu 牙籌譜
Gamō Kumpei 蒲生君平
gedō 外道
Gemmei (female sovereign) 元明
Genji 源氏
genrō 元老
Genroku 元禄
Genshō (female sovereign) 元正
Godaigo (emperor) 後醍醐
go-ikō 御威光
gokumon 獄門
Gomi Fusen 五味釜川
Gomizuno-o (emperor) 後水尾
Gomurakami (emperor) 後村上
gōnō 豪農
Goshirakawa (ex-emperor) 後白川
Gotoba (ex-emperor) 後鳥羽
Goyōzei (emperor) 後陽成
gōzoku 豪族
Gukanshō 愚管抄
gunken/hōken 郡県封建
gunkoku no sei 軍国の制
gyo/go/on 御
gyosui gattei 魚水合体

Hachiman Bosatsu 八幡菩薩
Hagiwara Motoe 萩原元克
hakuryō gyofuku 白竜魚服
Han 漢
Han Fei Tzu / Kampishi 韓非子
hangyaku 叛逆

Harima no jō　播磨掾
Hatchōbori-Nagasawachō　八丁堀長沢町
Hatsuon ryaku　発音略
Hattori Nankaku　服部南郭
Hayashi Fusao　林房雄
Hayashi Razan　林羅山
Heian　平安
heiran　兵乱
hioku hōzubeshi　比屋可封
Hiraizumi　平泉
Hiraizumi Kiyoshi　平泉澄
Hirohito / Yūnin　裕仁
Hoashi Banri　帆足万里
hōbatsu　放伐
Hōgen-Heiji　保元平治
hohitsu　輔弼
Hōjō Yasutoki　北条泰時
　　　Yoshitoki　義時
Hōken taiki　保建大記
hōraku　炮烙
Hōreki　宝暦
Hosaka　保坂
Hosokawa Morisada　細川護貞
Hou Han shu　後漢書
Hou Kuang　霍光
Hsia　夏
Hsia Yu　夏育
Hsiang (duke)　襄
hsing / kei　形
Hsun Tzu　荀子
Huang Hsien　黄憲

I (duke)　懿
i (increase, benefit)　益
Ieharu　家治
Ienobu　家宣
Ieshige　家重
Ii Naosuke　井伊直弼
Iji hatsuran　医事撥乱
Ikeda Mitsumasa　池田光政
ikkun banmin　一君万民
Imbe　忌部

ishin　維新
ito no gotoku　綫のごとく
Jien　慈円
jigi　時宜
jikiso　直訴
Jimmu (emperor)　神武
jindai　神代
Jingū (female sovereign)　神功
Jinnō shōtōki　神皇正統記
Jinshin　壬申
jitō　地頭
Jitō (female sovereign)　持統
jō　丞
jogen　助言
jōi　攘夷
Jōkyū　承久
jōruri　淨瑠璃
jotei　女帝
Juei-Bunji　寿永文治
jun / gyaku　順逆
junshi　殉死
Juntoku (emperor)　順徳
jūshin　重臣
jutsu-chi　術知

kabuki　歌舞伎
Kagami Ōu　加賀美桜塢
Kai　甲斐
Kaien yawa　解寃夜話
Kaiho Seiryō　海保青陵
kakikudashibun　書下文
kakyo no hō　科挙の法
Kamakura bakufu　鎌倉幕府
Kamanashi　釜無
kambun　漢文
Kamo no Mabuchi　賀茂真渕
kampaku　関白
kanji　漢字
Kansei　寛政
Kao-tsu　高祖
Kao Yao　皋陶

karō 家老
Katsushika 葛飾
Katsuura 勝浦
Kawachi 河内
Keichū 契沖
Keikō (emperor) 景行
Keizai roku 経済録
Kemmu 建武
Kenkyū 建久
Kingaku hakki 琴学発揮
kinnō 勤王
Kira Yoshinaka 吉良義央
Kitabatake Chikafusa 北畠親房
Kobayashi Shinsuke 小林新介
Kōbun (emperor) 弘文
Kōfu 甲府
kōgō 皇后
Kojiki 古事記
Kōkaku (emperor) 光格
Kōken (female sovereign) 孝謙
kokka 国家
Kōkō (emperor) 光孝
kōkoku shikan 皇国史観
koku 石
kokubun 告文
Kokugaku 国学
kokumu 国務
kokutai 国体 (國體)
Koma 巨摩
Komagatake 駒嶽
Komiyo 小美夜
Konoe Fumimaro 近衛文麿
Kose 巨勢
Kōzuke 上野
Ku-shih 賈師
kudari 下り
Kujō Yoritsune 九条頼経
Kumaso 熊襲
Kumazawa Banzan 熊沢蕃山
kung (tax) 貢
kunshin gattei gyosui no gi 君臣
合体魚水の儀
Kuo Wei 郭隗

Kuriyama Sempō 栗山潜鋒
Kurizaki Michiari 栗崎道有
Kusaka Genzui 久坂玄瑞
Kusunoki Masashige 楠木正成
kyobun 虚文
kyōshu 共主
Kyōhō 享保
Kyoto 京都

li 里
li/ch'i 理／気
Ling (king) 霊
Liu Pang 劉邦
Liu T'ao 六韜

Makita Giemon 蒔田儀右衛門
Marubashi Chūya 丸橋忠弥
Matsubara Gundayū 松原郡太夫
Matsudaira Sadanobu 松平定信
　　　　　Nobutsuna 信綱
Matsumiya Kanzan 松宮観山
Matsuo Bashō 松尾芭蕉
Matsuzaka 松坂
meakashi 目明
mei-jitsu/ming-shih 名実
mei-kei/ming-hsing 名形
Meiji 明治
Meiwa 明和
Meiwa fudoki 明和風土記
Meng Pin 孟賁
Miao 苗
Mikami Sanji 三上参次
Minamoto no Yoritomo 源頼朝
Ming T'ai-tsu 明太祖
minshūshi 民衆史
Mitogaku 水戸学
Miyake Kanran 三宅観瀾
Miyazaki Sachimaro 宮崎幸麿
Mommu (emperor) 文武
Momonoi Kyūma 桃井久馬
Mondō sho 問答書
Mononobe 物部
Mōri 毛利

Motoori Norinaga　本居宣長

mou　畝

Mu-yeh　莫邪

muhon　謀叛

muhonnin　謀叛人

Murakami-Genji　村上源氏

Murao Jirō　村尾次郎

Murase Gunji　村瀬郡司
　　　Kiyozaemon Tamekiyo
　　　村瀬清左衛門為清
　　　Kiyozaemon Tamenobu　為信

Muro Kyūsō　室鳩巣

Muromachi bakufu　室町幕府

Nakajima Kumakichi　中島久万吉

Nakatomi　中臣

Nawa Nagatoshi　名和長年

nengō　年号

Nihon shoki　日本書紀

Ninigi no mikoto　瓊瓊杵命

Ninnaji　仁和寺

Nishikawa Joken　西川如見

Nitta Yoshisada　新田義貞

nobori　上り

nōhei　農兵

Nozawa Sawaemon　野沢沢右
衛門
　　　Tarōzaemon　太郎左衛門

nuhi　奴婢

Ōama (prince)　大海

Obata　小幡

Oda Nobuhide　織田信栄
　　　Nobukuni　信邦
　　　Nobunaga　信長

ōdai　王代

ōdō　王道

ōdo ōmin　王土王民

Ogyū Sorai　荻生徂徠

Ōjin (emperor)　応神

Okada Keisuke　岡田啓介

okappiki　岡引

Ōoka Tadamitsu　大岡忠光
　　　Tadasuke　忠相

Ōshio Heihachirō　大塩平八郎

Otokoyama-Yawata　男山八幡

Ōtomo (clan)　大友

Ōtomo (prince)　大伴

Ototachibana　弟橘媛

Pan Ku　班固

pi-chien-shou　比肩獣

pi-yi-niao　比翼鳥

p'i (stagnation)　否

Po Lo　伯楽

Po-ssu　波斯

Rai Sanyō　頼山陽

Rangakusha　蘭学者

renkoku no moto　輦轂の下

Ritsu　律

riyō kōsei　利用厚生

rōjū　老中

rōnin　浪人

ryō　両

Ryōgoku　両国

Ryū　柳

Ryūō　竜王

Ryūshi shinron　柳子新論

sakan　大目

Sakanoue no Tamuramaro　坂上田
　　　村麻呂

Sakaori　酒折

Sakatomi Masakage　鈇富昌景

sakayaki no daijin　月代の大臣

sakoku　鎖国

Sango　産語

seii taishōgun　征夷大将軍

Seikei tōta　星経淘汰

Seimeiron　正名論

Seimu (emperor)　成務

Seiwa (emperor)　清和

sengoku　戦国

sengoku no sei　戦国の制

sesshō 摂政

Shang 商

Shang-han lun 傷寒論

Shao 召

Shih chi 史記

shikibu 式部

Shimabara 島原

Shimane 島根

Shimazu 島津

shimin 四民

Shimōsa 下総

shinchoku 神勅

Shinkokinshū 新古今集

Shinohara 篠原

Shinron 新論

shishi 志士

Shittan moji kō 悉曇文字考

Shizen shin'ei dō 自然真営道

shōbu 尚武

shōen 荘園

shōkoku 勝国

shokunin 職人

Shōmu (emperor) 聖武

shōri 正理

Shōtoku (female sovereign) 称徳

Shōtoku Taishi 聖徳太子

Shōwa 昭和

Shu 蜀

Shu-sun T'ung 叔孫通

shugo 守護

Shun 舜

Shuo yuan 説苑

Soga 蘇我

sōhatsu 総髪

Songō 尊号

sonnō 尊王

sōshi 草紙

Ssu-ma Ch'ien 司馬遷

      Kuang 光

Ssu-shih 司市

Sugawara no Michizane 菅原道真

Sugita Gempaku 杉田玄白

Suiko (female sovereign) 推古

suke 介

sukegō 助郷

sun (decrease) 損

Sun Tzu 孫子

Sung 宋

T'ai (Mt.) 泰

t'ai (security) 泰

T'ai Chia 太甲

Taiheiki 太平記

Taihō 大宝

Taika 大化

Taira no Kiyomori 平清盛

       Masakado 将門

taisei 大政

Taishō 大正

Taishōgun 大将軍

Tajima-dayū 但馬太夫

Takatenjin 高天神

Takeda Katsuyori 竹田勝頼

Takenouchi Shikibu 竹内式部

Takkoku no Iwa 達谷窟

Takumi no kami 内匠頭

Tanaka Takashi 田中卓

T'ang (dynasty) 唐

T'ang (king) 湯

T'ang (sage) 湯

Tao te ching 道徳経

Tayū (-dayū) 太夫

Temmu (emperor) 天武

Tendai 天台

ten'i 天意

tenka 天下

Tenkei hatsumō 天経発蒙

Tenji (emperor) 天智

Tenjin-sama 天神様

tennō shinsei 天皇親政

T'ien-ching huo-wen 天経或問

tōbaku 倒幕

Tokiwabashi 常盤橋

Tokutomi Sohō 徳富蘇峰

tono (-dono) 殿

Toyosatomimi no mikoto　豊聡
　耳皇
tozama　外様
Tso chuan　左伝
Tsuchimikado　土御門
Tsuda Sōkichi　津田左右吉
tsui/sui　椎／推
tsuiro　椎魯
Tsunayoshi　綱吉
Tung Chung-shu　董仲舒
Tzu-hsia　子夏
Tzu-lu　子路
Tzu-yu　子游

Usui　碓氷
Utsunomiya Mokurin　宇都宮黙霖

wakadoshiyori　若年寄
Wang Chu　王蠋
Wani/Wang Jen　王仁
Warashina Shōhaku　藁科松伯
Watsuji Tetsurō　和辻哲郎
Wei (duke)　衛
Wei (state)　魏
Wen-yen　文言
Wu Huo　烏獲

yabuhebi　藪蛇
Yamada Yoshio　山田孝雄
Yamaga Sokō　山鹿素行
Yamagata Daini　山県大弐
　　Ichirōzaemon　一郎左衛門
　　Itsuki　斎宮
　　Masasada　昌貞
　　Taika　大華
　　Yamasaburō　山三郎
Yamagata jinja　山県神社
Yamaguchi-gumi　山口組

Yamanashi　山梨
Yamashiro　山城
Yamato　大和
Yamatotakeru　日本武
Yamazaki Ansai　山崎闇斎
Yao　尭
Yaso no oshie　耶蘇の教
Yen　燕
Yi Yin　伊尹
Yin (dynasty)　殷
yin-yang　陰陽
Yōmei (emperor)　用明
Yonai Mitsumasa　米内光政
yonaoshi　世直
Yonezawa　米沢
yoriki　与力
Yosa Buson　与謝蕪村
Yoshida Sadafusa　吉田定房
　　　Gemba　玄番
　　　Shōin　松陰
Yoshimune　吉宗
Yoshino　吉野
Yoshino-Anō　吉野賀名生
Yōzei (emperor)　陽成
Yu I　游藝
Yu Meng　優孟
Yu　禹
Yu chien p'ien　玉鈴篇
Yuan　元
Yueh　越
Yui Shōsetsu　由井正雪
Yūki Chikatomo　結城親朝
yūmin　遊民
Yusa Bokusai　遊佐木斎

za　座
zuryō　受領

Bibliography

All Japanese publishers are in Tokyo unless otherwise shown.

Primary Sources

Arai Hakuseki 新井白石. *Buke kan'i shōzoku kō* 武家官位装束考. In Ichijima Kenkichi, 市島健吉, ed., *Arai Hakuseki zenshū* 新井白石全集, vol. 6, n.p., 1907, pp. 465–481.

———. *Dokushi yoron* 読史余論. In Matsumura Akira 松村明 et al., eds., *NST 35: Arai Hakuseki* 日本思想大系 35 新井白石. Iwanami shoten 岩波書店, 1975, pp. 183–431.

———. *Oritaku shibanoki* 折たく柴の記. In Odaka Toshio 小高敏郎 and Matsumura Akira, eds., *NKBT 95: Taionki, Oritaku shibanoki, Rantō kotohajime* 日本古典文学大系95 戴恩記折たく柴の記 蘭東事始. Iwanami shoten, 1964, pp. 147–450.

Asaka Tampaku 安積澹泊. *Dainihonshi sansō.* 大日本史賛藪. In Matsumoto Sannosuke 松本三之介 and Ogura Yoshihiko 小倉芳彦, eds., *NST 48: Kinsei shiron shū* 日本思想大系 48 近世史論集. Iwanami shoten, 1974, pp. 11–319.

Buyō Inshi 武陽隠士. *Seji kembun roku* 世事見聞録. In Harada Tomohiko 原田伴彦, ed., *Nihon shomin seikatsu shiryō shūsei* 日本庶民生活資料集成 vol. 8, San'ichi shobō 三一書房, 1979.

Chikamatsu Monzaemon 近松門左衛門. *Kokusenya kassen* 国性爺合戦. In Shuzui Kenji 守随憲治 and Ōkubo Tadakuni 大久保忠国, eds., *NKBT 50: Chikamatsu jōruri shū ge* 日本古典文学大系 50 近松浄瑠璃集 下. Iwanami shoten, 1959, pp. 227–292.

———. *Yōmei tennō shokunin kagami* 用明天皇職人鑑. In Shuzui Kenji and Ōkubo Tadakuni, eds., *NKBT 50: Chikamatsu jōruri shū ge.* Iwanami shoten, 1959, pp. 57–120.

Date Chihiro 伊達千広. *Taisei santenkō* 大勢三転考. In Matsumoto Sannosuke and Ogura Yoshihiko, eds., *NST 48: Kinsei shiron shū.* Iwanami shoten, 1974, pp. 385–461.

Dazai Shundai 太宰春台. *Akō shijū roku shi ron* 赤穂四十六士論. In Ishii Shirō 石井紫郎, ed., *NST 27: Kinsei buke shisō* 近世武家思想. Iwanami shoten, 1974, pp. 404–411.

————. *Bendōsho* 弁道書. In Inoue Tetsujirō 井上哲次郎 and Kanie Yoshimaru 蟹江義丸, eds., *Nihon rinri ihen 6: Kogakuha no bu, ge* 日本倫理彙編 6 古学派の部 下. Ikuseikai 育成会, 1902, pp. 204–299.

————. *Bunkai zakki* 文会雑記. In Hayakawa Junzaburo 早川純三郎, ed., *Nihon zuihitsu taisei* 日本随筆大成, vol. 7. Yoshikawa kōbunkan 吉川弘文館, 1927, pp. 551–711.

————. *Keizai roku* 経済録. In Takimoto Seiichi 滝本誠一, ed., *NKS 6* 日本経済叢書 6. Nihon keizai sōsho kankōkai 日本経済叢書刊行会, 1914, pp. 1–286.

————. *Sango* 産語. In Takimoto Seiichi, ed., *NKS 6*. Nihon keizai sōsho kankōkai, 1914, pp. 309–369.

Fujita Yūkoku 藤田幽谷. "Seimeiron" 正名論. In Kikuchi Kenjirō 菊地謙二郎, ed., *Yūkoku zenshū* 幽谷全集. Kōbunsha insatsusho 康文社印刷所, 1940.

Fukuchi Gen'ichirō 福地源一郎. *Yamagata Daini* 山県大弐. Shun'yōdō 春陽堂, 1892.

Fukunaga Mitsuji 福永光司, ed. *Sōshi gaihen, jō, chū, ge* 荘子外篇 上中下. 3 vols. *Chūgoku kotensen 13, 14, 15: Sōshi gaihen* 中国古典選13, 14, 15 荘子外篇. Asahi shimbunsha 朝日新聞社, 1978.

————, ed. *Sōshi naihen* 荘子内篇. *Chūgoku kotensen 12: Sōshi naihen* 中国古典選 12 荘子内篇. Asahi shimbunsha, 1978.

————, ed. *Sōshi zappen jō, ge* 荘子雑篇 上下. 2 vols. *Chūgoku kotensen 16, 17: Sōshi zappen* 中国古典選 16, 17 荘子雑篇. Asahi shimbunsha, 1978.

————, ed. *Rōshi jō, ge* 老子 上下. 2 vols. *Chūgoku kotensen 10, 11: Rōshi* 中国古典選10, 11 老子. Asahi shimbunsha, 1978.

Gamō Kumpei. 蒲生君平 "Bengiroku" 弁疑録. In Hirose Kōichi 広瀬広一, ed., *YDSJS* 山県大弐先生事蹟考資料. Kōfu 甲府: Shōkokumin shimbunsha 少国民新聞社, 1931, pp. 25–29.

————. "Kaien yawa" 解冤夜話. In Hirose Kōichi, ed., *YDSJS*, pp. 24–25.

Gomizuno-o 後水尾. "Shinkan gokyōkun sho" 宸翰御教訓書. In Miura Tōsaku 三浦藤作, ed., *Rekidai shōchoku zenshū* 暦代詔勅全集. Vol. 4. Kawade shobō 河出書房, 1941, pp. 198–199.

Gotō Tanji 後藤丹治, Okami Masao 岡見正雄, and Kamata Kisaburō 釜田喜三郎, eds., *Taiheiki jō, chū, ge* 太平記 上中下. 3 vols. In *NKBT 34, 35, 36: Taiheiki* 日本古典文学大系 34, 35, 36 太平記. Iwanami shoten, 1960–1962.

Gunji Masakatsu 郡司正勝, ed. *Kanjinchō* 勧進帳. In *NKBT 98: Kabuki jūhachiban shū* 日本古典文学大系98 歌舞伎十八番集. Iwanami shoten, 1965, pp. 176–192.

Hayashiya Tatsusaburō 林屋辰三郎 et al., eds. *Shiryō taikei Nihon rekishi 4: Kinsei I* 史料大系日本歴史 4 近世 I. 8 vols. Osaka: Osaka shoseki 大阪書籍, 1977–1981.

Hiraga Gennai 平賀源内. *Fūryū shidōken den* 風流志道軒伝. In Nakamura Yukihiko 中村幸彦, ed., *NKBT 55: Fūrai sanjin shū* 日本古典文学大系 55 風来山人集. Iwanami shoten, 1961, pp. 152–224.

Hirose Kōichi 広瀬広一, ed. *YDSJS* 山県大弐先生事蹟考資料. Kōfu 甲府: Shōkokumin shimbunsha 少国民新聞社, 1931.

Honda Wataru 本田済, ed. *Eki* 易. *Shintei Chūgoku kotensen 1: Eki* 新訂中国古典選 1 易. Asahi shimbunsha, 1966.

———, ed. *Chūgoku koten bungaku taikei 13: Kanjo, Gokanjo, Sangokushi retsuden sen* 中国古典文学大系 13 漢書後漢書 三国史烈伝選. Heibonsha 平凡社, 1968.

Hori Keizan 堀景山. *Fujingen* 不尽言. In Takimoto Seiichi, ed., *NKS 11*. Nihon keizai sōsho kankōkai, 1915, pp. 271–355.

Hosokawa Morisada 細川護貞. *Hosokawa nikki jō, ge* 細川日記 上下. 2 vols. Chūōkōronsha 中央公論社, 1989.

Ichihara Kyōkichi 市原亨吉, Imai Kiyoshi 今井清, and Suzuki Ryūichi 鈴木隆一, eds. *Raiki jō, chū, ge* 礼記上中下. 3 vols. *Zenshaku Kambun taikei 12, 13, 14: Raiki* 全釈漢文大系 12, 13, 14 礼記. Shūeisha 集英社, 1976–1979.

Ichii Saburō, *Rekishi no shimpo towa nanika* 歴史の進歩とは何か. Iwanami shoten, 1971.

Ichiko Teiji 市古貞治 and Ōshima Tatehiko 大島健彦, eds. *NKBT 88: Soga Monogatari* 日本古典文学大系 88 曽我物語. Iwanami shoten, 1966.

Ikeda Suetoshi 池田末利, ed. *Shōsho* 尚書. *Zenshaku Kambun taikei 11: Shōsho* 全釈漢文大系 11 尚書. Shūeisha, 1976.

Inoue Mitsusada 井上光貞 et al., eds. *Ritsu* 律. In *NST 3: Ritsu-ryō* 日本思想大系 3 律令. Iwanami shoten, 1976, pp. 16–484.

Ishida Ichirō 石田一良 and Kanaya Osamu 金谷治, eds. *NST 28: Fujiwara Seika, Hayashi Razan* 日本思想大系 28 藤原惺窩 林羅山. Iwanami shoten, 1975.

Ishii Shirō 石井紫郎, ed. *Buke shohatto* 武家諸法度. *NST 27: Kinsei buke shisō* 日本思想大系 27 近世武家思想. Iwanami shoten, 1974, pp. 454–462.

Jien 慈円. *Gukanshō* 愚管抄. In Okami Masao 岡見正雄 and Akamatsu Toshihide 赤松俊秀, eds., *NKBT 86: Gukanshō* 日本古典文学大系 86 愚管抄. Iwanami shoten, 1967.

Kajiwara Masaaki, 梶原正昭, ed. *Gikeiki* 義経記. In *Nihon koten bungaku zenshū 31: Gikeiki* 日本古典文学大系 31 義経記. Shōgakkan 小学館, 1971.

Kamata Tadashi 鎌田正 et al., eds. *Saden* 左伝. *Shinshaku Kambun taikei 30–33: Shunjū sashiden* 新釈漢文大系 30–33 春秋左氏伝. Meiji shoin 明治書院, 1971–1981.

Kanaya Osamu 金谷治, ed. *Mōshi* 孟子. *Shintei Chūgoku kotensen 5: Mōshi* 新訂中国古典選 5 孟子. Asahi shimbunsha, 1966.

————. *Sonshi* 孫子. Iwanami shoten, 1963.

Kanaya Osamu 金谷治, Sagawa Osamu 佐川修, and Machida Saburō 町田三郎, eds. *Junshi jō, ge* 荀子 上下. 2 vols. *Zenshaku Kambun taikei 7-8: Junshi* 全釈漢文大系 7, 8 荀子, Shūeisha, 1973–1974.

Kawakami Kizō 川上喜蔵, ed. *Utsunomiya Mokurin, Yoshida Shōin ōfuku shokan* 宇都宮黙霖 吉田松陰 往復書翰. Kinseisha 錦正社, 1972.

Kishi Shōzō 貴志正造, ed. *Zen'yaku Azuma kagami* 全訳吾妻鏡. 2 vols. Shin jimbutsu ōraisha 新人物往来社, 1979.

Kitabatake Chikafusa 北畠親房. *Jinnō shōtōki* 神皇正統記. In Iwasa Tadashi 岩佐正 et al., eds., *NKBT 87: Jinnō Shōtōki, Masukagami* 日本古典文学大系 87 神皇正統記 増鏡. Iwanami shoten, 1965, pp. 37–211.

Kondō Keizō 近藤圭造, ed. "Yamagata Daini oshioki ikken" 山県大弐御士置一件. In his *Kaitei shiseki shūran* 改訂史籍集覧, vol. 16, Kondō kappansho 近藤活版所, 1902, pp. 399–406.

Kondō Mitsuo 近藤光男, ed. *Sengokusaku jō, chū, ge* 戦国策 上中下. 3 vols. *Zenshaku Kambun taikei 23, 24, 25: Sengokusaku* 全釈漢文大系 23, 24, 25 戦国策. Shūeisha, 1975–1979.

Kōno Yukitaka 河野幸孝, ed. *Yamagata jinja shi* 山県神社誌. Tsukagawa meibun sha 塚川明文社, 1972.

Konoe Fumimaro 近衛文麿. *Ushinawareshi seiji* 失はれし政治. Asahi shimbunsha 朝日新聞社, 1951.

Kumazawa Banzan 熊沢蕃山. *Shūgi washo* 集義和書. In Gotō Yōichi 後藤陽一 and Tomoeda Ryūtarō 友枝竜太郎, eds., *NST 30: Kumazawa Banzan* 日本思想大系 30 熊沢蕃山. Iwanami shoten, 1971, pp. 7–403.

Kuriyama Sempō 粟山潜鋒. *Hōken taiki* 保建大記. In Matsumoto Sannosuke and Ogura Yoshihiko, eds., *NST 48: Kinsei shiron shū*. Iwanami shoten, 1974, pp. 321–348.

Kusaka Genzui 久坂玄瑞. "Shisai takuroku" 俟采擇錄. In Fukumoto Yoshisuke 福本義亮, ed., *Kusaka Genzui zenshū* 久坂玄瑞全集. Tokuyama 徳山: Matsuno shoten マツノ書店, 1978.

Meiwa fudoki 明和風土記. Manuscript in the University of Tokyo Library.

Motoori Norinaga 本居宣長. *Hihon tamakushige* 秘本玉くしげ. In Ōkubo Tadashi 大久保正, ed., *Motoori Norinaga zenshū* 本居宣長全集. Vol. 8. Chikuma shobō 筑摩書房, 1972, pp. 327–369.

————. Letter to Hagiwara Motoe 萩原元克. In Ōkubo Tadashi, ed., *Motoori Norinaga zenshū*, vol. 17, pp. 109–110.

Muro Kyūsō 室鳩巣. *Akō gijin roku* 赤穂義人録. In Ishii Shirō, ed., *NST 27: Kinsei buke shisō*. Iwanami shoten, 1974, pp. 272–342.

————. "Yusa Jirōzaemon ni kotauru no sho" 遊佐次郎左衛門に答ふるの書. In Araki Kengo 荒木見吾 and Inoue Tadashi 井上忠, eds., *NST 34: Kaibara Ekken, Muro Kyūsō* 日本思想大系 34 具原益軒室鳩巣. Iwanami shoten, 1970, pp. 233–253.

Nagasawa Kikuya 長沢規矩也, ed. *Nan pei ch'ao k'an pen Erh ya* 南北朝刊本爾雅. Kyūko shoin 汲古書院, 1973.

———, ed. *Wakokubon seishi Kanjo* 和刻本正史漢書. 2 vols. Kyūko shoin, 1972.

Nishikawa Joken 西川如見. *Chōnin bukuro* 町人裏. In Nakamura Yukihio 中村幸彦, ed., *NST 59: Kinsei chōnin shisō* 日本思想大系 59 近世町人思想. Iwanami shoten, 1975, pp. 85-173.

Numata Jirō 沼田次郎, et al. eds. *NST 64: Yōgaku jō* 日本思想大系 64 洋学 上. Iwanami shoten, 1976.

Ogyū Sorai 荻生徂徠. *Rongochō* 論語徵. In Imanaka Kanji 今中寛司 and Naramoto Tatsuya 奈良本辰也, eds., *Ogyū Sorai zenshū* 荻生徂徠全集. Vol. 2. Kawade shobō shinsha 河出書房新社, 1978, pp. 9-365.

———. *Seidan* 政談. In Yoshikawa Kōjirō 吉川幸次郎 et al., eds., *NST 36: Ogyū Sorai* 日本思想大系 36 荻生徂徠. Iwanami shoten, 1973, pp. 257-445.

———. *Sorai sensei tōmonsho* 徂徠先生答問書. In Imanaka Kanji and Naramoto Tatsuya, eds., *Ogyū Sorai zenshū*. Vol. 6. Kawade shobō shinsha, 1973, pp. 167-214.

———. *Sorai shū* 徂徠集. In Yoshikawa Kōjirō et al., eds., *NST 36: Ogyū Sorai*. Iwanami shoten, 1973, pp. 487-546.

———. "Utsunomiya Sankin ni atauru sho" 宇都宮三近に与ふる書. In Bitō Masahide 尾藤正英, ed., *Nihon no meicho 16: Ogyū Sorai* 日本の名著 16 荻生徂徠. Chūōkōronsha, 1974, pp. 283-285.

———. "Yakusha kiyaku" 訳社規約. In Bitō Masahide, ed., *Nihon no meicho 16: Ogyū Sorai*. Chūōkōronsha, 1974, pp. 238-240.

Ōshio Heihachirō 大塩平八郎. *Gekibun* 檄文. In Okamoto Ryōichi 岡本良一, *Ōshio Heihachirō* 大塩平八郎. Sōgensha, 創元社, 1975, pp. 101-104.

Rai Sanyō 頼三陽. *Nihon seiki* 日本政記. In Uete Michiari 植手通有, ed. *NST 49: Rai Sanyō* 日本思想大系 49 頼三陽. Iwanami shoten, 1977.

Sakamoto Tarō 坂本太郎 et al., eds. *NKBT 67, 68: Nihon shoki jō, ge* 日本古典文学大系 67, 68 日本書記 上下. 2 vols. Iwanami shoten, 1967.

Shimada Kenji 島田虔二, ed. *Daigaku, Chūyō* 大学中庸. *Shintei Chūgoku kotensen 4: Daigaku, Chūyō* 新訂中国古典選 4 大学中庸. Asahi shimbunsha, 1967.

Sugita Gempaku 杉田玄白. *Nochimigusa* 後見草. In Mori Senzō, 森銑三, ed., *Enseki jisshū* 燕石十種. Vol. 2. Chūōkōronsha, 1979, pp. 107-153.

———. *Yasō dokugo* 野叟独語. In Numata Jirō et al., eds., *NST 64: Yōgaku jō*. Iwanami shoten, 1976, pp. 291-313.

Takeuchi Teruo 竹内照夫, ed. *Kampishi jō, ge* 韓非子 上下. 2 vols. *Shin-*

shaku Kambun taikei 11, 12: Kampishi 新釈漢文大系 11, 12 韓非子.
Meiji shoin, 1960–1964.

Takizawa Bakin 滝沢馬琴. Koike Tōgoro 小池藤五郎, ed., *Nansō Satomi hakken den* 南総里見八犬伝. 8 vols. Iwanami shoten, 1937.

Tsukamoto Tetsuzō 塚本哲三, ed. *Shikyō, Shokyō, Ekikyō* 詩経 書経 易経. Yūhōdō 有朋堂, 1924.

Yamada Yoshio 山田孝雄 et al., eds. *NKBT 23: Konjaku monogatari 2* 日本古典文学大系 23 今昔物語 2. Iwanami Shoten, 1960.

Yamaga Sokō 山鹿素行. *Takkyo dōmon* 謫居童問. In Hirose Yutaka 広瀬豊, ed., *Yamaga Sokō zenshū shisō hen* 山鹿素行全集思想篇. Vol. 12. Iwanami shoten, 1940, vol. 12, pp. 14–495.

———. *Takkyo zuihitsu* 謫居随筆. In Hirose Yutaka, ed., *Yamaga Sokō zenshū shisō hen*. Vol. 12. Iwanami shoten, 1940.

Yamagata Daini 山県大弐. *Ryūshi shinron* 柳子新論. In Inoue Tetsujirō 井上哲次郎 and Kanie Yoshimaru 蟹江義丸, eds. *Nihon rinri ihen 7: Shūshi gakuha no bu, jō* 日本倫理彙編 7 朱子学の部 上. Ikuseikai 育成会, 1902, pp. 584–618.

———. *Ryūshi shinron*. In Kawaura Genchi 川浦玄智, ed., *Ryūshi shinron*. Iwanami bunko, 1943, pp. 15–143.

———. *Ryūshi shinron*. In Naramoto Tatsuya 奈良本辰也, ed., *NST 38: Kinsei seidō ron* 日本思想大系 38 近世政道論. Iwanami shoten, 1976, pp. 391–419.

———. *Ryūshi shinron*. In Nishida Taichirō 西田太一郎, ed., *NS 17: Fujiwara Seika, Nakae Tōju, Kumazawa Banzan, Yamazaki Ansai, Yamaga Sokō, Yamagata Daini shū* 日本の思想 17 藤原惺窩 中江藤樹 熊沢蕃山 山崎闇斎 山鹿素行 山県大弐集. Chikuma shobō, 1970, pp. 341–428.

———. *Ryūshi shinron*. In Takimoto Seiichi, ed., *NKS*, vol. 26. Nihon keizai sōsho kankōkai, 1915, pp. 63–102.

Yamaguchi-ken kyōikukai 山口県教育会, ed. *Yoshida Shōin zenshū* 吉田松陰全集. 12 vols. Iwanami shoten, 1940.

Yoshikawa Kōjirō 吉川幸次郎, ed. *Rongo jō, ge* 論語 上下. 2 vols. *Shintei Chūgoku kotensen 2, 3: Rongo* 新訂中国古典選 2, 3 論語. Asahi shimbunsha, 1965.

Yusa Bokusai 遊佐木斎. *Yusa Bokusai shokan* 遊佐木斎書簡. In Araki Kengo and Inoue Tadashi, eds., *NST 34: Kaibara Ekken, Muro Kyūsō*. Iwanami shoten, 1970, pp. 341–386.

Secondary Sources

Ackroyd, Joyce, trans. *Lessons from History: Arai Hakuseki's Tokushi Yoron*. St. Lucia: University of Queensland Press, 1982.

———. *Told Round a Brushwood Fire: the Autobiography of Arai Hakuseki*. Princeton: Princeton University Press, 1979.

Akamatsu Toshihide 赤松俊秀. "Kaisetsu" 解説. In Okami Masao and Akamatsu Toshihide, eds., *NKBT 86: Gukanshō*. Iwanami shoten, 1967, pp. 3–34.

Aoki Kōji 青木虹二. *Hyakushō ikki no sōgō nenpyō* 百姓一揆の総合年表. San'ichi shobō 三一書房, 1975.

Asao Naohiro 朝尾直弘 "Bakuhansei to tennō" 幕藩制と天皇. In *TNKS 3: Kinsei* 大系日本国家史 3 近世. Tokyo daigaku shuppankai 東京大学出版会, 1975, pp. 187 – 222.

Beasley, W. G. *The Meiji Restoration*. Stanford: Stanford University Press, 1972.

Beckmann, George M. *The Making of the Meiji Constitution*. Westport, Conn.: Greenwood Press, 1975.

Bitō Masahide 尾藤正英. "Arai Hakuseki no rekishi shisō" 新井白石の歴史思想. In Matsumura Akira et al., eds., *NST 35: Arai Hakuseki*. Iwanami shoten, 1975, pp. 555–568.

———. "Dazai Shundai no hito to shisō" 太宰春台の人と思想. In Rai Tsutomu 頼惟勤, ed., *NST 37: Sorai gakuha* 日本思想大系 37 徂徠学派. Iwanami shoten, 1972, pp. 487–514.

———. *Nihon no rekishi 19: Genroku jidai* 日本の歴史 19 元禄時代. Shōgakkan 小学館, 1975.

———. "Sonnō jōi shisō" 尊王攘夷思想. In *IKNR 13: Kinsei 5* 岩波講座日本歴史 13 近世 5. Iwanami shoten, 1977, pp. 41–86.

Borgen, Robert. *Sugawara no Michizane and the Early Heian Court*. Cambridge: Harvard University Press, 1986.

Brown, Delmer. *Nationalism in Japan*. New York: Russell & Russell, 1971.

Brown, Delmer, and Ishida, Ichirō, trans. *The Future and the Past*. Berkeley and Los Angeles: University of California Press, 1979.

Chan, Wing-tsit, ed. *A Sourcebook of Chinese Philosophy*. Princeton: Princeton University Press, 1963.

Creel, Herlee G. *What Is Taoism?* Chicago: University of Chicago Press, 1970.

Earl, David Magarey. *Emperor and Nation in Japan: Political Thinkers in the Tokugawa Period*. Seattle: University of Washington Press, 1964.

Fukaya Katsumi 深谷克己. "Bakuhansei kokka to tennō" 幕藩制国家と天皇. In Kitajima Masamoto 北島正元, ed., *Bakuhansei kokka seiritsu katei no kenkyū* 幕藩制国家成立過程の研究. Yoshikawa kōbunkan 吉川弘文館, 1978, pp. 221–274.

———. "Kinsei no shōgun to tennō" 近世の将軍と天皇. In Rekishigaku kenkyūkai 歴史学研究会 and Nihonshi kenkyūkai 日本史研究会, eds., *KNR 6: Kinsei 6* 講座日本歴史 6 近世 6. Tokyo daigaku shuppankai 東京大学出版会, 1985, pp. 45–77.

———. "Ryōshu kenryoku to buke kan'i" 領主権力と武家官位. In Fukaya Katsumi and Katō Eiichi 加藤栄一, eds., *KNKS 1: Bakuhansei kokka no seiritsu* 講座日本近世史 I 幕藩制国家の成立. Yuikaku 有斐閣, 1981.

Gauntlett, John Owen, trans. *Kokutai no Hongi: Cardinal Principles of the National Entity of Japan*. Cambridge: Harvard University Press, 1949.

Hall, John. *Tanuma Okitsugu: Forerunner of Modern Japan*. Cambridge: Harvard University Press, 1955.

Harootunian, H. D. *Toward Restoration*. Berkeley and Los Angeles: University of California Press, 1970.

Hayashi Fusao 林房雄 and Kobayashi Hideo 小林秀雄. "Rekishi ni tsuite" 歴史について. In Koyama Atsuhiko 小山敦彦, ed., *Fukuroku ban: Shōwa daizasshi senchū hen* 復録版昭和大雑誌戦中篇. Ryūdō shuppan 流動出版, 1978, pp. 110-121.

Hayashi Motoi 林基. "Hōreki-Tenmei ki no shakai jōsei" 宝暦天明期の社会状勢. In *IKNR 11: Kinsei 4* 岩波講座日本歴史 11 近世 4. Iwanami shoten, 1963, pp. 103-154.

Hirose Waiku 広瀬和育 and Hirose Kōichi 広瀬広一. *YDSJ* 山県大弐先生事蹟考. Kōfu 甲府: Rōgetsudō shoten 朗月堂書店, 1931.

Hori, Ichirō 堀一郎. *Wagakuni minkan shinkōshi no kenkyū* 我国民間信仰史の研究. 2 vols. Sōgen shinsha, 創元新社, 1966.

Hoshino Mamoru 星野恒. *Takenouchi Shikibu gimi jiseki kō* 竹内式部君事迹考. Fūzambō 富山房, 1899.

Hucker, Charles O. *A Dictionary of Official Titles in Imperial China*. Stanford: Stanford University Press, 1989.

Ichii Saburō 市井三郎. "Ishin henkaku no shisō" 維新変革の思想. In Shisō no kagaku kenkyūkai 思想の科学研究会, ed., *Kyōdō kenkyū Meiji ishin* 共同研究 明治維新, pp. 97-150. Tokuma shoten 徳間書店, 1967.

———. *Meiji ishin no tetsugaku* 明治維新の哲学. Kōdansha 講談社, 1967.

———. "Yamagata Daini no shisō" 山県大弐の思想. *Seikei daigaku kenkyū hōkoku* 成蹊大学研究報告 3 (March–September 1965): 1-12.

Ienaga Saburō 家永三郎. *Sensō sekinin* 戦争責任. Iwanami shoten, 1985.

Iizuka Shigetake 飯塚重威. *Yamagata Daini seiden* 山県大弐正伝. Mitsui shuppan 三井出版, 1943.

Imanaka Kanji 今中寛司. "Ryūshi shinron to sono shisōshiteki keiretsu ni tsuite" 柳子新論とその思想史的系列について. *Bunka shigaku* 文化史学 15 (1960): 50-63.

Inoue Kiyoshi 井上清. *Nihon gendaishi I: Meiji ishin* 日本現代史 I 明治維新. Tokyo daigaku shuppankai 東京大学出版会, 1951.

Irokawa Daikichi 色川大吉. *Meiji no seishin* 明治の精神. Chikuma shobō 筑摩書房, 1968.

Ishii Ryōsuke 石井良助. *Shimpen Edo jidai mampitsu jō, ge* 新編江戸時代漫筆上下. 2 vols. Asahi shimbunsha, 1979.

————. *Tennō: Tennō tōchi no shiteki kaimei* 天皇 天皇統治の史的解明. Kōbundō 弘文堂, 1950.

Ishii Susumu 石井進. *Nihon no rekishi 7: Kamakura bakufu* 日本の歴史 7 鎌倉幕府. Chūōkōronsha, 1965.

Itō Takashi 伊藤隆 and Ōe Shinobu 大江志乃夫. "Rekishiteki 'sekinin' no shozai" 歴史的「責任」の所在. *Asahi jaanaru* 朝日ジャーナル (25 Jan. 1989): 43–49.

Iwahashi Junsei 岩橋遵成. *Sorai kenkyū* 徂徠研究. Meicho kankōkai 名著刊行会, 1969.

Kamata Shigeo 鎌田重雄. *Dare nimo wakaru Kokutai no hongi* 誰にもわかる國體の本義. Kenkyūsha 研究社, 1944.

Keene, Donald, trans. *The Battles of Coxinga*. London: Taylor's Foreign Press, 1951.

Kidani Hōgin 木谷蓬吟. *Chikamatsu no tennō geki* 近松の天皇劇. Tanseidō shuppan 淡清堂出版, 1947.

Kinugasa Yasuki 衣笠安喜. "Buke shohatto no ideorogii" 武家諸法度のイデオロギー. *RK 歴史公論* 2(4) (April 1976): 82–93.

————. *Kinsei jugaku shisōshi no kenkyū* 近世儒学思想史の研究. Hōsei daigaku shuppankyoku 法政大学出版局, 1976.

Kiryū Yūyū 桐生悠々. *Chikushōdō no chikyū* 畜生道の地球. Chūōkōronsha 中央公論社, 1989.

Kitajima Masamoto 北島正元, ed. *Taikei Nihonshi sōsho: Seijishi II* 大系日本史叢書政治史 II. Yamakawa shuppan, 1965.

Kitayama Shigeo 北山茂夫. *Nihon no rekishi 4: Heian-kyō* 日本の歴史 4 平安京. Chūōkōronsha, 1965.

Kodama Kōta 児玉幸多. "Mibun to kazoku" 身分と家族, In *IKNR 10: Kinsei 2* 岩波講座日本歴史 10 近世 2. Iwanami shoten, 1963, pp. 225–271.

————. *Nihon no rekishi 18: Daimyō* 日本の歴史 18 大名. Shōgakkan, 1975.

Koyama Atsuhiko 小山敦彦, ed. *Fukuroku ban Shōwa daizasshi, senchū hen* 復録版昭和大雑誌 戦中篇. Ryūdō shuppan 流動出版, 1978.

Lau, D. C., trans. *Confucius: The Analects*. Middlesex: Penguin Books, 1979.

————. *Mencius*. Middlesex: Penguin Books, 1970.

————. *Lao Tzu: Tao Te Ching*. Middlesex: Penguin Books, 1963.

Maruyama, Masao 丸山真男. *Nihon seiji shisōshi kenkyū* 日本政治思想史研究. Tokyo daigaku shuppankai 東京大学出版会, 1952.

————. *Studies in the Intellectual History of Tokugawa Japan*. Translated by Mikiso Hane. University of Tokyo Press, 1974.

Mase Kumiko 間瀬久美子. "Kinsei no minshū to tennō" 近世の民衆と天皇. In Fujii Shun sensei kiju kinenkai 藤井駿先生喜寿記念会, ed., *Okayama no rekishi to bunka* 岡山の歴史と文化. Okayama: Fukutake shoten 福武書店, 1983, pp. 229–266.

Mass, Jeffrey. *Warrior Government in Early Medieval Japan*. New Haven: Yale University Press, 1974.

Matisoff, Susan, trans. *The Legend of Semimaru*. New York: Columbia University Press, 1978.

Matsumoto Sannosuke 松本三之介. *Kinsei Nihon no shisōzō* 近世日本の思想像. Kembun shuppan 研文出版, 1984.

———. *Kokugaku seiji shisō no kenkyū* 国学政治思想の研究. Miraisha 未來社, 1972.

Mikami Sanji 三上参次. *Sonnōron hattasu shi* 尊王論発達史. Fūzambō 風山房, 1941.

Mitamura Taisuke 三田村泰助. "Manshū kara kita ōchō" 満州からきた王朝. In Tamura Jitsuzō 田村実造, ed., *Sekai no rekishi 9: Saigo no Tōyōteki shakai* 世界の歴史 9 最後の東洋的社会. Chūōkōronsha 中央公論社, 1975, pp. 187–216.

Miura Tōsaku 三浦藤作, ed. *Kokutai no hongi: Seikai* 國體の本義精解. Tōyō tosho 東洋図書, 1937.

Miyagi Kimiko 宮城公子. *Ōshio Heihachirō* 大塩平八郎. Asahi shimbun-sha, 1977.

Miyaji Masato 宮地正人. *Tennōsei no seijishiteki kenkyū* 天皇制の政治史的研究. Azekura shobō 校倉書房, 1981.

Miyazaki, Ichisada. *China's Examination Hell*. Translated by Conrad Shirokauer. New Haven: Yale University Press, 1981.

Mizubayashi Takeshi 水林彪. "Bakuhan taisei ni okeru kōgi to chōtei" 幕藩体制における公儀と朝廷. In Asao Naohiro 朝尾直弘 et al., eds., *Nihon no shakai shi: Ken'i to shihai* 日本の社会史 3 権威と支配. Tokyo daigaku shuppankai 東京大学出版会, 1987.

Moriyama Shigeo 森山重雄. *Chikamatsu no tennō geki* 近松の天皇劇. San'ichi shobō, 1981.

Nagahara Keiji 永原慶二. *Kōkoku shikan* 皇国史観. Iwanami shoten, 1983.

Nagahara Keiji and Ōsumi Kazuo 大隅和雄. "Chūsei no rekishi kankaku to seiji shisō" 中世の歴史感覚と政治思想. In Nagahara Keiji, ed., *Nihon no meicho 9: Jien, Kitabatake Chikafusa* 日本の名著 9 慈円 北畠親房. Chūōkōronsha, 1971, pp. 7–64.

Najita, Tetsuo. *Japan*. Englewood Cliffs, N.J.: Prentice-Hall, 1974.

———. "Nakano Seigō and the Spirit of the Meiji Restoration in Twentieth-Century Japan." In James Morley, ed., *Dilemmas of Growth in Prewar Japan*. Princeton: Princeton University Press, 1971.

———. "Ōshio Heihachirō (1793–1837)." In Albert M. Craig and Donald H. Shively, eds., *Personality in Japanese History*. Berkeley: University of California Press, 1970.

———. "Restorationism in the Political Thought of Yamagata Daini (1725–1967)." *Journal of Asian Studies* 31(1) (November 1971): 17–30.

Nakai, Kate Wildman. "The Naturalization of Confucianism in Tokugawa Japan." *HJAS* 40(1) (June 1980): 157–199.

———. *Shogunal Politics*. Cambridge: Harvard University Press, 1988.

———. "Tokugawa Confucian Historiography." In Peter Nosco, ed., *Confucianism and Tokugawa Culture*. Princeton: Princeton University Press, 1984, pp. 62–91.

Nakamura, Takafusa. *Economic Growth in Prewar Japan*. Translated by Robert A. Feldman. New Haven: Yale University Press, 1983.

Nakayama, Shigeru. *A History of Japanese Astronomy*. Cambridge: Harvard University Press, 1969.

Naramoto Tatsuya 奈良本辰也. *Nihon no rekishi 17: Chōnin no jitsuryoku* 日本の歴史 17 町人の実力. Chūōkōronsha, 1966.

Nezu Masashi ねずまさし. *Tennō to Shōwa shi (jō, ge)* 天皇と昭和史 (上下) 2 vols. San'ichi shobō, 三一書房 1976.

Noguchi Sadao 野口定男 et al., trans. *Shiki jō, chū, ge* 史記上中下. 3 vols. *Chūgoku kotenbungaku taikei 10, 11, 12: Shiki* 中国古典文学大系 10, 11, 12 史記. Heibonsha, 1968–1971.

Noguchi Takehiko 野口武彦. "Ōdō to kakumei no aida" 王道と革命の間. *BG* 文学 44(7) (July 1976): 81–97.

———. "Tō-Bu hōbatsu no aporia" 湯武放伐のアポリア. *BG* 文学 49(7) (July 1981): 43–62.

Nosco, Peter. *Remembering Paradise*. Cambridge: Harvard University Press, 1990.

Oda Makoto 小田実. *Yonaoshi no rinri to ronri (jō, ge)* 世直しの倫理と論理 (上下). 2 vols. Iwanami shoten, 1972.

Ohnuki-Tierney, Emiko. *The Monkey as Mirror*. Princeton: Princeton University Press, 1987.

Ōishi Shinzaburō 大石慎三郎. *Edo jidai* 江戸時代. Chūōkōronsha, 1977.

———. *Nihon no rekishi 20: Bakuhansei no tenkan* 日本の歴史 20 幕藩制の転換. Shōgakkan, 1975.

———. "Nōmin tōsō yori mita Genroku-Kyōhō-Meiwa ki ni tsuite" 農民闘争よりみた元禄享保明和期について. *RGK* 歴史学研究 260 (December 1961): 14–21.

———. "Tanuma Okitsugu ni kansuru jūrai no shiryō no shimpyōsei ni tsuite" 田沼意次に関する従来の史料の信憑性ついて. *NR* 日本歴史 237 (February 1968): 24–62.

Ono Shinji 小野信二. "Bakufu to tennō" 幕府と天皇. In *IKNR 10: Kinsei 2*. Iwanami shoten, 1963, pp. 313–356.

Ooms, Herman. *Tokugawa Ideology*. Princeton: Princeton University Press, 1985.

Ōuchi Tsutomu 大内力. *Nihon no rekishi 24: Fashizumu e no michi* 日本の歴史 24 ファシズムへの道. Chūōkōronsha, 1967.

Ozawa Eiichi 小沢栄一. *Kinsei shigaku shisōshi kenkyū* 近世史学思想史研究. Yoshikawa kōbunkan, 1974.

Reischauer, Edwin O., and John K. Fairbank. *East Asia: The Great Tradition*. Boston: Houghton Mifflin, 1960.

Sansom, George. *A History of Japan: 1615–1867*. Stanford: Stanford University Press, 1963.

Sasayama Haruo 笹山晴生. *Kodai kokka to guntai* 古代国家と軍隊. Chūōkōronsha, 1975.

Satō Shin'ichi 佐藤進一. *Nihon no rekishi 9: Nambokuchō no dōran* 日本の歴史 9 南北朝の動乱. Chūōkōronsha, 1965.

Shively, Donald. "Tokugawa Tsunayoshi, the Genroku Shōgun." In Albert M. Craig and Donald H. Shively, eds., *Personality in Japanese History*. Berkeley: University of California Press, 1970.

Taga Munehaya 多賀宗隼. *Jimbutsu sōsho 15: Jien* 人物叢書 15 慈円. Yoshikawa kōbunkan, 1959.

Tahara Tsuguo 田原嗣郎. "Kinsei chūki no seiji shisō to kokka ishiki" 近世中期の政治思想と国家意識. In *IKNR 11: Kinsei 3*. Iwanami shoten, 1976, pp. 297–329.

Takahashi Hiroshi 高橋紘 and Suzuki Kunihiko 鈴木邦彦 *Tennōke no mitsushi tachi* 天皇家の密使たち. Bungei shunjūsha 文芸春秋社, 1989.

Takahashi Takashi 高橋崇. *Sakanoue no Tamuramaro* 坂上田村麻呂. Yoshikawa kōbunkan, 1959.

Takano Toshihiko 高埜利彦. "Bakuhan taisei ni okeru kashoku to ken'i" 幕藩体制における家職と権威. In Asao Naohiro et al., eds., *Nihon no shakaishi 3: Ken'i to shihai*. Tokyo Daigaku shuppankai, 1987, pp. 234–276.

Tokutomi Iichirō (Sohō) 徳富猪一郎(蘇峰). *Kinsei Nihon kokuminshi 22: Hōreki-Meiwa hen* 近世日本国民史 22 宝暦明和篇. Meiji shoin 明治書院, 1936.

———. *Kinsei Nihon kokuminshi 23: Tanuma jidai* 近世日本国民史 23 田沼時代. Meiji shoin, 1936.

Tōyama Shigeki 遠山茂樹. *Meiji ishin* 明治維新. Iwanami shoten, 1951.

———. "Watashi no rekishi kenkyū to tennōsei" 私の歴史研究と天皇制. *Gendai to shisō* 現代と思想 15 (March 1974): 118–120.

Tsuji Tatsuya 辻達也. *Ōoka Echizen no kami* 大岡越前守. Chūōkōronsha, 1964.

———. "*Seidan* no shakaiteki haikei" 「政談」の社会的背景. In Yoshikawa Kōjiro et al., eds., *NST 36: Ogyū Sorai*. Iwanami shoten, 1973, pp. 741–785.

Tsuji Zennosuke 辻善之助. *Tanuma jidai* 田沼時代. Iwanami shoten, 1980.

Tsukamoto Manabu 塚本学. *Shōrui o meguru seiji* 生類をめぐる政治. Heibonsha, 1983.

Uchiyama Mikiko 内山美樹子. "Meiwa hachi-nen no Chikamatsu Hanji" 明和八年の近松半二. *BG* 54 (September 1986): 67–81.

Ueda Masaaki 上田正昭. *Jimbutsu sōsho 49: Yamatotakeru no mikoto* 人物叢書 49 日本武尊. Yoshikawa kōbunkan, 1960.

Uete Michiari 植手通有. *Nihon kindai shisō no keisei* 日本近代思想の 形成. Iwanami shoten, 1974.

Ueyama Shumpei 上山春平. *Kamigami no taikei* 神々の体系. Chūōkōron-sha, 1972.

Varley, H. Paul, trans. *A Chronicle of Gods and Sovereigns: Jinnō Shōtōki of Kitabatake Chikafusa.* New York: Columbia University Press, 1980.

Wakabayashi, Bob Tadashi. *Anti-Foreignism and Western Learning in Early-Modern Japan: The New Theses of 1825.* Cambridge: Harvard University Press, 1986.

———. "In Name Only." *Journal of Japanese Studies* 17(1) (Winter 1991): 25–57.

———. "Katō Hiroyuki and Confucian Natural Rights, 1861–1870." *HJAS* 44(2) (December 1984): 469–492.

———. "Tokugawa Sociopolitical Thought." In Richard Bowring and Peter Kornicki, eds., *The Cambridge Encyclopedia of Japan.* Cambridge: Cambridge University Press, 1993.

Watanabe Hiroshi 渡辺浩. *Kinsei Nihon shakai to Sōgaku* 近世日本社会 と宋学. Tokyo daigaku shuppankai, 1985.

———. *Seiji shisō II: Kinsei Nihon seiji shisō* 政治思想 II 近世日本政治 思想. Nihon hōsō shuppan kyōkai 日本放送出版協会, 1985.

Watanabe Osamu 渡辺治. *Sengo seijishi no naka no tennōsei* 戦後政治史 の中の天皇制. Aoki shoten, 青木書店, 1990.

Watson, Burton, trans. *The Complete Works of Chuang Tzu.* New York: Columbia University Press, 1968.

———. *Han Fei Tzu: Basic Writings.* New York: Columbia University Press, 1964.

———. *Hsun Tzu: Basic Writings.* New York: Columbia University Press, 1963.

———. *Records of the Historian: Chapters from the Shih chi of Ssu-ma Ch'ien.* New York: Columbia University Press, 1965.

Webb, Herschel. *The Japanese Imperial Institution in the Tokugawa Period.* New York: Columbia University Press, 1968.

Wilhelm, Richard, and Baynes, Cary F., trans. *The I Ching or Book of Changes.* Princeton: Princeton University Press, 1967.

Yamada Tadao 山田忠雄. "Kinsei ni okeru 'hōbatsu' shisō no oboegaki" 近世における「放伐」思想の覚書. *RH* 歴史評論 314 (June 1976): 36–41.

Yamaguchi Kazuo 山口和夫. "Shokunin zuryō no kinseiteki tenkai" 職人 受領の近世的展開. *NR* 日本歴史 505 (June 1990): 57–74.

Yasuda Tokiko 安田富貴子. "Kinsei zuryō kō" 近世受領考. In *Kojōruri*

seihonshū 古浄瑠璃正本集. Kadokawa shoten 角川書店, 1967, pp. 591–650.

Yokoyama Seiji 横山政治. "Meiwa jiken kō" 明和事件考. In Tsuda Hideo 律田秀男, ed., *Kinsei kokka no tenkai* 近世国家の展開. Hanawa shobō 稿書房, 1980, pp. 200–241.

Yokota Kōichi 横田耕一. *Kempō to tennōsei* 憲法と天皇制. Iwanami shoten, 1990.

Yoshikawa Kōjirō 吉川幸次郎. *Jinsai, Sorai, Norinaga.* 仁斎 徂徠 宣長. Iwanami shoten, 1975.

Index

Note: Italicized page numbers refer to the text of the translation of Ryūshi shinron.

About the Author

Bob Tadashi Wakabayashi is currently an associate professor of history at York University, Toronto. After graduating from the University of California, Los Angeles, he spent 1972–1979 in Japan at Tokyo Kyōiku Daigaku and Tokyo Daigaku. He received his Ph.D. from Princeton University in 1982. Professor Wakabayashi is the author of *Anti-Foreignism and Western Learning in Early-Modern Japan: The New Theses of 1825*. His articles have appeared in *Journal of Japanese Studies, Monumenta Nipponica, Harvard Journal of Asiatic Studies,* and *Sino-Japanese Studies.*

Production Notes

Composition and paging were done in
FrameMaker software on an AGFA AccuSet
Postscript Imagesetter by the design
and production staff of University of
Hawai'i Press.

The text typeface is Sabon and
the display typeface is Eras.

Offset presswork and binding were done by
The Maple-Vail Book Manufacturing Group.
Text paper is Writers RR Offset,
basis 50.